The Economic Factor in International Relations

THE ECONOMIC FACTOR IN INTERNATIONAL RELATIONS

Spyros Economides
&
Peter Wilson

I.B.Tauris *Publishers*
LONDON • NEW YORK

Published in 2001 by I.B.Tauris & Co Ltd
6 Salem Road, London W2 4BU
175 Fifth Avenue, New York NY 10010
Website: http://www.ibtauris.com

In the United States and Canada distributed by St. Martin's Press
175 Fifth Avenue, New York NY 10010

ISBN 1 86064 662 X hardback
         1 86064 663 8 paperback

A full CIP record for this book is available from the British Library
A full CIP record for this book is available from the Library of Congress

Library of Congress catalog card: available

Typeset in Janson by Dexter Haven, London
Printed and bound in Great Britain

CONTENTS

PREFACE

Economics is more important today than it has ever been. Foreign policy is increasingly driven by commercial considerations. Economic strength gives incomparably more political influence than military strength. Globalisation is irreversible. The conquest of markets is now much more important than the conquest of territory. Growing economic interdependence is rapidly rendering war obsolete. Economic interdependence, not military strategy, is today the chief guarantor of security. The information revolution is creating a borderless world in which the nation-state is no longer a meaningful unit of economic activity. The state, indeed, is becoming a 'nostalgic fiction'.[1]

These are just some of the grand claims that are made these days about the role of economics in world affairs. The cliche 'it's all about economics' caps them all. Together they signal the growth of a new, popular, economic determinism: economics is seen to be at the root of everything. Bold, ambiguous, tendentious: these statements exhibit all the hallmarks of the political slogan. Yet they are widely and enthusiastically believed.

It would be precipitous to dismiss them in their entirety. Like all cliches and slogans they contain some grains of truth. The key question is, how many? The purpose of this volume is to provide a beginning for those who wish to acquire the intellectual skills and empirical knowledge by which the veracity and utility of such statements can be effectively judged. It is aimed primarily at second- and third-year undergraduates studying for degrees in International Relations. It is based on a series of lectures given at the London School of Economics and Political Science between 1993 and 1999. It is written by an international relations theorist who specialises in the history of thought, and a foreign policy analyst with a special interest in the international politics of Western and Southern Europe. It is thus written from the viewpoint of the student of politics rather than that of the professional economist or political economist. It is felt that this may bring certain benefits to a field – often called International Political Economy (IPE) – dominated by those who are primarily interested in economics, politics being a factor rather than the focus.

Inspired by such excellent short books as E.H. Carr's *Nationalism and After,* Joseph Frankel's *The National Interest,* and Michael Donelan's *Elements of International Political Theory,* it aims to provide a brief readable, introduction to a complex and important subject: an introduction that will provide enquiring students with a good basis for tackling more detailed and advanced works in the field. It also seeks to emulate these short books in combining a brief introduction to a subject with a line of argument, a 'position' or 'thesis', with which the reader may find him- or herself not entirely in agreement. This is fine. The authors have no desire to convert, only to encourage their readers to examine their subject carefully, critically, and as dispassionately as the sometimes emotionally highly-charged subject matter will allow. The line of argument, simply put, is that statements about the growing significance of economic factors need to be handled with considerable care. They are often open to a variety of interpretations. One observer's understanding of what, precisely, is being claimed is often quite different to another's. They often conceal an ideological commitment to one way of viewing the world vis-a-vis another. They are also often based on a range of assumptions the validity of which is, at best, unproven. The authors' general position is that while sometimes profound and decisive, the role of economic factors in determining international relationships is often much exaggerated.

The book is divided into three parts. Part I outlines and examines the three main approaches – sometimes called 'theories', 'ideologies' or 'paradigms' – to the relationship between politics and economics at the international level. Chapter 1 takes a general look at the economic factor in international relations and asks whether it is true, as some have claimed, that professional analysts of international relations have, over the years, tended to ignore this factor. Chapter 2 looks at the evolution of classical liberalism and the doctrine of *laissez-faire.* This doctrine has its origins in the writings of Adam Smith in the late eighteenth century. It stresses the possibility and desirability of separating economics from politics. Chapter 3 deals with the theory and practice of mercantilism and economic nationalism. These closely connected doctrines have characterised certain historical epochs, notably the seventeenth and eighteenth centuries and the inter-war period. They take as their basic premise the impossibility of separating economics from politics. Chapter 4 examines Marxist theories of 'the international'. These explain the links between economics and politics in terms of class struggle and the exploitation and domination of the weak by the strong. The chapter also examines the concept of imperialism, a concept central to much radical thinking, Marxist and non-Marxist, on international political economy.

Part II looks at the institutional structure of the post-war liberal international economic order. Chapters 5 and 6 deal with the establishment and evolution of the Bretton Woods system of international monetary management, the development of the General Agreement on Tariffs and Trade (GATT), and its replacement in 1994 by the World Trade Organisation (WTO). Chapter 7 examines the challenge to the rules and institutions of the liberal international order by the developing countries of the 'South'. It investigates the institutional, political, and intellectual origins of this challenge. It also examines the main interpretations of its purpose, or 'real' purpose, and the reasons behind its failure.

Part III looks at four key issues concerning the relationship between politics and economics in the contemporary world. Chapters 8 and 9 looks at the two most important, and controversial, economic instruments of foreign policy: economic aid and economic sanctions. These are the principal economic means by which states seek to alter the international and domestic behaviour of other states. The efficacy of these instruments is widely disputed. There are also serious disputes over their moral validity and whether, or to what extent, they can be seen as 'non-violent' alternatives to the use of force in international relations. Chapters 10 and 11 examine two concepts, and phenomena, that have provoked much excitement in recent years: regionalism and globalisation. Some have seen in the growth of 'exclusive' regional organisations and arrangements the dawning of a new age of mercantilism. The more pessimistic among them envisage the gradual division of the world into three or four huge, mutually antagonistic, commercial blocs, with profound implications for the maintenance of international order. Others, however, see regionalism not as an obstacle in the way of greater world unity and 'globalisation', but a stepping stone on its path. They point out that these groupings do not aspire to self-sufficiency and the creation of what Friedrich List (see Chapter 3) called the 'closed commercial state'. On the contrary, they are often forged in order to facilitate greater openness in economic relations and have evolved *pari passu* with broader international agreements and institutional developments designed to encourage greater international economic co-operation and, in particular, freer international trade. Finally, Chapter 11 examines the broad and controversial subject of globalisation. It enquires into the coherence of the concept of globalisation and critically assesses the two general accounts – liberal and Marxist – of its nature and significance. It concludes that there is a sense in which the concept of globalisation is all things to all men – at least to those who see it as the latest and most direct route to the achievement of a community of mankind. It still, however, might signal the emergence of a new and profound force in international life.

In writing the book we have incurred a number of debts of gratitude. We would like to thank Michael Donelan and James Mayall for encouraging us to take responsibility for the university course out of which it emerged, despite the fact that our main field of expertise lay elsewhere. Attending their lectures while studying for postgraduate degrees at the LSE in the late 1980s provided us with an ideal platform from which to launch our own explorations of the subject. We would like to thank Charles Jones, David Long, James Mayall and a fourth (anonymous) reviewer for their many incisive comments and suggestions on an earlier draft. Finally, we are much indebted to our students for providing a conducive environment in which to test many of the ideas contained in these pages. They have constantly challenged us to find better, simpler ways of expressing often complex points. They have frequently seen through assertions and theories that fire the imagination, promise the earth, but do not bear close scrutiny.

Note on Preface

1   The last three assertions are taken from Kenichi Ohmae, *The Borderless World: Power and Strategy in the Interlinked Economy* (London, HarperCollins, 1990), xii; *The End of the Nation State: The Rise of Regional Economies* (London, HarperCollins, 1995), viii, 12.

ACRONYMS

ACP	African, Caribbean and Pacific countries
APEC	Asia-Pacific Economic Co-operation forum
CAP	Common Agricultural Policy
CMEA	Council for Mutual Economic Assistance (or COMECON)
ECLA	Economic Commission for Latin America
EEC	European Economic Community
EFTA	European Free Trade Area
EU	European Union
FTA	free-trade agreement
GATT	General Agreement on Tariffs and Trade
GNP	gross national product
GSM	global system model
HST	hegemonic stability theory
IAEA	International Atomic Energy Agency
IBRD	International Bank for Reconstruction and Development (or World Bank)
IMF	International Monetary Fund
IPE	International Political Economy
IR	International Relations (academic discipline)
ISI	import substitution industrialisation
ITO	International Trade Organisation
Mercosur	'Southern Cone' common market
MITI	Ministry of International Trade and Industry (Japan)
MNC	multinational corporation
NAFTA	North American Free Trade Agreement
NATO	North Atlantic Treaty Organisation
NIEO	new international economic order
NTB	non-tariff barriers
OECD	Organisation of Economic Co-operation and Development
OMA	orderly marketing agreement
OPEC	Organisation of Petroleum Exporting Countries
RTA	regional trade arrangement
Stabex	Stabilisation of Exchange scheme (EU–ACP)

TCC	transnational capitalist class
TNC	transnational corporation
TRIM	trade-related investment measure
UN	United Nations
UNCTAD	United Nations Conference on Trade and Development
VER	voluntary export restraint
WTO	World Trade Organisation

PART I

QUESTIONS, CONCEPTS, THEORIES

CHAPTER 1

The Economic Factor in International Relations

The somewhat hackneyed statement that economics are more important in international relations today than they have ever been contains more than a few grains of truth. Some of the most important issues on the current international agenda, though not exclusively concerned with economics, revolve around or hinge upon economic questions: how best can the West assist the growth of democracy and facilitate the transition from a centrally planned to a market economy in Eastern Europe and the former Soviet Union? Do economic sanctions work? What are the merits and demerits of further integration within the European Union and the creation of a single European currency? What role can foreign investment play in under-pinning the PLO–Israeli Peace Accords, democracy and reconciliation in South Africa, the reconstruction of Bosnia, and the peace process in Northern Ireland?

It should also be remembered that the questions that most exercise the minds of governments are those concerned with economic growth, development, price inflation, unemployment and other economic considerations. These, after all, are the questions upon which the future electoral success of those governments by and large depend. Even non-democratic governments, those not burdened with the inconvenience of elections and electorates, need to pay attention to these matters if they are to maintain their legitimacy with key domestic groups such as the armed forces, business elites, tribal leaders and the urban proletariat.

In addition, there is a range of international issues that seem to have little, if anything, to do with economics, but which, if one scrapes below the surface, clearly involve some fairly weighty economic considerations. Take for example UN peacekeeping, or the nuclear non-proliferation regime, or international environmental co-operation. The success of all of these things depends at least in part on proper financing. This, in turn, depends on the health of the international economy. A sluggish international economy bodes ill for a range of problems that states, and other important actors on the international stage, would like, ideally, to solve.

General Questions

There are a number of more general questions that can be asked about the relationship between economics and politics at the international level. It is important to make them explicit because it is impossible to make progress in any line of enquiry unless we are clear about the questions we are asking. 'What are the important questions?' is perhaps the most important question a social scientist can ask. Among these general questions, the following have received considerable attention from specialists in the field of International Political Economy (IPE):

- Does an open, liberal, international economic order require a hegemon to lay down and enforce the rules? That is, does the efficient functioning of a liberal order depend on the existence of a state with the power, resources and willingness to perform a leadership or 'policing' role?
- What are the implications of uneven growth, which inevitably accompanies such an order, for the power distribution between states?
- What are the implications of the relative rise and decline in the prosperity of nations for the maintenance of international order?
- How important is the question of economic justice? When thinking about this question is it justice between individuals we should be concerned with, or justice between states?
- Does rapid change in the international economic system (say, the growth of interdependence) inevitably bring about change in the international political system (say, the decline of the state as the chief repository of political power)?
- In what ways does the international political system constrain the development of the international economic system?

- Can economic instruments of foreign policy, such as economic aid or sanctions, be a substitute for the use of force, or do they work only when backed up by force?
- Is free trade utopian (as E.H. Carr famously claimed)? Is protectionism the natural condition of the international economic system (as maintained by Robert Gilpin)?

This list of questions is far from exhaustive, but it serves to illustrate the range and nature of questions asked in the growing field of IPE. To answer them is important for a proper understanding of the relationship between economics and politics at the international level. But it is also important for a proper understanding of international relations *in toto*. To this extent, the division between IPE and the other sub-fields of International Relations (IR) and Political Science, such as Foreign Policy Analysis and Comparative Politics, is an artificial one. It is best seen not as a reflection of any such division existing 'out there', empirically, in the real world of facts, but as a scholarly division of labour: a dividing up of tasks in order to make the study of a broad subject ('world politics') practicable.

Although it is possible to survey the field of IPE and identify those general questions most frequently asked, it is important to note that there is little agreement on which among them are the most important. The importance of a question depends to a large extent on the philosophical or ideological prejudices of the investigator. In this regard, three broad perspectives on the relationship between politics and economics at the international level have been identified: economic liberalism, economic nationalism and Marxism (or sometimes, more contentiously, 'structuralism'). These schools of thought differ not only with respect to the answers they give, but also with respect to the questions they ask. For instance, Marxists ask questions about historical structures, the reproduction of social relations, the commodification of labour, and the exploitation by the 'core' of the world economy of the 'periphery' that are by and large meaningless to economic liberals. Similarly, liberals ask questions about the maximisation of global efficiency, the economic utility of military spending, and how to achieve an 'optimal' international division of labour, that economic nationalists consider largely irrelevant.

The 'Neglect' of Economics

Though some of the questions asked are different, there is no doubt that all three traditions see the economic factor as immensely important. Given this, it is perhaps surprising that until about 25 years ago IR scholars paid little attention to economic matters. There were some studies in the 1950s and 1960s of the Marshall Plan, economic integration within the European Economic Community (EEC), the economic interactions of former communist-bloc countries of the Council for Mutual Economic Assistance (CMEA or 'Comecon'), and the economic aspects of the relationships between certain pairs or small groups of countries (in Latin America or the Middle East for example). But there were no studies of international economic relations in general.[1]

Yet if we cast our minds back further, to the time before IR became a highly professionalised discipline in the post-1945 period, a different picture emerges. The so-called inter-war 'idealists' took economic factors very seriously. Norman Angell wrote a series of popular books on interdependence and the irrationality of war under modern conditions. J.M. Keynes wrote famously on the economic consequences of the Versailles peace. Philip Noel-Baker wrote in great detail about *The Private Manufacture of Armaments*, arguing quite convincingly that private arms manufacturers had a vested interest in war and used their financial power and political muscle to provoke arms races and incite international hostility. Liberals like J.A. Hobson, socialists like Leonard Woolf, and Marxists like Rosa Luxemburg and, of course, Vladimir Ilyich Lenin, wrote extensively on 'economic imperialism'. David Mitrany, one of the most influential theorists of international organisation, wrote one of the first books on economic sanctions, and developed his theory of functionalism. It may be worthwhile to dwell for a few moments on this theory. Its central contention was that the state, as a mode of political and economic organisation, was becoming obsolete. It was increasingly unable to perform the welfare tasks demanded of it by its citizens. As a consequence, it needed to be complemented, and to a large extent superseded, by technical bodies above and below the state which, utilising modern scientific, social and economic knowledge, would be better able to satisfy human needs. In doing so, loyalty to largely militaristic states would be diffused. In its prediction of the decline of the nation-state, and its prescription that new sub-national and transnational bodies needed to be created to manage the powerful, perhaps inexorable, economic and social forces responsible for this decline, Mitrany's theory of functionalism has clear echoes in contemporary theories of 'globalisation' (see Chapter 11).[2]

So there was plenty of interest in the economic factor in the first part of this century among observers of international relations. It should also be noted that E.H. Carr, who attacked many of these writers in his classic work *The Twenty Years' Crisis*, also considered economic factors to be of vital importance. His 'crisis' of international relations was at least in part an economic crisis – a crisis brought on by the continued promulgation, by the 'utopian' intellectuals of the inter-war period, of the nineteenth-century liberal doctrine of *laissez-faire* at a time when it no longer had any relevance. The world, he felt, had moved on to new forms of social, economic and political organisation, characterised chiefly by large-scale production, the big trade union, the welfare state and economic planning.[3]

It should also be pointed out that – in contrast to later fellow 'realist' thinkers, but in common with many of the 'utopian' thinkers of the time – Carr considered economic and political factors to be inextricably linked. Carr asserted, for example, that political power contained three elements: military power, economic power and power over public opinion.[4]

The period between 1945 and the early 1970s can thus be seen as the exception rather than the rule. Both before and since, IR scholars have given much attention to economic factors. Given this, what explains the 'neglect', as Susan Strange called it, of economics? Three factors can be put forward.

First, the central fact of the period was the Cold War, and the central task was to avoid a nuclear confrontation between East and West. At the time, most observers saw the Cold War in terms of political, military and ideological competition. As a result, little attention was given to the economic dimension of the struggle. Economics, in the classic realist formulation, was relegated to the realm of 'low politics', to be contrasted with the 'high politics' of state security and military strategy.[5]

The second factor concerns methodology. During this period an attempt was made to build a 'science' of international politics. In doing so, 'economics' was either consciously or unconsciously left out of the equation. Hans Morgenthau – in his influential text, *Politics Among Nations*, for example – made a sharp separation between economics and politics. The former, he contended, was about wealth, the latter about power. The former was based on the assumption of *homo economicus* (the utility-maximising man), the latter was based on an assumption of *homo politicus* (the power-maximising man). Though Morgenthau recognised that states could and did use economic means to enhance their power, and though he saw 'economic resources' as an important component of 'national power', he tended to assume that economic intercourse between peoples was not a part of international politics. He gave the example of Switzerland. This country, he suggested, was an important participant in international economic relations because of its long history of involvement in international finance and the strength and repute of its banks. It was also an important participant in international social relations due to its humanitarian work and its role as host to a wide range of international economic, technical and humanitarian agencies. But because it abstained from the balance of power through its traditional stance of neutrality, and because it was not concerned to increase its power vis-a-vis the power of other states, it was not a participant in international politics.[6]

The third factor concerns US hegemony. The hegemonic position of the US in the post-war international economy served further to entrench the assumption that international politics is separable from international economics. America emerged from the war unrivalled in its industrial and financial strength. It was in a position both to determine the rules of the post-war economic game and ensure, through a range of threats and inducements, that these rules met with compliance. Coupled with the need for the Western democracies to maintain their unity in the face of the Soviet challenge, this position of economic hegemony ensured that intra-alliance disputes were settled relatively smoothly. This meant that potential differences, disagreements and disputes did not become actual differences, disagreements and disputes. This, in turn, led to the illusion that international economic relations, at least in the Western camp, were fairly un-contentious, that is, they did not raise questions of a political nature.

This neglect of economics in IR came to an end in the 1970s. Nothing less than an explosion of interest occurred around 1973, with books on interdependence, transnationalism, international economic organisations, 'regimes', the multinational corporation, economic sanctions, the Bretton Woods system, 'dependency', and the politics of foreign aid.[7] Again it can be asked, what accounts for this sudden explosion of interest in economic factors in the 1970s? Three reasons are particularly important.

First, the bulk of scholarly writing on IR is American in origin. With the demise of the Bretton Woods system and the oil crisis of the early 1970s, many observers reached the conclusion that the US had suddenly lost its grip on the world economy. Not surprisingly, these writers started to look for an explanation for this sudden change. Primary among the explanations given was that the world had become highly interdependent. There followed a massive amount of interest in the idea of economic interdependence and related phenomena such as transnationalism and international regimes, i.e., 'sets of implicit or explicit principles, norms, rules and decision-making procedures around which actor expectations converge in a given issue-area of international relations'.[8]

The important thing to note in this connection is that there is nothing new about these phenomena. They did not suddenly emerge with the collapse of the Bretton Woods system and the oil embargo by the Organisation of Petroleum Exporting Countries (OPEC). A number of writers in the US, however, assumed that they were new, partly as a result of their uncritical and unreflective acceptance of America's economic supremacy: their uncritical acceptance of America's 'place in the sun', and its rightful position as leader of the free world, blinded them to the fact that these forces had been at work from the very onset of the Industrial Revolution.

Second, in the early 1970s the campaign for a new international economic order (NIEO) began. It was felt that the classical model of economic development had not worked. Trade was not proving to be the 'engine of growth'. Allowing the market to be the principal means by which resources were allocated around the globe had not led to wealth 'trickling down' from the rich North to the poor South. On the contrary, the vast inequalities of wealth between North and South were increasing. As a consequence, Third World states called for a radical overhaul of the international economic system, involving the regulation and relegation of the market, and the introduction of radical redistributive mechanisms. This gave rise to the North–South debate (see Chapter 7) and the NIEO became one of the most important issues on the international agenda. There was consequently a rise in interest in economics, because this debate was one explicitly concerned with the way the international economy should be organised.

Third is the pioneering role of certain individuals in putting the sub-field of IPE on the academic map. Professor Susan Strange, Montague Burton Professor of International Relations at the London School of Economics, 1980–90, criticised IR, as we have seen, for neglecting economic factors. In particular, she drew attention to the possibility that the rapid changes occurring in the international economy could have profound implications for the international political system. She did not believe that the role and power of the state was diminishing, as some contested. But she did argue that certain forms of power (financial power, and the power that comes from having exclusive access to certain types of knowledge) were increasing in importance, and that new mechanisms would have to be developed in order to manage this rapid change. In putting across these ideas, in spelling out, as E.H. Carr had done 30 years before her, the ever intimate connections between international economic processes and institutions and international political processes and institutions, she played an important role in rekindling an interest in economic factors in the IR discipline. Note should also be made of the contribution of Fred Hirsch. A British economist working for the World Bank in Washington during the crises of the mid-1970s, Hirsch returned to the UK to found a department of International Studies at the University of Warwick. There, IPE, not international politics, or strategy, or international history, formed the intellectual core of the syllabus from the outset.

Economic Power

It has been mentioned that E.H. Carr viewed economic power as an important component of political power. But what is economic power? The possession of considerable economic power is implicit in the notion of 'hegemony'. We take it for granted – at least we have done since the revolutions of 1989 – that the Cold War revolved around the issue of economic power; that the industrial and financial might of the US vis-a-vis the Soviet Union was a crucial factor in its outcome. We also take it for granted that the Southern challenge to the post-war liberal economic order constructed and maintained by the North revolved around economic power: the desire of the South to have more of it and the use of it by the North to frustrate this desire. On analysis, however, the concept of economic power turns out to be much more complicated than it first appears. At least three types of economic power can be identified.

First, there are those types of economic power relating to 'war potential'. This is the form of economic power most discussed in texts of a realist or economic nationalist persuasion. The focus is on a country's industrial capacity, the size and skill-level of its population, its degree of technological advancement, and the degree to which it is self-sufficient in food and vital raw materials. All of these factors contribute to a state's 'war potential', that is its ability to prevail in a military conflict. The conclusion is usually drawn that highly industrialised states large enough to have a high degree of autarky (i.e. economic self-sufficiency), like the US, are the ones most likely to prevail.[9]

Second, there are those types of economic power not directly related to war potential but which may provide a state with extensive international influence. Certain states, for example, possess 'financial power' by virtue of their ability to support or undermine another state's currency, and their ability to help or hinder another state's investment plans. This may involve having a large say in the running of international financial organisations such as the International Monetary Fund (IMF) or World Bank. Some countries have 'production power' by virtue of their ability to invest directly in other countries. Other countries have 'market power' by virtue of their possession of a large and lucrative market. In order to achieve certain political or economic objectives, for example, a country with production power could threaten to prevent its firms from investing in another country. Similarly, a country with market power could impose tariffs or quotas on another country's exports, or by other means prevent or restrict access to its large and lucrative market in the pursuit of its economic and political goals.

Third, there are those types of economic power which result from certain 'structural' advantages. This is not 'relational power' (the ability of state A to get state B to do something that it otherwise would not do), nor 'Godfather power' (the ability of State A to make State B an offer that it cannot refuse). Rather it is the ability to determine an agenda, shape the context and environment in which any decision is made, to determine opportunities or a range of choices. Structural power involves unconscious rather than conscious exercise of power.[10] It is sometimes said, for instance, that despite balance-of-payments and budget deficits and falling competitiveness in the 1970s and 1980s, the US still possessed and wielded immense structural power. This was due to a range of factors, including the influence of American corporations on business practices, consumption patterns, values, attitudes and tastes worldwide; the leading role that the US plays in international financial institutions, which gives it a large say in their mode of operation, recruitment practices, and 'ethos' or 'guiding philosophy'; and the sheer size of the American economy, which often means, as one economist once said, that when America sneezes, the world catches a cold.

Economic Factors

As intimated at the beginning of this chapter, the assertion that economics is more important today than it has ever been is something of a cliche. It may contain grains of truth, but if we are to proceed any further, if we are to acquire a deeper understanding of the economic and political forces that are shaping the modern world, we need to get a much firmer grip on the nature of the claim being made. When it is said that economics are more important today than they have ever been, 'economics' can mean one, or more, of the following four things: economic means, economic ends, economic implications and economic causes. It may mean, therefore, that economic means (tariffs, quotas, currency manipulation, aid, sanctions) are now more important; or that economic ends (full employment, low inflation, growth, 'development') have assumed more importance; or that political and other acts today have far greater economic implications or consequences; or that a greater number of significant political and other acts and events, including the achievement of peace and the outbreak of war, have economic causes. It is important to bear in mind this four-fold distinction when examining statements about the role of economic factors in modern-day international relations. With it, a good deal of the dross that one hears in political speeches, reads in the press or sees on television can be safely done away with.

Notes on Chapter 1

1 Susan Strange, 'International Economics and International Relations: A Case of Mutual Neglect', *International Affairs* 46, 2 (1970).

2 Norman Angell, *The Great Illusion, 1933* (London, Heinemann, 1933); J.M. Keynes, *The Economic Consequences of the Peace* (London, Macmillan, 1920); Philip Noel-Baker, *The Private Manufacture of Armaments* (London, Gollancz, 1936); J.A. Hobson, *Imperialism: A Study*, 3rd ed., (London, George Allen and Unwin, 1938); Leonard Woolf, *Economic Imperialism* (London, Swarthmore Press, 1920); Rosa Luxemburg, *The Accumulation of Capital* (London, Routledge and Kegan Paul, 1951 [1913]); Vladimir Ilych Lenin, *Imperialism, The Highest Stage of Capitalism* (Peking, Foreign Language Press, 1975 [1917]); David Mitrany, *The Problem of International Sanctions* (London, Oxford University Press, 1925); David Mitrany, *A Working Peace System* (London, Royal Institute for International Affairs, 1943). The thought of many of these authors is discussed in David Long and Peter Wilson (eds), *Thinkers of the Twenty Years' Crisis: Inter-War Idealism Reassessed* (Oxford, Clarendon Press, 1995).

3 E.H. Carr, *The Twenty Years' Crisis, 1919–1939: An Introduction to the Study of International Relations*, 2nd ed., (London, Macmillan, 1946); *Conditions of Peace* (London, Macmillan, 1942); *The New Society* (London, Macmillan, 1951). See also Peter Wilson, 'The New Europe Debate in Wartime Britain', in Philomena Murray and Paul Rich (eds), *Visions of European Unity* (Boulder, CO, Westview Press, 1996); "E.H.Carr: The Revolutionist's Realist", www.theglobalsite, December 2000.

4 Carr, *Twenty Years' Crisis*, 102–45.

5 A caveat is required here. The ideological battle between East and West was in part a battle between communism and capitalism, i.e. between two competing economic systems, although it was most commonly portrayed as a battle between dictatorship and democracy, 'totalitarianism' versus the 'free world'. The point being made here is that while the importance of these two systems as models of economic development and efficiency cannot be denied, the relegation of economics by the dominant realist paradigm to the realm of 'low politics' in effect removed international economic interaction as a class of human activity from the purview of specialist observers of international relations.

6   Hans J. Morgenthau, *Politics Among Nations: The Struggle for Power and Peace*, 5th ed., revised (New York, NY, Alfred A. Knopf, 1978), 16–41.

7   Most prominently, Robert O. Keohane and Joseph S. Nye (eds), *Transnational Relations and World Politics* (Cambridge, MA, Harvard University Press, 1971); Robert O. Keohane and Joseph S. Nye, *Power and Interdependence: World Politics in Transition* (Boston, MA, Little Brown, 1977); Stephen D. Krasner (ed.), *International Regimes* (Ithaca, NY, Cornell University Press, 1983); Robert Gilpin, *US Power and the Multinational Corporation: The Political Economy of Foreign Direct Investment* (New York, NY, Basic Books, 1975); John White, *The Politics of Foreign Aid* (London, Macmillan, 1974).

8   Stephen Krasner, 'Structured Causes and Regime Consequences: Regimes as Intervening Variables', *International Organization* 36, 2 (1982), 1.

9   See Paul Kennedy, *The Rise and Fall of the Great Powers: Economic Change and Military Conflict from 1500–2000* (London, Fontana, 1989), for the most detailed and persuasive account to date of the importance in history of the economic and technological 'sinews of war'.

10   For an excellent general analysis see Steven Lukes, *Power: A Radical View* (London, Macmillan, 1974).

Select Bibliography

Baldwin, David, *Economic Statecraft* (Princeton, NJ, Princeton University Press, 1985), especially Chs 1–4, 7. Empirically rich and analytically astute, the leading text on the economic instruments of foreign policy.

Carr, E.H., *The Twenty Years' Crisis, 1919–1939: An Introduction to the Study of International Relations*, 2nd ed. (London, Macmillan, 1946), especially Ch. 8. The most important book in the field of IR. Provocative, incisive and excoriating attack on the 'utopian' thinking of the inter-war period; but one with, paradoxically, strong utopian leanings. Influential, much misunderstood, and ultimately deeply flawed. Essential reading for the careful reader.

Gilpin, Robert, *The Political Economy of International Relations* (Princeton, NJ, Princeton University Press, 1985), especially Ch. 1. The leading American textbook in the field of IPE. Sets out and defends the perspective of 'benign mercantilism'. Comprehensive and analytically sharp.

Garnett, John, 'States, State-Centric Perspectives, and Interdependence Theory', in J. Baylis and N.J. Rengger (eds), *Dilemmas of World Politics* (Oxford, Clarendon Press, 1992). Lucid overview from a state-centric perspective.

Maddock, R., 'The Global Political Economy', in J. Baylis and N.J. Rengger (eds), *Dilemmas of World Politics* (Oxford, Clarendon Press, 1992).

Pollard, Sidney, *The International Economy Since 1945* (London, Routledge, 1997). Highly readable and concise overview of the main developments in the international economy since 1945.

Strange, Susan, *States and Markets: An Introduction to International Political Economy*, 2nd ed. (London, Pinter, 1995), especially Part 1. Highly readable statement from a pioneer in the field, based on forty years' teaching and writing experience.

Strange, Susan, 'International Economics and International Relations: A Case of Mutual Neglect', *International Affairs* 46, 2 (1970). Pioneering article making the case for a separate field of IPE.

Underhill, Geoffrey R.D., 'Conceptualizing the Changing Global Order', in Richard Stubbs and Geoffrey R.D. Underhill (eds), *Political Economy and the Changing Global Order* (London, Macmillan, 1994).

CHAPTER 2

Economic Liberalism

The first point to note about economic liberalism is that it is an exceedingly broad doctrine – broader than economic nationalism and even Marxism. Adam Smith, David Ricardo, J.S. Mill, J.A. Hobson, J.M. Keynes, David Mitrany, Friedrich Hayek, J.K. Galbraith, Milton Friedman, Robert Keohane – all of these influential political economists are considered to be liberals.

They are a motley bunch. Smith, Ricardo, Hayek and Friedman, strongly advocate *laissez-faire*, free trade and minimal state intervention in the 'natural' working of the economy. By contrast, Hobson, Keynes, Galbraith and Keohane advocate quite extensive state intervention in the economy both domestically and internationally.

Some thinkers, indeed, have been advocates of both *laissez-faire* and state intervention. In the early years of their respective careers, Hobson and Keynes, for example, were both staunch supporters of *laissez-faire* and free trade. However, first Hobson (in the 1910s) and then Keynes (in the 1920s) abandoned their earlier beliefs and became proponents of a 'new', interventionist, form of liberalism.[1] This transformation in their thought was based on a growing awareness that certain profound changes were taking place in the world economy.

First, the invention of the assembly line had revolutionised production. Goods could now be rapidly manufactured in vast quantities for the mass market. This innovation also enabled firms to maximise 'economies of scale' and dramatically increase productivity. The law of economies of scale holds that, up to a point, the larger the scale of production the lower the cost of each unit produced (that is the lower the 'marginal cost' of production). Later somewhat tendentiously called 'Fordism', after the great American automobile manufacturer, this revolutionary development involved breaking down the manufacture of complicated modern machinery into a series of highly specialised and repetitive tasks. Each worker would concentrate on the performance of one of these minute tasks. His level of skill, and consequently degree of training, only needed to be small. Only a tiny proportion of workers required knowledge of the production process as a whole or the engineering principles at work. Unit cost could, as a result, be dramatically cut. Previously expensive goods could be mass-produced for the newly emerging mass market.

This new technique of production, which soon became the method of manufacture of all goods except the most specialised and luxurious, was highly capital-intensive. Although it increased labour productivity (output per worker), it also led to the redundancy of large sections of the labourforce (at least in the short run). In addition, capital-intensive techniques of production led to wealth being concentrated in fewer and fewer hands. As well as raising certain ethical questions about justice and democracy, such a development had far-reaching implications for economic stability. As income inequality increases, so does the ratio of aggregate savings to consumption, due to the higher propensity to save of higher income groups. But if consumption does not keep pace with output, what happens to the goods being turned out of the factories in ever larger quantities? The answer, according to Hobson and Keynes, was some kind of economic crisis. For Hobson this manifested itself in imperialism, as industrialists and financiers were forced increasingly to look overseas for new markets and fields of profitable investment. For Keynes, it manifested itself in increasing market disequilibria and a need to rethink the fundamentals of domestic and international economic policy.

Second, monopolies and cartels were becoming increasingly salient features of the world economic landscape. Collaboration between firms to divide up markets was increasingly replacing free competition between firms within the market.

Third, the scale and sophistication of advertising had grown to new, previously unimagined, heights. Corporate executives, especially in America, were quick to spot the commercial potential of new mass media, such as the radio and television. Through such media, information about products could be instantaneously communicated to an ever larger, and largely captive, audience of consumers. Sales techniques could be refined utilising the latest findings from new fields of scientific enquiry, such as behavioural psychology. The new economy had the means not only to satisfy demand, but artificially to create and sustain it.

Fourth, Hobson and Keynes were alarmed by the increasing ability of foreign firms to gain a decisive competitive advantage in world markets by 'sweating' (that is exploiting) their non-unionised labourforce. The relative degree of protection afforded by the state to workers within its jurisdiction, and the relative strength of the trade union movement from one country to another, was becoming an increasingly important factor in national competitiveness. By suppressing trade unions and rejecting workers' demands for employment rights and regulation of the workplace, some countries were able to force down the price of labour. This enabled their firms to steal a competitive advantage over rivals operating in more humane, socially progressive countries.

A fifth development was the tremendous success of certain countries in building up immense industrial strength behind high protective walls. This was contrary to the teachings of classical economics, which held that the short-term benefits of interference in the 'natural' workings of the economy were always bought at a high long-term price. The nineteenth-century experience of Germany and the US suggested otherwise.

Finally, in an era of mass democracy, governments were increasingly obliged to respond to the ebb and flow in the economic fortunes of their countrymen, particularly as they affected the level of employment. It is an important but widely unappreciated fact that until the extension of the franchise in the nineteenth and early twentieth centuries, unemployment had not been a significant political issue. Within the space of a generation it became one of the most important issues on the political agenda.

These six developments suggested to Hobson and Keynes, among others, that the classical economic model of 'perfect competition' between relatively small producers had become obsolete. Economic activity was now characterised by 'oligopolistic competition', meaning competition, and often collaboration, between a diminishing number of large-scale producers (whose operations, incidentally, were increasingly international in scope). The implication of this was that the state would have to assume greater responsibility in the economic realm if the well-being of the consumer, the worker and the small-scale producer were to be protected, and the welfare goals of society as a whole achieved. The market, as a method of allocating resources in society, was far from dead. But it could no longer be allowed to operate in the unfettered way advocated by the classical political economists.

Core Characteristics

Given the variety of liberal thought, the question arises, what are its distinguishing characteristics? Three broad features can be identified. Firstly, faith in the market as the most efficient means of allocating resources, or at least a relatively efficient means of allocating resources, provided that the state successfully performs its role of establishing the conditions – preventing, for example, the growth of monopolies – upon which the successful operation of the market depend. Secondly, individualism: the belief that the individual is the basic unit of society and that the acid test of any set of institutions is the degree to which they promote individual liberty and welfare (as opposed to the welfare of a clan, class, business elite, ethnic or some other group). Thirdly, scepticism towards state, or central, control of economic activity. Some liberals, 'new', 'left' or 'welfare' liberals, contend that management and regulation of economic activity is increasingly needed in modern industrial conditions. But all liberals believe that direct central control of economic activity is only justified in the most extreme circumstances – during war, for example, or in the face of acute market failure – and then only temporarily.

But one has to be careful even with this very broad way of looking at things. Mitrany, for instance, is generally regarded as a liberal theorist of international relations, but his 'working peace system' contains very little scope for the operation of market forces. He shared the Marxist view that freedom of choice in a capitalist society meant freedom to exploit. He distrusted the market, believing it to be an increasingly unstable and inequitable method of economic exchange. In its place Mitrany put science. He believed, in particular, that the production and distribution of goods and services should be based on rational, scientifically identifiable, 'human needs'. Only by this revolutionary method could the instability and inequity which had become an endemic feature of modern industrial society be avoided.[2] In some of Hobson's writings a similar distrust of the market and faith in 'rational' economic planning can be observed. Indeed, he extended this faith to the world as a whole in his plans for international economic government.[3]

It is important to note, however, that these two thinkers were not statists: they did not view state intervention in and organisation of economic activity as some kind of panacea. They certainly believed in regulating economic activity, and planning in such areas as investment and production. But they did not think that the state should be the only organ performing these tasks. On the contrary, they envisaged an extensive role for specialised agencies, public corporations, co-operatives, guilds and other non-state entities. These bodies would be staffed by technical experts. Like many of their generation, Mitrany and Hobson shared the Fabian faith in the ability of the specially trained technical expert to solve a range of technological, economic, social, even political, problems.

It is because of their distrust of the market and their belief in certain forms of economic planning that certain writers have declined to regard them as *bona fide* members of the liberal tradition.[4] It is largely a matter of where one draws the line between liberalism and reformist socialism, a line much blurred by the revitalisation (some would say degradation) of liberal doctrine in the early part of the twentieth century by such men as Hobson, Mitrany and, in particular, Keynes. The general view, however, is that they should be considered as liberals because of their faith in meliorism and the possibility of reform without revolution, because of their belief in 'pluralism' – that is in multi-association governance of human society – and because their ultimate unit of analysis was the individual. For them, as with other writers in the liberal tradition, it was individual welfare that mattered, and any value that the various groups and associations they recommended possessed was a by-product of their success in delivering individual human welfare.

Classical Liberalism

The roots of most liberal ideas can be found in classical liberalism, which emerged with the writings of Adam Smith in the late eighteenth century. It is important to understand this doctrine if we are to understand later liberal theories.

Classical liberals share six core beliefs. First, they claim there are laws of human behaviour comparable to natural laws. Just as there are objectively existing physical laws, for example the law of gravity, there are objectively existing social laws, for example the laws of supply and demand. These laws are objective because they are not products of thought or consciousness, they are not 'socially reproduced' attitudes, values or norms. Rather they exist external to ourselves, even though 'irrational' governments may sometimes choose to suppress them (as they did during the 'mercantilist' period – see Chapter 3). The word 'irrational' is important. According to classical liberals, these laws not only exist but can be discovered through reason. Governments and societies that made no attempt to discover them, or who ignored them, were thus acting irrationally. To illustrate: just as it would be irrational to ignore the laws of physics when building a bridge, it would be irrational, classical liberals claim, to ignore the laws of economics when seeking to create wealth. If the laws of physics are ignored when building a bridge, the bridge will collapse. If the laws of economics are ignored when seeking to acquire wealth, the result will be poverty. It is because classical liberals believe in the existence of such laws that classical liberalism has been called a 'theory of social physics'.

Secondly, classical liberals claim that wealth consists of production, and especially industrial production. This contrasts with the mercantilist view, which maintained that wealth resided in precious metals. The significance of this disagreement is considerable. Whereas for mercantilists wealth was finite, for classical liberals it is infinite, at least in principle. The world enjoys only a finite supply of precious metals, whereas the only limit to the number of goods and services that can be produced is human imagination and ingenuity. The social and political implications of this belief are profound. For mercantilists, economics is a struggle for wealth, a 'zero-sum game'. For classical liberals, economics is a competitive activity the outcome of which is wealth for all, a 'positive-sum game'.

A third belief of classical liberalism is that self-interest is central to the operation of these economic laws. Smith felt that in itself self-interest was not a good thing. Indeed, in his famous work, *The Wealth of Nations*, there are a number of references to the 'mean rapacity' of the rising commercial class and, by virtue of this, their 'unfitness' for government. However, though not a good thing in itself, the pursuit of self-interest has social value: the unbridled pursuit of economic self-interest, by consumers and producers, leads, through the operation of the 'hidden hand', to the most efficient possible allocation of resources in society as a whole. In a typically acute and droll passage Smith described his idea thus: 'It is not from the benevolence of the butcher, the brewer, or the baker that we expect our dinner but from their regard to self-interest. We address ourselves, not to their humanity, but to their self-love, and never talk to them of our necessities, but of their advantages.'[5]

Fourthly, classical liberals also emphasise the importance of specialisation through a division of labour. This can operate both nationally and internationally. Individuals should produce the things that they are best at producing and exchange them in the market-place. Production and consumption are thereby increased. Similarly, nations should concentrate on producing those things they are best endowed to produce, and exchange them in the international market-place. It was in light of this that David Ricardo developed his notion of 'comparative advantage', which he famously illustrated with his tale of Portuguese wine and English cloth. Though Portugal was more efficient at producing both of these commodities, Ricardo argued that it would be better from the point of view of the welfare of both Portugal and England, and indeed the welfare of the world as a whole, if Portugal concentrated on the production of wine, and England on the production of cloth. Though Portugal had an absolute advantage in the production of both commodities, England had a comparative advantage in the production of cloth. The reason for this was simple. Though its climate inhibited England from ever becoming an efficient producer of wine, the skills, ingenuity, and industriousness of its workforce suggested that it could become an efficient producer of cloth: if not as efficient – at least for the time being – as Portugal. Basing production on comparative, as opposed to absolute, advantage would lead to the maximisation of aggregate production.[6]

Fifthly, classical liberals maintain that maximum efficiency is not the only benefit of *laissez-faire* and free trade. Two further benefits are maximum liberty and peace. Liberty is achieved because individuals are perfectly free to pursue their interests as they define them: not for nothing did Adam Smith call the market economy 'the system of perfect liberty'. Peace is achieved because the 'harmony of interests' immanent in nature is allowed to manifest itself unimpeded by state meddling.

Finally, classical liberals advocate the minimal or 'nightwatchman' state. In the eighteenth and nineteenth centuries, the state was seen by many liberals as synonymous with 'privilege', with the landed aristocracy, with corruption, and with mercantilism. As the intellectual spokesmen of the rising commercial class, Smith and Ricardo, among others, wanted to reduce the role of the state to an absolute minimum. It is not the case, however, that they argued for no state at all. There were certain functions, essential to the operation of the market, that only the state could perform, for example the provision of law and order, defence, the protection of 'inalienable' property rights, and the maintenance of the value of the currency.

'The International Man': Richard Cobden

The chief exponent of the classical liberal doctrine that free trade leads to peace is Richard Cobden. Indeed, he is often credited with being the first person to politicise Smith's doctrine, in that he devoted much of his life to describing and propagating the political virtues that flowed from *laissez-faire* and free trade. A member of parliament for Stockport (and later Camden Town), and leader with John Bright of the 'Manchester Capitalists' and the Anti-Corn Law League, Cobden argued that the most important prerequisite of international peace was unfettered commerce between nations.

He advanced two arguments. Firstly, like Smith and Ricardo before him, he argued that commerce made societies mutually dependent on one another. Commerce bound nations together in a common endeavour – the common endeavour of maximising trade and wealth. Peace would result, since all states benefited from a system of free commerce. No state had an interest in breaking these beneficial ties by going to war. Cobden felt that free trade was nothing short of a divine law: 'One country has cotton, another wine, another coal, which is proof that, according to the Divine Order of things, men should fraternise and exchange their goods and thus further Peace and Goodwill on Earth'.[7] Cobden also described free trade, in characteristically grandiloquent terms, as 'God's diplomacy' and 'the grand panacea'. It brought in its wake not only peace but prosperity, liberty, moral improvement and civilisation.

But free trade brought peace in another way. At the heart of Cobden's theory is what Kenneth Waltz has labelled a 'second image' analysis of international relations: the idea that war is a product of the domestic structure or constitution of the state.[8] Cobden believed that conflict and war was a conspiracy of the aristocratic ruling class. This class, in Cobden's view, had an interest in monopoly, protectionism, colonialism, the balance of power and foreign intervention. And these things led to international jealousy, hostility, and, ultimately, to war – from which no one benefited except the ruling classes.

The highly restrictive corn laws were the outstanding symbol of the old order. This high tariff on imported corn not only created hostility and retaliation from corn exporting countries, but also raised the costs of domestic industry; created a shortage of sterling abroad, thereby hindering British exporters; lined the pockets of the ruling elite, thereby consolidating their power; and enabled the ruling elite to continue their military, colonial and diplomatic adventures which, since they did not pay, landed the country deeper and deeper into debt. In addition, involvement in war enabled the ruling class to justify increases in taxation, which further eroded the capital available for investment in, and the production of, socially more useful commodities.

Cobden argued that free trade would undermine the political dominance of the old order. Restrictions on commerce would be eradicated, and interference, meddling and coercion by the state would be superseded by the principle 'as little intercourse as possible betwixt *governments*, as much connection as possible between the *nations* of the world'.[9]

The Impact of Economic Liberalism

The impact of economic liberalism has been very considerable, if not in the pure form advocated by Cobden. Firstly, free trade became one of the central goals of British foreign policy between 1846 and 1880. During this time, Britain had far more influence than any other power on the shape of the international economic order. Other countries, advanced and backward, were encouraged and cajoled to open their markets. The gold standard ensured international economic stability, if sometimes at a high domestic social price (see Chapter 5). The world went from economic strength to strength under the 'benign financial autocracy' of the City of London.[10]

Secondly, from the 1880s onwards there was a general drift towards protectionism, especially with respect to colonial possessions. Free trade was suspended during the First World War. Economic controls were introduced by all the major combatants, as was planning for the production of vital war materials. The status of *laissez-faire* and free trade as the normal method of economic organisation was not, however, seriously challenged. The third of President Wilson's 'Fourteen Points' called for the removal, as far as possible, of economic barriers between nations. But despite widespread intellectual adherence to these principles, most countries, due to the devastation they had suffered during the war, and the political need to give employment a high priority, found it difficult to implement them in practice. It should also be noted that the notorious reparations clauses of the Treaty of Versailles were in direct contradiction to the principle of free trade: a throw-back, indeed, to the dark days of mercantilism.[11] In addition, the new system had from the outset one notable defector. Bolshevik Russia denounced all treaties, including commercial ones, as instruments of capitalism, and condemned free trade as the doctrine of the bourgeois imperialist powers.

Thirdly, economic liberalism formed an essential part of the diplomacy of US Secretary of State Cordell Hull in the 1940s, and the international economic order created after the Second World War was founded on its principles: openness; non-discrimination; multilateralism; and convertibility of currencies. More than anyone involved in the negotiations at Dumbarton Oaks, San Francisco, Bretton Woods and Havana, Hull held faith with the classical liberal vision. This was in sharp contrast to Keynes, the chief British negotiator, who advocated *inter alia* state trading in commodities, international cartels for 'necessary' manufactures, and quantitative import restrictions for non-essential manufactures.

What John Gerrard Ruggie has termed the 'compromise of embedded liberalism' has been the cornerstone of the international economic order since 1945.[12] Notwithstanding the intellectual victories of the New Right of the 1980s, and the subsequent deregulation of many aspects of economic life – especially financial markets – around the world, the multilateral management of the international marketplace, through a wide variety of international institutions and agreements, is still the dominant norm of the system. There is room for argument about the precise ratio of 'state' to 'market' in the current configuration of the international economic system, but the centrality of liberal ideas of one kind or another cannot be denied. Indeed, with the end of the Cold War and the collapse of Soviet communism, Francis Fukuyama proclaimed the 'unabashed victory' of economic liberalism as a central part of his thesis on the 'End of History'.[13]

It is certainly true that, for the time being, economic liberalism does not have any serious ideological rivals. But Fukuyama's bold thesis needs to be qualified in at least two ways. First, it should be noted that economic liberalism comes in a wide variety of forms. The aggressively 'individualistic capitalism' of the US (where private profit comes first, and the well-being of the nation is a by-product), can be contrasted with the 'collective capitalism' of Japan and the newly industrialising countries of East and South East Asia (where the nation comes first, and private profit second). This, in turn, can be contrasted with the 'welfare capitalism' of the EU, characterised by a social contract between capital, labour and the state (though one, it should be noted, that has suffered considerable erosion in recent years with the ascendancy of free-market thinking and the gathering pace of globalisation).

Second, a distinction should be made between economic liberalism in theory and economic liberalism in practice. While virtually all of the world's leading politicians extol the virtues of free trade, every government without exception protects its home market from foreign competition to a lesser or (usually) greater degree. There is therefore a wide gulf between the rhetoric and the reality of economic liberalism.[14]

The Prevalence of Protectionism

One of the main institutions of the post-war order, the General Agreement on Tariffs and Trade (GATT), has been highly successful in bringing down tariffs on manufactured goods (see Chapter 6). Yet a wide range of non-tariff barriers (NTBs) have grown up in their place, including voluntary export restraints (VERs), orderly marketing agreements (OMAs), so-called 'anti-dumping' and licensing laws, and onerous health and safety regulations.[15] Why, despite speaking the language of free trade, have states without exception continued to employ protectionist measures? The broad answer is that they do not have the courage of their convictions: while subscribing to the theory of free trade, believing in its general virtues, they constantly find it difficult to implement in practice, exceptions to the general rule always seeming to get in the way. States have thus resorted to protectionist measures of one kind or another to protect a wide variety of industries: 'infant' industries that otherwise would not otherwise get off the ground; 'senile' industries that would otherwise go bust, with dire consequences for jobs; industries of strategic importance, such as steel-making and shipbuilding; industries of cultural importance, such as film-making and agriculture; and industries with political influence, such as French agriculture or American automobiles. They have also resorted to protectionist measures for a host of other more general reasons, such as to stave off balance-of-payments crises, to increase government revenue and to reduce unemployment.

To these market distortions must be added the myriad ways in which modern governments intervene in order to make their economies more competitive. Such measures include: strategic trade policies; education and training policies; tax holidays; enterprise zones; export credits; subsidies; industrial policies; and regional policies.

Rethinking Free Trade?

Given the numerous, often subtle and complex ways in which the modern state interferes with the economic life of its citizens, some analysts have contended that the concept of free trade needs to be reformulated. Free trade, they say, no longer has the same meaning as it did in the days of Smith, Ricardo and Cobden.

It is now widely accepted that comparative advantage no longer depends on natural endowments but is policy-created. There are some obvious exceptions to this rule: mineral extraction; the growing of vines, olives, citrus and tropical fruits; tobacco and cotton growing; various kinds of farming, and so on. But the general point stands: the 'commanding heights' of the modern industrial economy are dominated by such products as consumer electronics, financial services and information technology. The key factor of production in all of these industries is knowledge. In principle, the products they produce can be manufactured or delivered anywhere in the world. The key variable is the 'policy environment' – a favourable tax regime, the availability of skilled and relatively cheap labour, political stability, support for 'enterprise', capital mobility – of one location vis-a-vis another.

Given this secular change in the nature and operation of the modern economy, the traditional notion of free trade becomes problematic. The old idea was that resources should flow to those parts of the world where they could be most effectively utilised, free of the distortions to market forces wrought by governments. But now governments are involved in creating the very conditions which determine whether such resources can be used effectively or not. They are, for good or ill, an intrinsic part of the economic landscape. This presents a huge problem for the traditional notion of free trade, predicated as it is on the absence of the state and other public authorities from the equation. Free trade meant trade 'free' of government meddling: the free flow of resources according to 'rational', that is apolitical, economic criteria. Regardless of whether they existed in the past, the existence of such rational, apolitical, economic criteria can certainly be doubted today. To take one example: to what extent can the state provide education and training before such provision becomes an unfair subsidy of domestic producers and exporters? If knowledge is a key factor of production, the provision of education and training by the state – in particular university education and advanced, highly specialised, technical training – becomes, according to the old model, irrational interference in the free working of the market. There must be something very wrong, some have contended, with a concept the application of which to current circumstances leads to such perverse conclusions.[16]

Cobden and Peace

If economic liberalism has played such a large role in shaping the contemporary world, why, it might be asked, has this world been so bloody and conflictual? Why has not free trade brought peace? One answer to this, of course, is that free trade has never been achieved. Although it is true that, at the beginning of the twenty-first century, we have freer trade in more goods and services than we have had at any time since the late nineteenth century, it is also true that many 'market imperfections' exist, and governments continue to 'interfere' with the operation of the market in all sorts of complex and often subtle ways: perhaps inevitably so.

Doubt can also be cast on the validity of Cobden's original thesis. It can certainly be cast on its relevance to contemporary circumstances.

It now seems clear, for example, that commerce and interdependence do not in themselves lead to peace. Indeed, greater commerce leads to greater contact and communication, and more, not less, opportunity for tension and disagreement.[17] Yet it is true that commerce and interdependence can contribute to peace indirectly by enabling states to increase their prosperity. If states are increasing their prosperity they are more likely to be stable domestically and less likely to seek revision of the status quo internationally. Commerce also gives states access to commodities vital to their well-being that they cannot produce themselves. They do not, therefore, have to fight in order to get them.

Yet there may be certain respects in which the effects of economic liberalism on peace are not so favourable. The extension of economic interests worldwide in the search for markets and fields of investment requires the extension of a certain political order. If that order is threatened by non-liberal states, protection of such 'global' economic interests may require the use of force. Force has been used by liberal states, for example, to protect direct foreign investments (witness the myriad interventions by the US in the domestic affairs of Latin American countries), and to ensure access to vital raw materials (witness US involvement in the Middle East, a result in part of Western reliance on a stable supply of oil at stable prices). In addition, liberal societies believe in freedom to travel. Citizens of these societies are the principal users of the world's airlines. They are therefore vulnerable to terrorist attacks and hostage-taking. Force may be used to rescue victims, protect potential victims and deter such undesirable activities.

More autarkic, mercantilist states are not so vulnerable as liberal states in these respects. They therefore, perhaps paradoxically, have less reason to resort to arms, and not more, as Cobden maintained. This is one of the reasons why Robert Gilpin has argued that, on balance, 'benign mercantilism' may be a more desirable approach to international economic relations than economic liberalism.[18]

One final point should be made on this issue. There is a sense in which economic liberalism in its purer forms depends on the conversion of all states to the liberal faith. All states have to be liberal for liberalism to work as intended. This is one of the reasons it has been condemned as utopian.

There is a curious parallel here with that other grand, totalising doctrine – Marxism. Lenin argued that revolution everywhere was the condition for the success of revolution anywhere. As with liberalism, all countries have to be Marxist for Marxism to work as intended. For this reason, Marxism too has been condemned as utopian.

Notes on Chapter 2

1   J.M. Keynes, 'My Early Beliefs', in *The Collected Writings of John Maynard Keynes*, ed. Donald Moggridge and Elizabeth Johnson, X, *Essays in Biography* (London, Macmillan, 1972), 433–50; J.A. Hobson, *Confessions of an Economic Heretic* (London, George Allen and Unwin, 1938).

2   See David Mitrany, *A Working Peace System* (London, Royal Institute of International Affairs, 1943); *The Functional Theory of Politics* (London, Martin Robertson, 1975).

3   See David Long, 'J.A. Hobson and Economic Internationalism', in David Long and Peter Wilson (eds), *Thinkers of the Twenty Years' Crisis* (Oxford, Clarendon Press, 1995), 179–83.

4   See Razeen Sally, *Classical Liberalism and International Economic Order* (London, Routledge, 1998), passim.

5   Quoted in Robert Heilbronner, *The Worldly Philosophers* (London, Penguin, 1983), 43.

6   For a more detailed account see Robert Gilpin, *The Political Economy of International Relations* (Princeton, NJ, Princeton University Press, 1987), 26–31, 172–80.

7   Quoted in Peter Cain, 'Capitalism, War and Internationalism in the Thought of Richard Cobden', *British Journal of International Studies* 5 (1979), 240.

8   Kenneth Waltz, *Man, the State, and War: A Theoretical Analysis* (New York, NY, Columbia University Press, 1959).

9   Quoted in Cain, 'Capitalism, War and Internationalism', 238.

10 See E.H.Carr, *The Twenty Years' Crisis*, 2nd Edition (London, Macmillan, 1946), 224; *The New Society* (London, Macmillan, 1951), Chs 3 and 5; *Nationalism and After* (London, Macmillan, 1945), 6–17.

11 Reparations is the term given to indemnities traditionally levied by victorious powers on defeated powers in compensation for damage done in war. The reparation clauses of the Versailles Treaty were a source of bitter resentment during the inter-war period. Germany was required to pay the huge sum of £6,500 million, which Keynes

famously decried as unsustainable and, in an interdependent world economy, counter-productive. Germany's allies were also required to hand over crippling sums. The debts were partly responsible for the financial collapse and ensuing monetary inflation in Germany and Austria in 1923 and 1929. In response to these crises, payments were rescheduled in the Dawes Plan of 1924 and the Young Plan of 1929, but effectively abandoned following the Lausanne Pact of 1932.

12 This involved embedding the operation of international market forces in a multilaterally agreed system of rules and norms. It was an attempt to avoid the subordination of domestic economic life to exchange-rate stability on the one hand, and the sacrifice of international stability to domestic policy autonomy on the other. For further details, see Chapter 5 and John Gerard Ruggie, 'International Regimes, Transactions, and Change: Embedded Liberalism in the Postwar Economic Order', *International Organization* 36 (1982).

13 Francis Fukuyama, 'The End of History?', *The National Interest* 16 (Summer 1989), 3–18.

14 See Chris Brown, '"Really Existing Liberalism" and International Order', *Millennium: Journal of International Studies* 21, 3 (1992).

15 VERs and OMAs are euphemistic terms for the negotiated agreements between the older industrial economies and the newly industrialised economies which limit the quantity of certain manufactures (notably motor cars) that can be exported in a given period from the latter to the former. These agreements, still in existence in many instances, have been weakly justified by reference to the 'serious injury to domestic industry' clause (Article XIX) of GATT.

16 See Ronald Dore, 'Rethinking Free Trade', in Roger Morgan (ed.), *New Diplomacy In the Post-Cold War World* (Basingstoke, Macmillan, 1993).

17 This point is well brought out in Jaap de Wilde, *Saved from Oblivion: Interdependence Theory in the First Half of the Twentieth Century* (Aldershot, Dartmouth Press, 1991), 8–40.

18 Robert Gilpin, *The Political Economy of International Relations* (Princeton, NJ, Princeton University Press, 1986), 394–408.

Select Bibliography

Cain, P.J., 'Capitalism, War and Internationalism in the Thought of Richard Cobden', *British Journal of International Studies* 5 (1979). Excellent short account of the political thought of Richard Cobden.

Fukuyama, Francis, *The End of History and the Last Man* (New York, NY, The Free Press, 1992). Development of the article that took the world – or at least Washington – by storm in 1989. Neo-Hegelian analysis of the triumph of economic and political liberalism.

Gallagher, J. and Robinson, R., 'The Imperialism of Free Trade', *Economic History Review* 4, 1 (1953). Seminal article on the relationship between free trade and empire. Essential reading.

Gilbert, Felix, 'The "New Diplomacy" of the Eighteenth Century', *World Politics* 4, 1 (1951). Classic article tracing the idea that war and conquest are irrational and peace and free trade rational back to the philosophers and physiocrats of the eighteenth century.

Hayek, F.A., *The Road To Serfdom* (London, Ark Paperbacks, 1986 [1944]). Classic attack on Marxists, social democrats, Fabians, state socialists and other 'totalitarians in our midst'. Powerful and eloquent restatement of the virtues of classical liberalism.

Heilbronner, Robert, *The Worldly Philosophers* (London, Penguin, 1983). Rightly celebrated overview of economic thought. Trenchant and engaging.

Hobson, J.A., *Richard Cobden: The International Man* (London, Ernest Benn, 1968 [1919]). Collection of Cobden's most important writings and speeches, and commentary from one of his foremost ideological descendants.

Keohane, Robert O., 'International Liberalism Reconsidered', in J. Dunn (ed.), *The Economic Limits to Modern Politics* (Cambridge, Cambridge University Press, 1990). Balanced recent account of the strengths and weaknesses of economic liberal from a contemporary point of view.

Keynes, J.M., *The End of Laissez-Faire* (London, Hogarth Press, 1925). Confessional, melancholic, and somewhat premature farewell to the unregulated market.

Markwell, D.J., 'J.M. Keynes, Idealism, and the Economic Bases of Peace', in David Long and Peter Wilson (eds), *Thinkers of the Twenty Years' Crisis* (Oxford, Clarendon Press, 1995). Highly useful overview of the great economist's thought on war and peace.

Mayall, James, 'The Liberal Economy', in James Mayall (ed.), *The Community of States* (London, George Allen and Unwin, 1983). Valuable introduction to the tensions between a society of states and a world economy of firms and individuals.

Mitrany, David, *A Working Peace System* (London, Royal Institute for International Affairs, 1943). Classic statement of the functionalist approach to international organisation. Sets out a non-state, non-market alternative vision of world order.

Sally, Razeen, *Classical Liberalism and International Economic Order* (London, Routledge, 1998). Erudite essays on the chief exponents of classical political economy.

Walter, Andrew, 'Adam Smith and the Liberal Tradition in International Relations', *Review of International Studies* 22, 1 (1996). Argues that Adam Smith is more of a realist in his approach to international politics than is conventionally supposed.

CHAPTER 3

Economic Nationalism

For liberals, commerce is a great force for good. It is a great emancipating, enriching, civilising and pacifying force – providing it is allowed to flow freely, or at least as freely as social and political circumstances allow.

For nationalists, this is a delusion. Economics and politics, according to the nationalist, can never be separated. The economic system is always created in the image of the dominant, hegemonic, power. By the same token, that power acquires its hegemonic status at least partly through its ability to manipulate economic forces to its advantage.

Terminology

Before discussing the tenets of economic nationalism, and its forebears, it may be helpful to say a few words on the terminology used in debates about this doctrine. Much confusion results from the fact that in such debates, both within and without the academy, a number of terms are employed which, on the surface, seem to have more or less the same meaning. It is important to stress that terms such as 'mercantilism', 'neo-mercantilism', 'economic nationalism', and 'protectionism', are not necessarily interchangeable. Some authors draw subtle but important distinctions between them.

Mercantilism, economic nationalism and 'neo-mercantilism' are often used to characterise certain historical *periods* in the world economy. Generally speaking, from the sixteenth to the late eighteenth century is known as the mercantilist period (or the period of 'classical'

34

mercantilism). The 'long nineteenth century' (1815–1914) is known as the economic liberal period or 'liberal interlude'. The 1930s are known as the period of economic nationalism. The post-war era from 1945 to the early 1970s is known as the Bretton Woods era, or that of 'embedded liberalism'. The 1980s have been widely termed the period of 'neo-mercantilism', 'neo-protectionism', or the 'new economic nationalism' due to increasing resort to novel kinds of protection (especially NTBs to trade such as VERs, anti-dumping legislation, and discriminatory government procurement policies). The period since the conclusion of the Uruguay Round of trade talks in the early 1990s, coinciding with the collapse of communism in the Soviet Union and Eastern Europe, and the deregulation of world financial markets, has not yet acquired the distinction of having its own appellation. The 'era of globalisation' might be a good bet.

But it is important to note that these 'isms' are also *doctrines*. That is, they are more or less coherent and distinct bodies of thought on how international economic relations actually work and how they should work. Protectionism, however, is the exception. This is not a doctrine but a general term for a range of measures that states can take to insulate its home market from foreign competition. Protectionism is, therefore, far from synonymous with mercantilism and economic nationalism. Although wide in variety, protectionist measures – tariffs, quotas, subsidies, anti-dumping laws, VERs, OMAs – are not the only measures that can be taken by an economically nationalistic or mercantilist state. Others include currency manipulation, 'Buy British' or 'Buy Canadian'-type campaigns, boycotts, tax holidays, dumping and war.

Classical Mercantilism

Classical mercantilism consists of a set of implicit or explicit beliefs of statesmen, merchants and political economists that were particularly prevalent from the sixteenth to the late eighteenth century. The following four beliefs are central. First, classical mercantilists held that the acquisition of wealth is a vital interest, not only for its own sake but in order to enhance state power. At a time when wars were fought by mercenary armies, the size of a state's 'war chest' was crucial. Princes and sovereigns needed a healthy war chest to pursue their ambitions, enhance their power and prestige, and ultimately in order to survive. Modern-day mercantilists continue to emphasise this relationship, arguing that a country's industrial strength and its security are intimately linked. Secondly, classical mercantilists believed that wealth consists of precious metals – the accumulation of gold and silver bullion – and is therefore finite. It follows from this that one state's gain is another state's loss and vice versa. Economics becomes a 'zero-sum' game.

Not surprisingly, given these first two beliefs, the pattern of international economic relations during the mercantilist period was fiercely competitive. Commercial rivalries often degenerated into war. Jean Baptiste Colbert (1619–83), statesman and finance minister of Louis XIV of France, described commerce as 'perpetual combat in peace and war among the nations of Europe as to who will gain the upper hand'.

Thirdly, classical mercantilism maintained that the first task of foreign economic policy is to secure a favourable balance of trade. Colbert said that 'it is only the abundance of money in a state that makes the difference as to its greatness and its power'. As a consequence of this view, exports were encouraged and imports discouraged. Exports were encouraged to increase the flow of bullion into the state, imports discouraged to keep to a minimum the flow of bullion out of the state. But commerce was not the only means by which money could be accumulated. It could also be accumulated through plunder (that is seizing by force property belonging to other nations). Significantly, no moral distinction was drawn between the two. Mercantilists held that both exchange and plunder were legitimate methods of amassing wealth. The only issue for mercantilists was the relative effectiveness of one method vis-a-vis another. Sir Josiah Child, seventeenth century merchant and economist, once said that 'all trade is a kind of warfare'.

Finally, classical mercantilists held that state regulation of economic activity is necessary and normal. That they should believe so is not surprising. The extension of the sovereign's power over the economic life of his subjects was one of the hallmarks of the transition from feudalism to modernity. The criss-crossing and overlapping jurisdictions of the feudal period were gradually replaced by the single jurisdiction of a sovereign power. In practice, this meant that, certainly by the late sixteenth century, sovereigns almost everywhere in

Europe claimed the exclusive right, within their territory, to raise taxes, impose duties, grant franchises, protect property rights and so on. Religious authorities – clerics, bishops, the Papacy – and local lords and barons were increasingly cut out of the equation. The regulation of economic activity is thus inextricably linked with the rise of the modern state. It should also be noted that these newly acquired sovereign prerogatives were not seen as 'interference' in the 'natural' working of the economy. Rather, they were immutable facts of life to be neither celebrated nor regretted.

Classical mercantilists, therefore, rejected the separation of economics and politics that underpins classical liberalism. They also reject the idea of a pre-existing harmony of interest between individuals or between nations. The economic realm, in their view, is indistinguishable from the political realm, and it is a realm of un-relenting struggle. Hence, Jacob Viner's characterisation of mercantilism as the pursuit of both power and plenty. Power was seen as a means to plenty; plenty was seen as a means to power. Both were entirely legitimate means and ends of policy.[1]

Economic Nationalism

Economic nationalism is the form that mercantilism has taken in an age of popular sovereignty and mass democracy – in an age, that is, in which government is conducted, at least in theory, in the interests of the people. The doctrine began to emerge in the early nineteenth century, partly as a product of the growth of political nationalism – the belief that nations exist objectively and have a right to self-determination – unleashed by the French Revolution; and partly as a reaction to the rise to prominence of economic liberalism (especially after economic liberalism became the ideology of the strongest economic power – Britain – in the mid-nineteenth century). Since then, economic nationalism has taken a number of different forms. One could contrast, for example, the aggressive economic nationalism of Johan Fichte in the early nineteenth century – the core ideas of which were later applied by Dr Schacht, Hitler's finance minister, in his attempt to build a 'new economic order' based on German supremacy in Europe – with the more defensive economic nationalism of modern-day writers such as Robert Gilpin. For Fichte, the economic stance of the nation was dictated by the political environment in which it operated. In a hostile environment of competing states, an aspiring nation, such as Germany in the nineteenth century, had no choice but to pursue an uncompromising economic foreign policy. Nationhood could not be acquired on the cheap, without injury to other nations. Its achievement and maintenance required unshakeable will and determination. Gilpin, on the other hand, advocates 'benign mercantilism'. The essence of this doctrine is that states regularly have to protect their economies from foreign competition in order to maintain high levels of employment, and general economic and social stability. The point of such measures is not to injure other parties, but to defend oneself. Modern democratic states in particular, he says, have no choice but to protect their citizens from the sometimes cruel vicissitudes of the international marketplace.[2]

Despite these wide differences, however, all economic nationalists contend that state intervention is needed to secure three goals: national identity and solidarity; national welfare; and national security.

The emphasis that economic nationalists have put on these goals is clearly revealed in the way that they have responded to the theory and practice of economic liberalism. Firstly, they have been sceptical of the notion that left to itself the market will, in the long run, reach a state of 'equilibrium' in which supply and demand of all goods and services in the marketplace are perfectly balanced. In their view, this notion is not so much theoretically invalid as socially and politically unrealistic. How long will it take before the market reaches equilibrium? Five years? Ten years? Twenty? As Keynes once sardonically said, 'In the long run we're all dead'. Governments cannot, in the opinion of economic nationalists, wait until markets achieve equilibrium. They must intervene. One reason for this is that the twentieth-century state, as a result of the rise of popular sovereignty and mass democracy, has increasingly assumed responsibility for the social and economic, as well as the physical, security of its citizens. Once this is done the state has no choice, Gilpin asserts, but to seek to cushion its citizens from the adverse effects of an interdependent international economy. If they do nothing, their popularity and ultimately their legitimacy will be undermined.

Secondly, economic nationalists have been sceptical of both the feasibility and desirability of free trade. E.H. Carr described free trade as 'an imaginary condition that has never existed'. This contrasts sharply with the fact of the sovereign state, and the fact of a plurality of states existing in an anarchical international system; that is, a system which lacks a central government. In such a system, states have to look after themselves. They cannot expect anyone else to do it for them. As a consequence, they are far more concerned with their own wealth, or their wealth vis-a-vis major rivals, than with the wealth of the world as a whole. For nationalists it is relative wealth and relative power that counts. Hence their contempt for the 'cosmopolitan' or 'utopian' liberal who looks at the international economy in terms not of national but of global welfare, and in doing so wishes away the nation-state. But the nation-state cannot be wished away, say nationalists, because it is the focal point of peoples' loyalties, and the central repository of power in the international system.

Carr also described free trade as the doctrine of the economic top dog. Free trade, he asserted, was not a universal interest (as Britain, France, the US and their official and unofficial 'utopian' spokesmen claimed during the inter-war period), but merely the particular interest of the strongest trading nations. This was because they were the ones who, because of their superior economic strength and efficiency, stood to benefit most from the existence of a free trading order. This line of attack has deep roots in economic nationalist thought, and can be traced back to the writings of Alexander Hamilton, and especially to those of Friedrich List.[3]

Thirdly, economic nationalists contend that liberals under-estimate the degree of interference in economic affairs required to preserve national security. Economic liberals, of course, do not ignore the question of national security. Smith declared that 'defence is more important than opulence'. He also threw his weight behind the navigation acts, a series of acts of parliament of the eighteenth century designed to protect the British shipbuilding industry and thus preserve Britain's maritime supremacy. Similarly, Cobden, though a non-interventionist, was certainly no pacifist. He was a firm supporter, for example, of the 'two-power standard' (the idea, central to British foreign policy in the nineteenth century, that the Royal Navy should be at least as strong as the navies of the next two strongest powers combined). However, economic nationalists have gone much further in their estimations of what an effective defence involves. They have naturally called for the protection of armaments industries. They have also called for the protection of the shipbuilding and iron and steel industries, coal mining, agriculture, high-technology industries, and even textile manufacture (to maintain morale, for instance, during a blockade). Obviously, the criteria for determining a strategically important good have changed *pari passu* with changes in the character of war (from small-scale conflicts between mercenaries to large-scale conflicts involving whole nations). Coal, for example, is not strategically important nowadays, but it was vital a hundred years ago. Oil was of minor importance a hundred years ago, today it is vital. The important point is that all economic nationalists define 'strategic importance' much more inclusively than liberals. Indeed this has often led to calls for a strategy of autarky.

Finally, some economic nationalists have opposed what might be called 'cosmopolitan liberalism' in principle; that is, not merely because leaving things to the market, they believe, will have certain undesirable practical consequences (for example the collapse of certain industries). This is because they feel that uncontrolled commerce can lead to the culture of the state being undermined and its national identity eroded. Romantic nationalists such as Fichte saw the nation as being prior to and constitutive of the individual. The nation, like the family, constituted an organic whole: it was a good in itself. It should therefore free itself from foreign influence as much as possible. He advocated national planning and the progressive reduction of foreign trade. Essential goods and raw materials previously acquired through trade would be provided for by the gradual expansion of the nation to its 'natural frontiers'.

Friedrich List

Few economic nationalists went as far as Fichte. List, author of *The National System of Political Economy* (1840), the most important economic nationalist text of the nineteenth century, put forward a strategy of 'selective self-reliance'. He argued that the pressure on developing countries to enter into an international economy dominated and shaped by the most developed countries was great. Such pressure, however, should be resisted, because integration would lead to dependence. Free trade, claimed List, was simply a device by which industrially advanced countries – Britain – maintained hegemony over newly industrialising countries – Germany. Latecomers, like Germany, should therefore pursue a policy of state-led national development involving protection, investment in infra-structure, the creation of a national system of education, and the formation of 'customs unions' with states at a similar stage of development.

For List, in contrast to Cobden, the power of producing wealth was infinitely more important than the wealth itself. Not surprisingly, therefore, he felt that the most important economic task of the state was to protect 'infant industries'. Only by ensuring that these young industries got off the ground could the future productive power of the nation be ensured.

It is important to note, however, that List advocated selective, not indiscriminate, protection. The state should not be gulled into protecting any industry at any price. On the contrary, it should protect only those industries earmarked for such privileged treatment according to a previously drawn-up national strategic plan.

It is also important to note that List did not reject economic liberalism in its entirety. In sharp contrast to Fichte, he felt that international trade was in the main a beneficial activity. But it was one from which weaker states sometimes had to abstain selectively in order to maintain their independence. Once an industry had reached an appropriate level of development, however, it should, indeed must, enter the international marketplace. This was the only way of ensuring that a country's industries did not become 'artificial' and that they kept pace with 'international standards'.

This partial acceptance of the benefits of market economics is evident in List's proposals for a German Zollverein, or customs union. He opposed the complicated system of tariff and custom duties that the various German states of the time maintained against each other. He proposed that they unify their tariffs and import levies into a single system. Members of the Zollverein would by such means protect themselves from foreign competition, especially from Britain. But competition would freely take place within the Zollverein. He thus sought to promote wealth through selective protection but within a competitive market system. This still constitutes the model of regional economic integration that informs such associations as the EU, the North American Free Trade Agreement (NAFTA), and the Economic Community of West African States (ECOWAS).

From an examination of Friedrich List's thought it can be seen that certain forms of economic nationalism are not necessarily incompatible with free trade. The nationalist can quite happily advocate free trade if he thinks it is consistent with the national interest of his country. By the same token, the supposed economic liberal sometimes uses the language of free trade as a cloak to conceal the pursuit of narrow national interest. If one looks closely at Cobden's writings, for example, one sees that one of his main concerns was to keep Britain 'in the front rank of nations' and to ensure her 'industrial predominance'. This is revealing, since it shows that even a true believer like Cobden – a man who elevated free trade into a kind of religion – championed free trade at least in part because it was a particular British interest. The disguise was all the more convincing for the unselfconscious way in which it was worn.

Economic Nationalism and the Post-war International Economic Order

The legacy of these ideas in the contemporary world is greater than sometimes imagined. The post-war international economic order, though almost invariably characterised as 'liberal', is in reality founded on a compromise between economic liberalism and economic nationalism. The idea was to combine the maximum degree of openness internationally (by progressively reducing barriers to trade, ending trade discrimination, establishing a multilateral payments system and so on) with a large degree of domestic autonomy (to manage 'demand', maintain full employment, build a welfare state, and stabilise prices).

This compromise is strongly implicit in the (1947) GATT. Whilst committing member states to the progressive reduction of barriers to trade, tariffs in particular, it also permits states to adopt protectionist measures in a number of circumstances. Article XII permits protection in the event of a chronic balance-of-payments crisis. This amounts to an implicit acknowledgement that the political commitment to full employment should, ultimately, take priority over the economic principle of comparative advantage. A payments crisis is a sign that an economy has become uncompetitive. Such an eventuality usually requires strong medicine to put things right. This often involves raising interest rates, cutting public expenditure, applying wage controls, devaluing the currency, and other methods to cut imports, boost exports and generally channel resources away from consumption towards investment. But Article XII allows states to postpone the day when such medicine needs to be taken – perhaps indefinitely. Protection is a relatively easy option for a government faced with a balance-of-payments crisis: one could say that it enables it to solve a short-term political problem – caused, say, by rising unemployment – by leaving the economic problem for some other government to deal with in the future. Article XVIII allows protection for infant industries for purposes of national economic development. Article XIX allows protection in the wake of unforeseen or 'serious injury' to domestic producers. Article XXI allows states to take protective measures for reasons of national security. And, perhaps most crucially, Article XXIV permits preferential trade (not permitted in any of the other articles) if the object is to create a customs union or free-trade area.

These articles demonstrate that, from the outset, the post-war liberal economic order made a number of substantial concessions to economic nationalism. Article XXIV alone suggests that the GATT agreement owes almost as much to List as it does to Cobden and Smith.

It should be stressed that universal free trade is not a stated aim of GATT. On the contrary, GATT implicitly concedes the right of states to protect their own markets. Its objects are the eradication of discriminatory treatment in international commerce, and 'substantial reductions' in, not elimination of, barriers to trade.

Economic Nationalism and War

The conventional wisdom has it that whereas economic liberalism leads to peace, economic nationalism leads to war. Protectionism, it is widely held, leads to retaliation, this leads to the growth of mutual animosity and distrust, which in turn leads to the greater likelihood of conflict and war. This wisdom can be challenged on a number of grounds.

Firstly, one has to take into account modern conditions. All the main industrial countries of today have so much to lose from war that war between them seems highly improbable. The costs, and therefore the improbability, of war are raised further when one bears in mind that a war between today's industrial powers would be one conducted with incredibly destructive weapons. The fact that a war between major industrial powers has not been fought for over 50 years, despite many differences and disagreements between them, provides at least partial evidence of an acute awareness of the risks and costs involved.

Secondly, the contention that increased protection leads to decreased trade and therefore an increase in economic instability and political tension can be refuted. Susan Strange has argued that the importance of the relationship between protectionism and trade is frequently overstated. GATT is often lauded for bringing about the vast increase in international trade that has occurred since 1945, and in so doing, for contributing to the generally peaceful relations that have prevailed between the world's major powers. But according to Strange, the availability of finance and credit accounts for the growth in post-war world trade, not the progressive reduction of trade barriers through GATT. As a consequence, GATT should not be praised for contributing to peace; nor should the name of protection be further besmirched. In Strange's view, price has not been the crucial factor in determining patterns of trade in the post-war period, but design, quality and performance. In other words, the goods that have sold best in world markets have not necessarily been the cheapest ones but those demanded by an increasingly sophisticated and discerning consumer. As a result, manipulating the marginal price of a good through the imposition of a tariff or restricting its supply through the imposition of a quota has not had the long-term effect on trade that many have supposed. In addition, the changing structure of international production has enabled firms to circumvent tariffs and other restrictive measures in a range of subtle ways. The growth of intra-firm trade (i.e. trade in goods and services between different branches of the same, conglomeratic, firm) and international production for the world market, for example, has enabled firms to circumvent protectionist measures by locating the manufacturing process in a variety of countries, the final product emanating from the one most conducive to maximising sales and profits.[4]

Thirdly, much depends on whether protectionist measures are offensive or defensive in nature and in intent. The vast majority of measures taken since the early 1980s have been of the latter, defensive, kind. Their object has been to defend jobs rather than purposefully to injure another country's economy. The transparency of many of the measures nowadays imposed to restrict imports is evidence of this fact. So, too, is the fact that many such restrictions, such as OMAs and VERs, are negotiated between the parties in advance.

Cordell Hull's famous statement that 'when goods can't cross borders, soldiers will' is thus at best a half-truth. The pursuit of economic nationalist policies may turn a healthy competitive relationship into an unhealthy adversarial one. But there are many other factors involved, not least the type of economic nationalist policies being pursued. The contention, therefore, that increased protection inevitably leads to decreased trade and an increase in the likelihood of conflict and war is one that needs to be treated with a fair amount of caution.

The Nature of the Terms

Having mentioned the good reputation of economic liberalism and the rather dark reputation of mercantilism and economic nationalism, a few words of caution should be uttered, by way of conclusion, on the nature of these words. 'Mercantilism' and 'economic nationalism' are not 'value-neutral' terms. They are to some extent 'loaded', that is they carry with them certain inferences or implications of a morally laudable or disreputable kind. 'Mercantilism' was not a term used by mercantilists themselves. Rather, it was a term selected for its negative connotations by later economic liberals in order to characterise a period of thought and practice of which they strongly disapproved. It is thus a pejorative word: a 'boo' word, to employ George Orwell's terminology, not a 'hooray' word.[5]

Economic nationalism is a 'boo' word too. It was popularised by liberal internationalists in the inter-war period in order to condemn, through association with the 'nationalism' that had caused the Great War, the restrictive and 'beggar-thy-neighbour' economic policies adopted by many states in the 1930s that they thought, not entirely errantly, would lead the world into another war. Nowadays, though many statesmen act in economically nationalistic ways, they rarely say that they are doing so, and never describe themselves as 'economic nationalists'. This is because liberals have been so successful in associating 'nationalism' with many of the most terrible ills of the twentieth century. It is also because these statesmen tend to see themselves as good, honest liberals when it comes to trade. It is the others, the foreigners, who are the selfish nationalists. Resort to protectionism is portrayed as a regrettable step, but a necessary one given the anti-social and selfish behaviour of others. Such measures are seen as short-term, to be abandoned as soon as such anti-social behaviour is terminated and any necessary economic adjustments made. Few statesmen see their policies as comprising a blend of economic nationalism and economic liberalism, despite the fact that protectionism and 'neo-protectionism' are without doubt enduring features of the international economic landscape, even in a supposedly 'rapidly globalising' world.

Notes on Chapter 3

1   Jacob Viner, 'Power Versus Plenty as Objectives of Foreign Policy in the Seventeenth and Eighteenth Centuries', *World Politics* I (1948). Carr characterised this as a trade-off between 'guns' and 'butter'. See E.H. Carr, *The Twenty Years' Crisis*, 2nd ed. (London, Macmillan, 1946), 119–20.

2   See Robert Gilpin, *The Political Economy of International Relations* (Princeton, NJ, Princeton University Press, 1987), 394–408.

3   See Alexander Hamilton, 'Report on Manufactures' and Friedrich List, 'Political and Cosmopolitan Economy', in George T. Crane and Abla Amawi (eds), *The Theoretical Evolution of International Political Economy* (Oxford, Oxford University Press, 1991), 35–54. The thought of List is discussed in more detail below.

4   Susan Strange, *States and Markets*, 2nd ed. (London, Pinter, 1995); 'Protectionism and World Politics', *International Organization* 39, 2 (1985).

5   The history of political words can tell us a lot about politics. Imperialism used to be a 'hooray' word but became, around the time of the First World War, a 'boo' word. Idealism used to be a 'boo' word but has recently, since the end of the Cold War, started to become a 'hooray' word. Realism has for most of its life been a 'hooray' word but has recently taken a turn for the worst. Socialism, one of the most prominent 'hooray' words of the twentieth century

(at least for considerable numbers of people), has taken such a terrible turn for the worst that one wonders whether it will ever recover. It is a curious fact, however, that in some shape or form most words usually do.

Select Bibliography

Carr, E.H., *Nationalism and After* (London, Macmillan, 1946). Brilliant short essay. Weaves together the many dimensions of nationalism with beguiling ease. Sanguine on 'After'.

Crane, George T. and Amawi Abla (eds), *The Theoretical Evolution of International Political Economy: A Reader* (Oxford, Oxford University Press, 1991). Useful collection of classic essays and excerpts from classic texts.

Dell, E., *The Politics of Economic Interdependence* (London, Macmillan, 1987).

Keynes, J.M., 'National Self-Sufficiency', *Yale Review* XXII (1933); reprinted in *The Collected Writings of John Maynard Keynes*, ed. Donald Moggridge and Elizabeth Johnson, XXI, (London, Macmillan, 1971–89). The apogee of Keynes's apostasy. Influential essay, written at the height of the Depression, in which he almost entirely abandons his earlier liberal faith.

Krasner, Stephen, *Defending the National Interest: Raw Materials Investments and US Foreign Policy* (Princeton, NJ, Princeton University Press, 1978).

Mayall, James, *Nationalism and International Society* (Cambridge, Cambridge University Press, 1990), especially Chs 3–5. The best modern account of the impact of nationalism on international relations. Especially strong on the compromises between economic nationalism and economic liberalism that states have repeatedly, if often reluctantly, struck in the post-war era.

Seers, Dudley, *The Political Economy of Nationalism* (Oxford, Oxford University Press, 1983). Refined, thought-provoking, lucid analysis.

Strange, Susan, 'Protectionism and World Politics', *International Organization* 39, 2 (1985). Iconoclastic attack on the liberal prejudice against protectionism.

Strange, Susan, 'Defending Benign Mercantilism', *Journal of Peace Research* 25, 3 (1988). Trenchant review of Gilpin.

CHAPTER 4

Marxism and Imperialism

With the completion of the decolonisation process and the collapse of the Soviet Union, it might be said that imperialism is a thing of the past. There are, however, several reasons why it is still an important concept. First, it is the central concept of the Marxist approach to international relations. Second, it has proved to be a remarkably resilient term. Despite the enormous changes in the last hundred years or so in the fortunes of empire as a mode of political organisation, the term is still an important one in the vocabulary of international politics (particularly in the vocabulary of radical states). This constitutes *prima facie* evidence that the term refers to certain enduring features of the international system.

The Problem of Definition

Imperialism is a notoriously difficult term to define. The meanings it has acquired since entering the political lexicon in the mid-nineteenth century are legion. In the early years of its history, 'imperialism' was used to describe the dictatorial form of government practised by Emperor Napoleon III of France. In the 1890s, it was used to describe the attempt by Germany to create a closed economic system protected from foreign competition by high tariff walls – the kind of system advocated by List. Not until the turn of the century did it acquire the meaning that it usually has today: the acquisition and control of undeveloped territories by advanced industrial countries. But conceptual innovation has continued unabated. Lenin famously defined imperialism not as the possession of overseas territories, but as a stage in the evolution of capitalism in his *Imperialism, the Highest Stage of Capitalism*. Half a century later, the social theorist Johan Galtung stretched the concept even further by, in effect, equating it with any form of international inequality.[1]

If we are to get a firm grip on this concept it is important to make a distinction between formal and informal imperialism. The former denotes the acquisition of and direct control over specific territories. This type of imperialism is indistinguishable from colonialism. Both involve overt administrative and political control of colonies, these colonies usually being part of a much wider empire. The latter denotes less explicit, even covert, control, influence or domination. It does not necessarily involve the destruction of a country's formal sovereignty, that is to say its constitutional independence. It can, for instance, take the form of a sphere of influence. It can be a product of unequal bargaining power, enabling one economically powerful state to determine the economic policies of another, much weaker, state. It can be even more diffuse than this: it is sometimes suggested that the US controls a 'transnational empire' by virtue of the strength of its multinational corporations and the influence of its culture.

This distinction between formal and informal imperialism is crucial because much confusion has resulted from a failure to separate them. It has been argued, for example, that Marxist theories of imperialism are invalid because they cannot account for the 'test case' of the 'scramble for Africa' in the 1880s. It is claimed that the growth of monopoly and the massive export of finance capital from the advanced capitalist countries to the unexploited parts of the world – key factors in the Marxist explanation of imperialism – occurred after, not prior to, the scramble. These things cannot, therefore, be said to be a cause.[2]

This may be true. But it does not disprove the Marxist case, since Marxists have been much more interested in informal than formal imperialism. They have paid much greater attention to Asia and Latin America than to Africa. This is significant because Asia was much less formally colonised than Africa, and most Latin American countries achieved formal independence as long ago as the early nineteenth century.

Marxist theories of imperialism have thus been judged on the basis of a definition of imperialism (that is formal as opposed to informal imperialism) that their proponents do not accept, and in the light of evidence from a part of the world (Africa) to which they have paid relatively little attention.³ It would also be true to say that Marxists have tended to view imperialism not simply in terms of a bilateral relationship between two countries, but as a condition of the entire world system.

At this point in the enquiry it might be asked: do the various definitions of imperialism share any common ground? Is it possible to identify any core characteristics? Two propositions can be advanced. First, imperialism involves domination. An imperialistic relationship entails more than 'influence' or 'persuasion', but it does not necessarily entail physical control. Second, imperialism involves domination by economically advanced, or powerful, countries of underdeveloped, or economically weak, countries.

Theories of Imperialism

As well as different definitions of imperialism, there are a number of different theories. Before looking at some of them, it is worth bearing in mind the following two points. Firstly, virtually all theories of imperialism are attempts to explain international political events in terms of economic factors. They are, in brief, economic explanations of foreign policy. Such an explanation has been given for every significant conflict of the twentieth century, from the First and Second World Wars, to the Vietnam War, the Gulf War, and the war between Britain and Argentina in the South Atlantic. The First World War has often been held out as the paradigmatic example of an imperialist war. It was a direct result of the increasingly ferocious competition among the major capitalist powers for new markets, new sources of raw materials and new fields of investment. For many years this was the standard view of the political left, whether Bolshevik, Fabian or Social Democratic. The Second World War has been seen as the culmination of capitalism in crisis. Nazism, Fascism, militarism and other phenomena commonly blamed for the war were merely the pathological manifestations of a decadent and decaying capitalist system. This was the underlying assumption of many of the books published in the 1930s by Victor Gollancz's famous Left Book Club: Nazism, Fascism and militarism were the 'immediate and superficial' causes of the war; the real cause was the 'crisis of capitalism', of which they were the symptoms. Similarly, it has been argued that American intervention in Vietnam was only superficially an attempt to defend democracy and contain the spread of communism. In reality it was an attempt by the US to secure the supply of vital raw materials and maintain its control over essential markets. It was also an attempt to 'make the world safe' for American capitalism. The Gulf War of 1991 has been portrayed as a war fought to ensure the continued flow of cheap oil from the Middle East to the US and her capitalist allies. The sovereignty of Kuwait, it is said, was an incidental factor. The coalition powers were not seriously interested in defending Kuwaiti sovereignty. Nor were they interested, despite strenuous propaganda to the contrary, in promoting democracy and human rights. Kuwait, after all, had no more claim to the status of democracy than her belligerent neighbour, Iraq. Nor did the coalition's other principal ally in the region, Saudi Arabia. If human rights had been an important concern, coalition powers such as the US, Britain and France would not have supported Iraq in her long, bitter and bloody conflict with Iran. Yet this support was substantial, and could not have but assisted the leader of Iraq, Saddam Hussein, in tightening his brutal grip on his people. Even the war between Britain and Argentina over the Falkland Islands in 1982 has been given an economic explanation. Though to many people a straightforward conflict about territory and sovereignty, some have interpreted it as a Thatcherite conspiracy to stave off an almost certain electoral defeat. At the time of the Argentinian invasion, the standing of Thatcher's Conservative government in the opinion polls was at an all-time low. Never had a British government been so unpopular. By going to war – a pointless, anachronistic, imperialist war – she cynically turned the electorate's attention away from unemployment, poverty and inner-city riots. Mrs Thatcher, no political innocent, knew that nothing unites a people like war. By opting for a violent solution to the Falklands dispute, she turned an almost certain electoral defeat into a landslide victory. She thus preserved the political ascendancy of the financial and commercial elite, the interests of whom it is the job of the Conservative Party to defend and promote.

The veracity of such economic explanations of foreign policy need not detain us. The point is to note how popular they are both in 'everyday' and academic debates.

A second preliminary point to make about theories of imperialism is that although most are Marxist in orientation, not all of them are. There is a 'realist' theory of imperialism. According to this theory, imperialism is not a modern but an age-old phenomenon, and it has nothing to do with capitalism or, necessarily, economics. It sees imperialism as an almost natural inclination on the part of independent states towards territorial expansion. International politics is a struggle for power and, in the words of Thucidydes, 'the strong do what they will and the weak do what they must'.[4]

There are also a number of liberal theories. The Austrian economist Joseph Schumpeter, for example, held that capitalism was inherently anti-imperialist. In his view, imperialism was caused by the survival, after the advent of capitalism and industrialism, of certain anti-democratic social groups who had a vested interest in conflict and war. The social groups generated by capitalism – the workers and the bourgeoisie – had no interest in imperial conquest, but sometimes supported it due to the survival of certain irrational, atavistic instincts. These anti-democratic groups and irrational instincts, he felt, would soon disappear from the scene (and imperialism along with them) once capitalism and industrialism took firm root.[5]

J.A. Hobson

In 1902, the English liberal economist and social theorist, J.A. Hobson, published one of the most important works on the subject, *Imperialism: A Study*. Hobson believed that imperialism was a product of novel developments in the structure of advanced capitalist economies. He observed that the economies of the leading capitalist countries were increasingly dominated by monopolies, trusts and cartels. These large businesses were able artificially to increase their profits, since they were not subject to the rigours of the market. Wealth was as a result being concentrated into fewer and fewer hands. Since the wealthy have a high propensity to save, the ratio of saving to consumption in the economy was increasing. But due to the unequal distribution of wealth, and consequently the limited purchasing power of the masses, there was little point in investing these savings domestically. Industrialists and financiers were thus compelled to look overseas for new fields of productive investment.

Hobson also observed that these industrialists and financiers exercised considerable political influence. By pushing a lever here, and pulling a string there, they were able to manipulate state policy. In particular they were able to gear the foreign policy of the state towards opening up these new fields of investment overseas: by peaceful means if possible, by coercion – even direct annexation – if necessary.

In this way the capitalist was able to 'use the public purse for the purposes of private profit'. Indeed, Hobson maintained that 'the growing pressure of the need for foreign investments must be regarded as the most potent and direct influence on our foreign policy'.

It is important to note that although undoubtedly a structural theory, Hobson's theory of imperialism is not a Marxist theory (though it is often erroneously described as such). The key to understanding it is the idea of 'underconsumption'. For Hobson, this was the 'tap-root' of imperialism. His solution was not revolution, but reform, in particular the redistribution of wealth from the rich to the poor. This would not only make society more equal and just, but more prosperous, and it would also remove the need for a costly and dangerous foreign policy of imperialism. Purchasing power would be put into the hands of the masses. The demand for goods and services would increase. Industrialists and financiers would no longer need to look abroad for an outlet for their excess capital. Capital could once more be safely invested at home.[6]

The Marxist Tradition

The Marxist tradition is a broad one, and analysis of it is hampered by the fact that there are some writers who have been heavily influenced by Marxist ideas who do not regard themselves as Marxists (for example Immanuel Wallerstein), and others on whom the influence is not so great who are nonetheless happy with the label (for example Johan Galtung).

The most fertile period of Marxist theorising took place in central Europe in the decade before the outbreak of the war in 1914. The theories developed during this time are often termed 'classical Marxist theories of imperialism'. The Austrian economist Rudolf Hilferding developed the concept of 'finance capital'. His central argument was that financiers, not industrialists, were responsible for the economic expansion occurring in the undeveloped parts of the world. The prominent radical thinker and political activist, Rosa Luxemburg argued that capitalism was inherently expansionary: it needed to expand in order to survive. Imperialism was inevitable, since sooner or later the capitalist countries would have to compete with one another for the last remaining territories not already subject to capitalist exploitation. The Bolshevik intellectual Nikolai Bukharin suggested that the main participants in the world economy were not individual firms, but increasingly states. This was due to the fact that competition within national boundaries was being progressively eliminated. Small businesses were being swallowed up by large ones and single, huge, 'state capitalist trusts' were in the making. These state capitalist trusts – 'Great Britain inc.', 'America inc.', 'Germany inc.' – would soon dominate the world economy. Bukharin gave the name 'imperialism' to the ferocious competition that was taking place between them.

It is important to note that Marx himself did not use the term 'imperialism', nor did he have a theory of it. Writers like Luxemburg and Bukharin, however, were profoundly influenced by his theory of capitalist development, and by his work on the impact of capitalism on non-European societies.

With respect to imperialism, two aspects of Marx's theory are particularly important. Firstly, though he did not have a theory of imperialism, he did have a theory of history in which capitalism plays a big part. This is sometimes called historical materialism. Its basic tenet is that history is a product of the social forces of production and the contradictions contained therein. The internal contradictions of feudalism led to its downfall and the establishment of capitalism. The internal contradictions of capitalism similarly lead to its downfall and the establishment of socialism.[7] Each stage is a necessary precursor to the next. The conditions for capitalism are established by feudalism and the conditions for socialism are established by capitalism. The historical role of capitalism was particularly important for Marx. Capitalism, unlike the modes of production it succeeded, was a dynamic force. It was driven by its own internal logic to expand to every corner of the globe. In doing so, backward, pre-capitalist modes of production and their attendant customs and habits, myths and superstitions would be dismantled, and the world united, for the first time, under a single socio-economic system. At the same time, capitalism would give rise to the formation of a worldwide urban proletariat, revolutionary class consciousness, and the conditions for the realisation of socialism. Capitalism is thus a disturbing, dislocating, destructive force, but also a progressive one with a vital historical task to perform: the destruction of backward social forms. This paradox, that capitalism is destructive but also progressive, although central to Marx's thesis, is one that later Marxists have found difficult to accept.

Secondly, it is important to note that Marx did not have much to say about the state. He regarded it as a product of more profound material forces: a 'superstructural' phenomenon. The state was thus an instrument of the dominant, ruling class, and state policy was always a reflection of its interests. Again, later Marxists have not been entirely happy with this view. Many came to feel that the state may have more autonomy than Marx allowed. If true, this is important, since it means that foreign policy cannot be reduced entirely to questions of social class.

The most famous Marxist book on imperialism is Lenin's *Imperialism, The Highest Stage of Capitalism*, first published in 1917. It might be said that just as Cobden dramatically illustrated the international political implications of Smith's analysis of the free market, Lenin dramatically illustrated the international political implications of Marx's analysis of capitalism.

Lenin's work is by and large not original. He borrowed heavily from other radical writers, Hobson and Hilferding in particular. He did, however, develop the important idea of the 'labour aristocracy'. Lenin attributed to this phenomenon the failure of the European working class to unite in opposition to war in 1914. Marxists were deeply puzzled when the plan of the Second International to resist war – an 'imperialist' war – through a general strike failed to materialise. Instead, the workers fell into line behind their respective national bourgeoisies, that is, they supported their national governments in their war preparations, rather than opposing such preparations in solidarity with their fellow workers across Europe. This was famously symbolised by the German Social Democratic Party voting for War Credits in the Reichstag. Nationalism had spectacularly triumphed over socialist internationalism. The dream of the Second International to bring capitalism crashing down through mass resistance to war was over. Lenin's explanation for this development, contrary to all the teachings of Marxism, was that certain sections of the proletariat

– skilled workers – had been co-opted by the bourgeoisie. The European proletariat had in effect been bribed to act contrary to its class interests. The European bourgeoisie was able to do this because of the extra profits they had reaped from decades of colonial exploitation.

Post-1945 Marxist and 'Neo-Marxist' Theories

Since the Second World War, a number of theories of imperialism have emerged from the Marxist tradition. The most prominent are dependency theory and world systems theory. By the 1960s it had become clear that the majority of Third World countries were not prospering, despite the fact that they had won their formal independence. Dependency theory and world systems theory offered new explanations for why this was so. The core contention was that a country's development is conditioned by the place it occupies in the capitalist system – a system characterised by a rigid division of labour from which a country cannot easily escape.

It is important to emphasise four novel features shared by these new theories. Firstly, considerable weight is attached to the concept of 'under-development'. This concept is used to denote the idea that capitalism plunders pre-capitalist economies. Resources and 'surplus value' are extracted, but nothing, except in certain small capitalist 'enclaves', is given in return. Development is, as a result, hindered rather than helped, contrary to the teachings of both liberalism and classical Marxism. Indeed, the areas being exploited are left in a worse state than they were before. Hence *under*-development.

Secondly, dependency and world systems theorists look at the world capitalist system as a whole rather than as a sequence of national economies, each developing in its turn. Crucially, they see this whole divided into a dominant centre and a dependent periphery. The centre develops at the expense of the periphery. In the words of André Gunder Frank, a chain of exploitation exists linking corporate headquarters in New York, London and Frankfurt to semi-subsistence cultivation in the most peripheral and poverty-stricken parts of the system.[8] This is a major departure from classical Marxism, which, as we have seen, sees capitalism as a progressive force. For dependency and world systems theorists, capitalism is progressive for some (advanced industrial countries), but regressive for others (primary producing countries). The only way for dependent countries to break out of this network of domination and exploitation is to sever completely their relations with the capitalist system.

This is difficult to do, however, because of the existence of a 'comprador'[9] class in the 'periphery'. This is the third novel feature of post-1945 neo-Marxist theories of imperialism. This class consists of westernised Third World elites with a stake in the existing system. In effect, they are in alliance with the 'core' or 'centre' countries because they have an interest in the exploitation of the 'periphery in the periphery'. The existence of a comprador class, or the 'core of the periphery', has ensured that attempts to break free from the world system have been few and far between.

Fourthly, dependency and world systems theorists define capitalism as a mode of exchange: basically, exchange for monetary profit on international or world markets. For Immanuel Wallerstein, the most prominent world systems theorist, the capitalist world system has been in existence since the sixteenth century. This contrasts sharply with Marx's view. For Marx, capitalism is a mode of production – 'generalised commodity production for the market where labour is itself a commodity' – rather than a mode of exchange. This mode of production only started to become dominant in the nineteenth century. Perhaps the most important difference between Marx and Wallerstein is that whereas Marx sees capitalism as taking root domestically and then spreading outwards – *Das Kapital* is primarily an analysis of capitalism in Britain – Wallerstein sees capitalism as a world system from the outset, and sees historical evolution not in terms of its spread, but in terms of its impact on its various component parts.

Critique of Classical Marxist Theories of Imperialism

Marxist theories have not gone uncriticised. The classical Marxist assumption that capitalism is a monolithic phenomenon has been challenged. As pointed out in Chapter 2, there may be several different kinds of capitalism, each with very distinct characteristics. Consequently, more than one theory may be needed to explain their evolution. It is also an interesting fact that if a 'monopoly stage' of capitalism ever existed, it reached some countries long before others. Take, for example, the US and Britain at the turn of the century. Of the two, the US was most advanced along the road of monopoly but had a small empire. Britain lagged far behind in monopoly terms but had an immense empire. According to classical Marxist theories, it should have been the other way around. Not unconnected with this, it is sometimes argued that Marxists overestimate the influence that financiers and capitalists have on foreign policy. They may be able to pull a string here and push a lever there, but so can the media, pressure groups (for example Amnesty International, Greenpeace), special constituencies (for example the Jewish lobby in the US, farmers in France), diplomats, generals, specialist advisors and so on.

An equally grave criticism of classical Marxism is that it under-estimated the capacity of capitalism to adapt to change. The highly regulated and rule-bound capitalism evident in most parts of the world today – even the US – is very different from the one that prevailed in the nineteenth century. Classical Marxists have underestimated the ability of the state to prohibit and dismantle cartels, monopolies and trusts; to manipulate aggregate supply and demand in order to correct periodic systemic malfunctions; to ameliorate suffering in periods of economic crisis; and to achieve certain economic and social goals through the redistribution of wealth. They have under-estimated the ability of organised labour to improve the incomes and conditions of the mass of working people and greatly enhance their political influence. Finally, they have underestimated the ability of capitalism to develop new and more productive technologies and generate fresh desires to motivate workers and capitalists alike. In sum, the 'immiseration of the masses' that Marx and his early disciples felt would bring down the capitalist system has not occurred. Capitalism has proved a highly resilient and adaptable system. Rather than immiserating the masses, in many parts of the world it has brought untold riches.

The success of the state in regulating and shaping economic processes and outcomes suggests that it is far from the slavish instrument of a homogeneous ruling class that classical Marxists assumed. The state has at least some degree of autonomy from the class structure of society. In addition, to the extent that a ruling class exists, the evidence suggests that it does not always speak with one voice on matters of foreign policy. Events such as the Spanish Civil War, the Vietnam War, and the Balkan wars of the 1990s provoked a variety of responses from all sections of society. The 'ruling class' in the principal capitalist countries proved just as divided on how to respond to these tragic events as other social and political groups. The assumption of homogeneity, therefore, is far from sound.

Finally, classical Marxist theories of imperialism have been criticised for being difficult to verify. What, it has been asked, is the object of these theories? To explain war? To explain the acquisition of territories? To explain the disarray of the Second International in 1914? To explain the periodic occurrence of crises in the international economic system? The focus, or *explanandum*, of these theories is far from clear. This has enabled their proponents conveniently to shift their ground when under attack. In the face of contradictory empirical evidence, they have been able to say: 'but the theory is not concerned with X, but rather with Y'. This may be a rhetorical asset, but it is a liability when it comes to promoting a clear understanding.

Critique of Neo-Marxist Theories

Neo-Marxists have been challenged over the concept of exploitation. It has been pointed out that this concept, so central to post-1945 Neo-Marxist thinking, is peculiarly difficult to define. It is said that while the prices of the manufactured goods of the industrialised 'North' have steadily risen, the prices of the primary products of the developing 'South' have fallen. The South therefore suffers from 'unfair terms of trade'. It has to export more and more of its primary produce in order to import the same amount of manufactures. But how does one calculate a fair price? How does one calculate the exchange-value of any given commodity without at least some reference to supply and demand, that is the price that the market is prepared to pay? Can all transactions in which one party benefits significantly more than another be deemed 'exploitative'?[10] Is it, indeed, true that Third World countries have suffered from adverse terms of trade? The prices of some commodities – for example oil, aluminium, chromium – have performed well relative to manufactures. In addition, empirical findings vary according to the year that is taken as the 'base' of the calculation. If one's analysis begins during a boom period for commodity prices, and terminates during a recession, it is likely to show that the terms of trade for these products has fallen. But if one's analysis begins during a recession, and terminates during a boom, it is likely to show the opposite. The available evidence suggests that the only safe conclusion that can be reached on commodity prices is that they have tended to be more volatile than the price of manufactures.[11] These and other concerns have not been satisfactorily addressed by contemporary Marxist writers. The confidence, therefore, with which the assertion that the Third World is a victim of continuous 'exploitation' has been expressed is far from entirely justified.

Similarly, the concept of 'dependency' is not entirely free of ambiguity. Dos Santos defines it as follows: 'By dependence we mean a situation in which the economy of certain countries is conditioned by the development and expansion of another economy to which the former is subjected'.[12] But what is meant by 'conditioned' and 'subjected'? Arguably, all Dos Santos does in his definition is replace one ambiguous term with two others.

Dependency theory has also been criticised for not paying sufficient attention to internal factors. Corruption, government mismanagement, nepotism and the systematic denial of civil liberties have been common ills in the body politic of many Third World states since they achieved their independence in the 1960s and 1970s. It is these ills, rather than 'structural imperialism', or the inherently exploitative nature of the world capitalist system, that account for their continued impoverishment. Dependency theory is, accordingly, simply a convenient means by which the plight of Third World countries can be dumped at the door of foreigners. It provides the government of these countries with a convenient excuse for not tackling problems the principal causes of which lie at home.

Finally, newer theories have been criticised for being un-Marxist. This is the thrust of Bill Warren's important study *Imperialism: Pioneer of Capitalism*. Warren argues that capitalist imperialism is exploitative, and it does involve some degree of subjugation. But it is also, as Marx said, historically necessary. Warren refutes empirically the central assertion of the dependency theorists that the Third World is not developing. He shows that it is developing, though at an uneven pace – a fact, he insists, that should surprise no one.

Notes on Chapter 4

1 Lenin, V.I., *Imperialism, The Highest Stage of Capitalism* (Peking, Foreign Language Press, 1963 [1917]); Johan Galtung, 'A Structural Theory of Imperialism', *Journal of Peace Research* 13, 2 (1971).

2 See A.J.P. Taylor, 'Economic Imperialism', in his *Essays in English History* (Harmondsworth, Penguin, 1976), 169–74; Kenneth Waltz, *Theory of International Politics* (Reading, MA, Addison–Wesley, 1979), 20–9.

3 The landmark contributions to the debate on imperialism are: John Gallagher and Ronald Robinson, 'The Imperialism of Free Trade', *Economic History Review* Second Series, 6, 1 (1953); D.K. Fieldhouse, '"Imperialism": An Historiographical Revision', *Economic History Review* Second Series, 14, 2 (1961); R.J. Hammond, 'Economic Imperialism: Sidelights on a Stereotype', *Journal of Economic History* 21, 4 (1961); Eric Stokes, 'Late Nineteenth-Century Colonial Expansion and the Attack on the Theory of Economic Imperialism: A Case of Mistaken Identity?', *Historical Journal* 12, 2 (1969); John Gallagher and Roland Robinson, with Alice Denny, *Africa and the Victorians: The Official Mind of Imperialism*, 2nd ed. (London, Macmillan, 1981); Norman Etherington, 'Reconsidering Theories of Imperialism', *History and Theory* 21, 1 (1982); D.K. Fieldhouse, *Economics and Empire 1839–1914* (London, Macmillan, 1984); P.J. Cain and A.G. Hopkins, *British Imperialism: Innovation and Expansion 1688–1914* (London, Longman, 1993); P.J. Cain and A.G. Hopkins, *British Imperialism: Crisis and Deconstruction 1914–1990* (London, Longman, 1993).

4 See Hans Morgenthau, *Politics Among Nations*, 5th ed. (New York, NY, Knopf, 1973), 48–76.

5 See Joseph Schumpeter, *Imperialism and Social Classes* (Oxford, Basil Blackwell, 1951); Lewis S. Feuer, *Imperialism and the Anti-Imperialist Mind* (London, Transaction, 1989), 16–25.

6 See J.A. Hobson, *Imperialism: A Study*, 3rd ed. (London, George Allen and Unwin, 1938); Michael Freeden (ed.), *J.A. Hobson: A Reader* (London, Unwin Hyman, 1988); David Long, 'J.A. Hobson and Economic Internationalism', in David Long and Peter Wilson (eds), *Thinkers of the Twenty Years' Crisis* (Oxford, Clarendon Press, 1995); David Long, *Towards a New Liberal Internationalism: The*

International Theory of J.A. Hobson (Cambridge, Cambridge University Press, 1996).

7   Lucid and insightful introductions to Marx's theory of history are provided by Donald MacRae, 'Karl Marx' in Timothy Raison (ed.), *The Founding Fathers of Social Science* (Harmondsworth, Penguin, 1969); and Robert Heilbronner, *The Worldly Philosophers* (London, Penguin, 1983), 105–30.

8   André Gunder Frank, 'The Development of Underdevelopment', *Monthly Review* (September 1966), 17–30.

9   This is a Portuguese term literally meaning an intermediary through whom a foreign firm trades with Chinese dealers.

10 One can also question from a classical Marxist perspective whether exploitation is always bad, certainly in broad historical terms. The Cambridge Marxist economist Joan Robinson once famously said, "The only thing worse than being exploited is not being exploited."

11 See Susan Strange, *States and Markets* (London, Pinter, 1988), 172–4.

12 Theotonio Dos Santos, 'The Structure of Dependence', *American Economic Review* 60 (1970), 231–6.

Select Bibliography

Brewer, Anthony, *Marxist Theories of Imperialism: A Critical Survey*, 2nd ed. (London, Routledge, 1990). The most comprehensive survey of Marxist theories in the field. Meticulous and lucid. Unlikely to be surpassed.

Cain, P.J., 'Hobson, Cobdenism and the Radical Theory of Economic Imperialism', *Economic History Review* 31, 4 (1978). A model of careful scholarship and tight analysis. Excellent short account of Hobson's political thought.

Etherington, Norman, *Theories of Imperialism: War, Conquest and Capital* (Beckenham, Croom Helm, 1984). Excellent account from lucid Australian historian. Traces the modern conception of imperialism back to the socialist Gaylord Wilshire and the jingoistic American press of the late 1890s.

Fieldhouse, D.K. (ed.), *The Theory of Capitalist Imperialism* (London, Longman, 1967). Highly useful anthology of classic essays compiled by one of the leading historians in the field.

Frank, André Gunder, *Capitalism and Underdevelopment in Latin America: Historical Studies of Chile and Brazil* (New York, NY, Monthly Review, 1969). Pioneering work of 'dependency' analysis.

Gill, Stephen, and Law, David, *The Global Political Economy: Perspectives, Problems and Policies* (London, Harvester, 1988). Leading textbook on IPE from a Marxist (in particular, Gramscian) perspective.

Hayter, Teresa, *Aid as Imperialism* (London, Verso, 1983). Radical analysis of the phenomenon of foreign aid. Short on counter-factuals. A strange blend of polemic and careful analysis.

Lall, Sanjaya, 'Is "Dependence" a Useful Concept in Analysing Underdevelopment?', *World Development* 3, 11 and 12 (1975). Trenchant if not conclusive empirical refutation of the central tenets of dependency theory.

McLellan, David, *The Thought of Karl Marx*, 2nd ed. (London, Macmillan, 1980). Still one of the best introductions.

Magdoff, Harry, *The Age of Imperialism: The Economics of US Foreign Policy* (New York, NY, Monthly Review, 1969). Influential revisionist text on the motivation of US foreign policy during the Cold War.

Rosenberg, Justin, *The Empire of Civil Society: A Critique of the Realist Theory of International Relations* (London, Verso, 1994). Erudite critique of realism from a historical materialist perspective. Room for argument on the accounts of Carr and Morgenthau.

Roxborough, Ian, *Theories of Underdevelopment* (London, Macmillan, 1979). Excellent overview of post-war thinking on development and underdevelopment.

Wallerstein, Immanuel, *Historical Capitalism* (London, Verso, 1983). Not everyone's favourite. Heroic and unsatisfactory abridgement of the author's monumental, multi-volume, *History of the Modern World System*.

Warren, Bill, *Imperialism: Pioneer of Capitalism* (London, Verso, 1980). Trenchant critique of dependency theory from a classical Marxist perspective. Detailed and cogent in analysis. An important restatement of the classical Marxist position.

PART II

INSTITUTIONS

CHAPTER 5

Bretton Woods and International Money Management

The Bretton Woods system, conceived of during and established immediately after the Second World War, contained two elements: a liberal international trading order and an international monetary regime. This chapter is concerned with the second of these elements and especially with the principles and institutions governing international monetary management. Two issues need to be addressed before examining the evolution of the Bretton Woods monetary arrangements and its central institution, the IMF. First is the role of 'international money' in the international system. Second is the historical, political and economic context of the creation of the Bretton Woods system, for it was not created in a historical vacuum and was intended to address the specific concerns of the immediate post-war era.

The Role of International Money

The last 300 years has seen a fundamental shift in the role and uses of money. Today we take its existence for granted. We chase, earn and spend it as a matter of routine. We acknowledge the existence of an international system of finance and investment, even though we are not always sure how it functions. We grant our leaders the right to manage our fiscal and monetary arrangements, both at home and abroad, as a matter of course. And it is taken for granted that there has always been a standard role of money internationally.

In the nineteenth century, money developed into the fundamental medium of exchange in the international economy. The late seventeenth and much of the eighteenth century, as we have seen, was dominated by so-called mercantilism, with its zero-sum outlook towards the international economy, and its assumptions of finite resources and wealth based on 'bullionism'. The progressive demise of this belief system and its gradual replacement by liberal ideas of free trade elevated the importance of money as a medium of exchange and established its centrality to the burgeoning international commercial system. Initially, money principally took the form of coinage, and derived its value from the material from which it was struck. As commercial transactions grew in bulk, so did the amount of money needed to fund these transactions. Consequently there was a progression, in the eighteenth and nineteenth centuries, towards the use of paper money as an accepted medium of exchange. This money was guaranteed by individuals and private institutions backed by their own reserves of gold and silver. States soon got in on the act, and paper currency was printed and circulated by governments, providing a greater degree of security that the bearer of the paper money could redeem its value. As well as being an accepted medium of exchange, money developed into a store, a measure of value, and a standard by which to judge national economies. More importantly, the printing and circulation of paper money by the state implied the creation of what Gilpin has called 'political money'.[1] Money now transcended the purely commercial realm and attained political attributes, since it could henceforth, in principle, be used by the state to influence the domestic and international economies. In turn, this ability to influence the domestic and international economies could have implications on the international system politically.

The growth in stature of *laissez-faire* economics and ideas of free trade by the mid-nineteenth century, in conjunction with the sheer growth in the volume of trade, meant that for the first time there emerged a widespread consciousness of an international monetary system supporting a wide and ever growing range of commercial activity. The growing awareness of the development of an international monetary system also generated a set of concerns about its management. One concern was to identify what sort of international monetary unit would be generally acceptable. A second touched on the methods that would have to be devised to enable balance-of-payments adjustments. A third concern related to the types of financial institutions that would be needed to manage these transactions.

Underlying these concerns was the need for the maintenance of stability internationally. This was seen as the key element of the emergent monetary system. Stability as the result of the management of capital and financial flows, and monetary institutions, would create the certainty essential for the smooth and efficient operation of an open commercial system. Nevertheless, these concerns were not simply economic in nature. As Scammel has argued, the international monetary system is defined by its political parameters, and it is within the context of these parameters that economic issues are discussed and resolved.[2] Hence, the belief that international economic stability is a fundamental precursor to a successful international monetary system cannot be viewed in isolation from the political activity required to set in place and maintain the conditions for stability. In fact, in attempting to manage the international monetary system, what is occurring is the political regulation of economic needs and processes.

If this is accepted, it becomes difficult to discuss the international economy as an entity separate from the broader international system. And while in the nineteenth century it became increasingly apparent that there was a move towards some form of management of the growing international economic system, it also became apparent that such attempts at management had potentially profound implications for state sovereignty, the cornerstone of the inter-state system.

From the middle of the twentieth century, a period that spawned international organisations such as the IMF, political control has been exerted over the international monetary system for three reasons: firstly, to provide a monetary framework to ease financial flows and assist the growth in volume of international trade; secondly, to stimulate and facilitate the process of foreign investment; thirdly, to promote and protect the process loosely called interdependence, which has both political and economic consequences (and to which we will return later). Within the system itself, the three main features requiring regulation to achieve stability, and thus facilitate the process outlined above, can be characterised as liquidity, adjustment and confidence. These features form the rationale behind the Bretton Woods system of international monetary management.

The Historical Antecedents to the Bretton Woods System

Bretton Woods is but the most recent attempt to impose order on the potentially chaotic flows of world money. Any attempt to understand the Bretton Woods system must examine its two immediate historical antecedents, the era of the gold standard and the troubled years between the two world wars.

It is no coincidence that the gold standard, which lasted from 1870 until 1914, operated at a time when *laissez-faire* liberalism was at its peak. It was a period of remarkable growth in the volume of world trade, and thus in the flow of capital needed to fund it. It was a period in which Ricardo's law of comparative advantage provided the main theoretical underpinning of international trade. A clear pattern of trade emerged, in which nations around the world progressively abandoned previous strategies of semi-autarchy and sought to produce, and sell, those goods in which they enjoyed a comparative advantage, and purchase those which could be produced comparatively more cheaply elsewhere. This was the heyday of the idea of trade and economic competition as a positive-sum game from which all could benefit, and a period in which the Cobdenite thesis that free trade was a boon for both prosperity and peace was at its most influential. In essence, it was a period in which the mercantilist notions of zero-sum international relations and inevitable conflict were subordinated to classical liberal views of the existence of a natural harmony of interests between nations, which could be achieved through competition and unfettered commerce.

The pre-eminence of these classical liberal views and the growth in volume of trade created the need for the establishment of the gold standard, which reflected the classical liberal belief in a natural harmony of interests by creating a co-operative regulatory mechanism to ensure international stability. Its functions were to: provide a base for currency in the form of a valuable commodity (gold); provide a means for adjusting the balance of payments; and establish a method for regulating, and if possible substantially reducing, fluctuations in exchange rates. Within this system, gold was universally accepted as a medium of exchange, that is as the international money. All national currencies were defined and valued in relation to gold, thus enabling currency stability through fixed exchange rates.

The gold standard operated in the following way. Gold would flow to surplus states and away from deficit states, leading to balance-of-payments adjustments and long-term equilibrium. That is, as money flowed out of states to pay for imports, so gold would similarly flow out to cover the financial deficit incurred by the outflow of money. The domestic effect of these outflows was a constriction in the money supply, resulting in deflation. In turn, this would reduce the demand for imports, and the tougher economic environment wrought by deflation would bring down prices, thus making exports more competitive. An adjustment in the balance of payments would automatically occur. Less would be imported, more exported, and the flow of money and gold would be thereby reversed.

This mechanism inevitably had serious implications for domestic economic welfare and stability. But external stability and adjustments in the balance of payments were seen as the more important considerations. The predominance of international concerns was made tolerable only by the fact that 'social uses of money' did not figure prominently on the domestic agenda. This would soon change. The system was also made tolerable by the additional factor of its truly co-operative nature, in which the participating states agreed to buy and sell gold to maintain stable exchange rates.

Parallel with the 'nightwatchman state' domestically, the gold standard did not stray into the realm of control, but rather provided an agreed element of regulation, these areas of regulation being the liquidity, adjustment and confidence already referred to. Liquidity effectively involved credit creation and the ability to do so within a system based on national currencies backed by gold. Adjustment to the balance of payments was provided by the mechanism of flows of gold outlined above. Finally, confidence was provided by a monetary system that allowed credit creation based on gold, and the free international movement of capital, as guaranteed by Great Britain and other great powers.

The economic merits of this system are palpable, and arguably it was this system that provided the requisite stability for the international economy to grow. Yet a more critical examination of the gold standard would emphasise the political nature of this regulatory arrangement. Did, for example, the success of the gold standard emanate from its co-operative regulatory function, or was it mainly a function of the power of the British Empire – in both its economic and military dimension – and its desire and ability to underpin the system? Great Britain, with its ability to draw on the immense resources and manpower of its imperial possessions, coupled with the supremacy of its maritime forces, could be said to be the hinge upon which the whole liberal international trading system and the gold standard rested.

This of course gives rise to a fundamental question: does the management of the international monetary system require a hegemon, akin to Great Britain, to lay down the rules? If the viability and stability of the gold standard depended solely on the supremacy and interests of the British Empire, then one could argue that any type of co-operative, regulatory mechanism for the international monetary and trading order relies on the interests and capabilities of a single powerful state for its existence. It could also be argued that economic co-operation in the form of the gold standard could only function when the political parameters had been agreed and set, either by the predominance of one state or through a political arrangement among states such as the nineteenth-century system of balance of power. Despite the effectiveness of the gold standard, the system was progressively eroded, through the turn of the century, by an increase in friction among the great powers and the associated rise in protectionism. The system came to an end with the onset of the First World War.

After the war, there was an attempt to revitalise the gold standard, especially between 1925 and 1931, when Great Britain returned to full sterling convertibility at the pre-1914 rate. This attempt was undermined not only by the onset of the great depression but also by the general turbulence of the inter-war period, in which states pursued their economic interests through means other than the co-operative arrangements embedded in the gold standard. The main reasons for this are to be found in the after-effects of the First World War. The total mobilisation, under state direction, of all aspects of the domestic economic life of the warring states, in pursuit of victory, created what has been referred to as the 'warfare state'.[3] With the end of the war, citizens' new found expectations of what the state should provide for them economically did not expire. This proved to be the beginning of the transformation of the 'warfare state' into the 'welfare state', a process speeded up by the influence of the ideas of Keynes: previously a staunch supporter of *laissez-faire* economics, he became increasingly sceptical of both the economic and political merits of an unregulated system. He proposed greater state intervention in the domestic economy and promoted policies such a full employment as goals for the post-war democracies. Under the influence of Keynesianism, there developed a general belief that the role of the state should be expanded into economic and social as well as political and military realms. The state, it was felt, should assume responsibilities for the economic and social well-being of its citizens, not only their defence and physical security. In achieving this goal, the state would have to protect the domestic economy from the vicissitudes of the international economy, thus sacrificing the basic principle of stability in the international monetary system in favour of domestic interests and autonomy. A good example of this is to be found in the 'New Deal' reforms embarked upon by President Roosevelt in the US to remedy the effects of the great depression. They centred on resuscitating the US economy through large programmes of publicly funded works. Through these means, the federal government directly put America back to work and reflated the US economy. The growth of discriminatory practices in trade was also an important feature of US economic policy in the 1930s.

But this was only one element of the inter-war international economic system, which was characterised by a succession of ad hoc, uncoordinated decisions by states concentrating on domestic adjustment and ignoring international stability. The domestic economic adjustments made by individual states were at odds with the system as a whole and resulted in general international disequilibrium. Great Britain could no longer perform its role as lender of last resort and chief regulator of the international economic system. Its war effort between 1914 and 1918 had drained it of the resources, both human and material, rendering it quite unable to maintain its role as guarantor of the system. In addition, the onset of the great depression spelt the end to international monetary co-operation. National self-sufficiency and the pursuit of domestic autonomy predominated over liberal internationalism, giving rise to a clash of national interests in the international arena. This clash of interests resulted in the complete break-down in the international monetary order into groups, or 'blocs', centred on the currencies of certain powerful states.[4] These currency blocs pursued conflicting goals, resulting in 'beggar thy neighbour' policies of trade conflict and economic warfare, primarily through the exportation of inflation and unemployment to other states. The 'natural harmony of interests' had given way to an international anarchy of very narrowly defined and conflicting national interests that did nothing to arrest the onset of the Second World War.

The Bretton Woods System

The Bretton Woods Agreement was signed in July 1944 and became operational in March 1947. The agreement aimed to put in place a set of rules and an institutional framework to ensure that the pitfalls of the gold standard and the turbulence of the inter-war period could be avoided. It was based, in principle, on the Mutual Aid Agreement signed by Great Britain and the US in 1942. This agreement stipulated that the basic goals of any post-war economic order should be the pursuit both of free trade internationally and full employment domestically. The turmoil of the inter-war period provided a strong incentive for the framers of the Bretton Woods system to tackle the issue of employment. The rise of political extremism in the 1930s, especially in Germany, was partly attributable to economic disarray caused by hyperinflation and resulting in mass unemployment. The vast numbers of disaffected unemployed proved easy prey for nationalist demagogues such as Hitler. The unemployed could be incited and manipulated through rhetoric that placed the blame for their economic ills squarely on the shoulders of other states, and more perniciously on Germany's Jewish population. This so-called 'scourge of unemployment', it was felt, should be removed forever.

Hence, the Bretton Woods Agreement attempted to achieve a compromise between domestic autonomy and international stability. In what has come to be know as 'the compromise of embedded liberalism'[5], Bretton Woods would allow states to pursue full employment and welfare policies at home, while providing the necessary regulation and management internationally to achieve stability and freer trade. This compromise directly addressed the problems encountered with both the gold standard and the economic disorder of the inter-war period. The gold standard had subordinated domestic economic activities to exchange-rate stability and the interests of international monetary order generally. In the inter-war period, international stability had been sacrificed in the name of self-sufficiency and domestic autonomy. Bretton Woods aimed to bridge the gap between these two extremes and allow states the possibility of pursuing policies that could be loosely described as 'Keynes at home and Smith abroad'. States would be allowed to pursue statist economic and social policies domestically, while simultaneously pursuing free trade and co-operative policies internationally.

The institution at the heart of the Bretton Woods monetary system was the IMF, its chief architect Keynes. It was he, while serving as an advisor at the British Treasury, who negotiated the system in conjunction with Harry D. White, an assistant to the US Treasury Secretary. These two architects of the system had differing plans, which reflected their respective countries' economic conditions. Keynes initially proposed an ambitious plan based on the creation of an 'International Clearing Union', which would function as a controller of the international demand for money. This system would work on the same premises as the common overdraft, in that the international agency would hold quotas (or an overdraft facility), for each signatory, which could be then drawn on by the state when facing balance -of-payments difficulties. This facility did not entail the lodging of any gold reserves with the international agency, or a reserve currency deposit, and would be repayable over an agreed period. Keynes's plan reflects Britain's status as debtor state towards the end of the Second World War, hence the desire to see more lenient adjustment policies.

White's plan, on the other hand, reflected the US position as a major creditor state with little dependence on foreign trade and the concomitant desire to see balance-of-payments deficits swiftly adjusted, and states operating within their 'incomes'. The main elements of White's plan were the creation of an 'International Stabilisation Agency'. Signatory states would lodge currency and gold reserves, calculated on the basis of their GNP and share of world trade. The size of their contribution would also determine their voting rights within the institution. In times of balance-of-payments crisis, states would have the right to draw foreign currency, calculated on their own share of funds lodged with the agency, to repay their debts. In return, their stock of currency lodged with the agency would be drawn upon by the same amount. States were obliged to replenish their share of the currency reserve once their balance of payments had returned to surplus.

In addition, the agency would have the right, in such times of crisis, to demand or impose measures on any member state to remedy any domestic causes of that crisis. At the heart of White's proposal was the notion of a fixed exchange rate for each participating state, which could not be changed unilaterally and would provide the requisite degree of stability in the international monetary system.

Though agreement on either of these plans was not forthcoming, they did have four factors in common, upon which the Bretton Woods system was ultimately based. These were that: exchange rates would be controlled by an international institution; international monetary reserves and liquidity would be created to supplement national reserves; there would be a mechanism for the multilateral clearing of accounts; and there would be some international regulatory powers for the international institution over domestic policies.

Therefore, when the Bretton Woods Agreement was finalised, it was based on the mechanism of fixed exchange rates and the transfer of currency reserves controlled by the newly created institution, the IMF, to meet any balance-of-payments disequilibria. The whole system of fixed exchange rates was based on the US dollar. This became the reserve currency, in that the price of gold was fixed at US$35 an ounce and all the other currencies were 'pegged' to the dollar within narrow bands. Some came to call this the 'gold exchange standard', since the value of currencies was tied, through the dollar, to gold, allowing some movement to reflect changes in economic circumstances. Initially these movements were restricted to 1 per cent above or below the agreed par value of the currency against the dollar. This band was later expanded to 2.5 per cent. In either case, movement of a currency beyond these bands could only be sanctioned by the IMF, and if a state willingly allowed a currency to break through these delineated restrictive values without authorisation, the IMF could take punitive action against that state. This fixed-exchange-rate system was intended to be more flexible than the gold standard in that it was based on the duality of gold and the US dollar, and was underpinned by a healthy US economy. It also created a framework that would diminish the impact of currency speculation – a major problem in the inter-war period – and thus reinforce international stability. In addition, when faced with balance-of-payments problems, member states could request capital support from the IMF, drawing on reserves lodged with it. In the face of fundamental disequilibria, some scope was permitted for the adjustment of par values if sanctioned by the IMF Board of Governors.

The system thus provided confidence through the fixed exchange rates that would limit currency speculation, and the fact that the system centred on the dollar – and hence drew on the strength of the US economy – and gold. It provided adjustment through the ability of states to draw on IMF reserves in time of crisis, by the possibility of the value of currencies fluctuating within the narrow bands prescribed, and by the possibility of a more substantial realignment with the Board's approval. Liquidity was provided by the availability of dollars, as the US concluded the war with huge gold and dollar surpluses. In addition, the IMF could disburse available funds in times of crisis, to meet a shortage or deficit.

The IMF in Action

It was this last area that dominated the workings of the IMF in the first 10 years of its existence, from 1947 to 1957. The main aim of the Fund in this decade was to find a way of recycling the huge reserves that had built up and continued to build up in the US Treasury. The provision of liquidity was not going to be as easy as had earlier been anticipated. The war-torn countries of Europe and Asia had little capacity to export. But they needed imports on a large scale to rebuild their economies. The US, on the other hand, had immense capacity to export, but required few imports. The outcome was a general and debilitating dollar shortage in the world economy. The IMF proved impotent to deal with the problem. It was only resolved through the supply of huge amounts of aid through the Marshall Plan of 1948.

In fact, it was only after 1959 that the Bretton Woods system started to function in the way envisaged by its architects. By 1959, the Western European economies had recovered sufficiently from the effects of the war to enable their currencies to be fully convertible into dollars. Marshall Aid, administered through the Organisation for European Economic Co-operation, and the European Payments Union played a crucial role in reconstructing the Western European economies to a level at which they could participate more equitably in the international economy.

In the 1960s, the objectives pursued through the Bretton Woods arrangements moved in the direction of a general increase in international liquidity, with the aim of stimulating a leap in international trade, and thus economic growth, through a boost to both exports and imports. The role of the dollar in this system of fixed exchange rates meant that the whole process was underwritten by the US economy, and hence US political leadership, which had to be committed to its maintenance. The US balance-of-payments deficit had to run at a sufficiently high level to keep enough dollars circulating in the world economy to maintain other balances, as all the other balances were calculated in dollars, the reserve currency. But the US deficit could not be allowed to spiral out of control, as this would mean a dollar glut, which would undermine confidence in the value of the dollar and hence the fixed-exchange-rate system as a whole. Similarly, US leaders could not tinker with the value of the dollar for domestic reasons, as the dollar was now not only a national currency but had also acquired the attributes of *the* international currency. All other currencies were valued against the dollar and had to sustain that value. Any change in the dollar's value, as a result of domestic reform in the US, would have a knock-on effect throughout the system.

This fundamental weakness in the system was first identified by the American economist Robert Triffin as early as 1960. He clarified that, as the system relied on the US balance-of-payments deficit to provide liquidity in the form of dollars, this deficit could not be allowed to climb chronically, since it would reach a point at which there would be a loss of confidence in the value of the dollar itself. That is, if there was a continuous and massive rise in dollars held outside the US, and these dollars became unredeemable at US$35 per ounce of gold, then confidence in the dollar (and hence the system) would plummet, destroying the monetary framework and international stability with it. While the US maintained sufficient gold reserves to cover its deficit, there would be no immediate problem. In 1958, US dollar liabilities accounted for only 80 per cent of the country's gold reserves. But by 1967, US gold reserves could cover only 30 per cent of liabilities. As Triffin had warned, the deficit had spiralled out of control, dollar liabilities massively outweighed US gold reserves, and confidence in the system began to subside.

The reasons for the immense growth in US dollar liabilities, and hence for the resultant crisis in confidence, were manifold. The majority of these reasons revolved around climbing US costs and expenditure, primarily abroad. The outflow of Marshall Aid and other US aid packages in the context of the Cold War accounted for some of these spiralling liabilities, as did the Vietnam War and general foreign US military commitments. In addition, foreign direct investment had grown rapidly as more markets opened up with recovery from the Second World War and the general growth in the post-war international economic system. Domestic costs in the US, especially those incurred by President Johnson's 'Great Society' programme, were also a significant factor.

The basic obstacle to counteracting this spiralling deficit was the central role of the US in the whole Bretton Woods system. As the US dollar could not be devalued, other short-term measures were introduced.[6] But these were only stop-gap measures, and did not tackle the major issue head-on.

The most important consideration was whether the US abused its power as the underpinner of the Bretton Woods system. The US was accused of benign neglect of the system. It did not want to make fundamental changes to its domestic economy for the sake of international stability – the traditional conflict between domestic economic autonomy and international order, or to put it otherwise the clash between national objectives and international order. Some would argue that in fact it was not benign neglect of the system on the part of the US, but rather a natural decline of that country's power and influence in the system that caused its collapse.

Throughout the post-war period, the US functioned as the international monetary system's hegemon. It was a 'benign hegemony', or what has been called an act of 'hegemonic benevolence'. The US provided leadership, stability and the opportunity for the world economy to flourish, through the pursuit of monetary management and freer trade. An inevitable consequence of the success of this hegemony, and the growth of the world economy, some would argue, was the relative dispersal of the power of the hegemon. As other states grew in economic strength and stature, and began to challenge the authority of the hegemon, so there was a relative decline in the ability of the US to lay down the law. It is this natural cycle of hegemonic decline that some pinpoint as the direct cause for the breakdown of the Bretton Woods system.

In August 1971, the US suspended dollar/gold convertibility, imposed a surcharge on imports, and pursued unilateral anti-inflationary domestic policies. By December of that year, the US dollar was devalued in the Smithsonian Agreement. This put an end to fixed exchange rates, thus ripping out the heart of the Bretton Woods monetary arrangement. Official recognition of the new state of affairs occurred with the introduction of floating exchange rates in 1973. The fixed exchange rate system was formally put to an end at the Jamaica Conference of 1976.

The demise of the adjustable peg system and the introduction of flexible exchange rates do not signify the end of the aim of imposing political management on the international monetary system. The idea of 'sound money' internationally still lives on, and is a particularly strong concern of the post-Cold-War era. Exchange rates are allowed to float freely, and currency speculation is rampant, but there persists a desire to coordinate economic policies, both domestic and international. This, it is still believed, is the key to the maintenance of that vital element called 'stability' in the international monetary system. While the mechanics of the Bretton Woods monetary arrangements came crashing down with a clash of national interests in the early 1970s, it could be said that the aspirations of the system live on. These aspirations were aided and abetted by the collapse of communism, which some characterised as the victory of liberalism. A new conventional wisdom swept through the major capitals of the world, certainly the Western world, in the early 1990s, which emphasised the abandonment of central planning, and the economics of statism and protectionism, in favour of a new liberal orthodoxy based on free markets and private investment. This wisdom came to be known as the 'Washington consensus'. The scope of this consensus extends to institutions such as the IMF and the World Bank, but also to Western governments, central bankers, international financiers and major opinion-formers. All these actors extol the virtues of liberalisation, privatisation, stable exchange rates and balanced budgets as the foundations for development and further growth in the international economy. And from the 1980s these virtues were adopted by or imposed upon developing states, emerging markets and transition economies, as the way forward. They do not go unchallenged, but they do provide an indication of a general coherence in thinking about the world economy.

The annual summits of the Group of Seven/Group of Eight (G7/8) leaders, in which they negotiate and endorse agreed measures, are but one indication that the ambitions behind the creation of the Bretton Woods system live on. So does the IMF, which is no longer confined to its specific Bretton Woods role, but has taken on the greater role of providing a channel for multilateral aid to the developing world and the transition economies of Eastern Europe and the former Soviet Union. In this role, the IMF has become increasingly active in the post-Cold-War era, imposing strict political as well as monetary and fiscal conditions on its aid packages, well beyond the economic reforms it could have imposed in the 1960s.

Concluding Remarks

Ultimately, the Bretton Woods system, as with its antecedents and successor systems, aimed to devise and manage an international monetary system. In doing so, it tried to circumscribe domestic autonomy and regulate the behaviour of a wide range of economic actors. As such, the growing importance of the economic factor in international relations was implicitly recognised, as was the need to strike a balance between economic efficiency and long-term stability, and between the economic ambitions of a growing number of actors in an increasingly global economy, and the political needs of a society of sovereign states.

Notes on Chapter 5

1   Robert Gilpin, *The Political Economy of International Relations* (Princeton, NJ, Princeton University Press, 1987), 122.
2   W.M. Scammel, *The International Economy since 1945* (Basingstoke, Macmillan, 1983).
3   Gilpin, *The Political Economy of International Relations*, 128.
4   The most powerful of these were the 'dollar bloc', centred on the US, and the 'sterling bloc', on Great Britain. France was the centre of the 'gold bloc', and the Fascist regimes in Italy, Germany and Japan attempted to create their own versions, centred on their respective currencies.

5   John Gerard Ruggie, 'International Regimes, Transactions, and Change: Embedded Liberalism in the Postwar Economic Order', *International Organization* 36 (1982), 399.
6   The General Agreement to Borrow, The Group of Ten, The Gold Pool, and Special Drawing Rights were the main measures agreed.

Select Bibliography

Block, Fred L., *The Origins of International Economic Disorder: A Study of the United States International Monetary Policy from World War II to the Present* (Berkeley, CA/London, University of California Press, 1977). Incisive and definitive examination of US international monetary policy in the Bretton Woods era.

Bordo, Michael D., and Barry J. Eichengreen (eds), *A Retrospective of the Bretton Woods System: Lessons from International Monetary Reform* (Chicago, IL, University of Chicago Press, 1993). Excellent re-examination of the implications of reform on the management of the international monetary system.

Cohen, Benjamin, 'Phoenix Risen: The Resurrection of Global Finance', *World Politics* 48, (1996).

Eichengreen, Barry J., *Globalizing Capital: A History of the International Monetary System* (Princeton, NJ, Princeton University Press, 1996). Examines why and how 'international money' has been managed. Detailed, penetrating analysis.

Frieden, Jeffrey A. and David A. Lake, *International Political Economy: Perspectives on Global Power and Wealth*, 4th ed. (Boston, MA, Bedford/St Martin's, 2000). Valuable, thorough textbook from team of leading American IPE analysts.

Gardner, Richard Newton, *Sterling–Dollar Diplomacy: Anglo–American Collaboration in the Reconstruction of Multilateral Trade* (Oxford, Clarendon Press, 1956). The deliberations and motivations behind Bretton Woods laid bare. Authoritative account still valuable 40 years on.

Kenen, Peter B. (ed.), *Managing the World Economy: Fifty Years After Bretton Woods* (Washington, DC, Institute for International Economics, 1994). Highly informative retrospective panorama. Broad analysis and wide-ranging views.

Keohane, Robert O., *After Hegemony: Cooperation and Discord in the*

World Political Economy (Princeton, NJ, Princeton University Press, 1984). Award-winning analysis of post-war international economic co-operation. Skilful and influential examination of the relative merits of functionalism, rational choice theory and hegemonic stability theory in explaining the persistence of co-operation into the post-Bretton-Woods era.

Walter, Andrew, *World Power, World Money: The Role of Hegemony and International Monetary Order* (New York, NY, Harvester Wheatsheaf, 1993). Elegant assessment of interplay between international finance and political power in the international system.

Williamson, John, *The Failure of World Monetary Reform 1971–1974* (Sunbury-on-Thames, Nelson, 1977). Meticulous account of the demise of the Bretton Woods system. Detached yet powerful critique of last-gasp reforms.

CHAPTER 6

GATT, WTO and Trade Relations

Trade issues occupy an elevated place on the international agenda at the turn of the century. G8 summits, which frequently have trade issues high on the agenda, and negotiations between states' trade representatives in various fora receive more attention than UN Security Council meetings and decisions. Governments and leaders devote more effort to developing trade policies and advocating them to their electorates than ever before. Some would argue that issues of international trade have become the 'high politics' of the twenty-first century. Yet the management of the international trading system is not a novel concept. States have attempted to reach agreement on the regulation of the international trading system for well over 50 years. In addressing the issue of the management and regulation of international trade since 1945, four areas need to be examined: firstly, the nature and role of international trade; secondly, the origins, aims and structure of GATT; thirdly, the problems of and challenges to GATT; fourthly, the revisions to GATT and the creation of the WTO.

The Nature and Role of International Trade

In simple terms, trade – that is the buying and selling or the exchange of goods – initially came about when certain resources and commodities could not be acquired locally or within specific societies. As societies grew and came into closer contact with one another, barter and trade became a fundamental form of economic interaction. The emergence of a European system of sovereign states, in conjunction with the discovery and exploration of new continents, and the gradual evolution and expansion of this system into one of nation-states, set the foundations for international trade. Increased links between peoples, and later states, that had control over different resources and commodities not readily available to all resulted in an increase in the exchange of these goods. The Industrial Revolution, and the spread of its fruit, industrialisation, led to the production and manufacture of goods, a process which required a variety of raw materials from a variety of sources at home and abroad. In addition, the production of goods in ever larger quantities required markets both at home and abroad. This further extended and deepened the channels of economic interaction.

As a consequence, international trade came about when essential raw materials were not available, or it was not economically efficient to manufacture goods domestically (or more accurately they could be produced more efficiently elsewhere). The cost of purchasing these foreign goods was cheaper than producing them at home. The latter part of this simple definition places the emphasis on economic factors. It concentrates on the idea of the efficiency in the allocation of resources and the production of goods. The emphasis is on economics, in that international trade is characterised as predominantly an economic activity with little political content, very much in the tradition of classical liberalism.

In the context of the twentieth century, this raises the fundamental question of whether it is possible to divorce economics from politics when discussing international trade. This is especially relevant as trade is conducted in the framework of an international system dominated by sovereign states. As long as the international system consists primarily of independent, sovereign states coexisting in an anarchical environment, and state policies for the most part concentrate on internal order and external security, the 'politicisation' of trade is inescapable.[1] The liberal ideal of free competition and the maximisation of efficiency, in this environment, can never be the sole goal of national policies or the simple result of market forces. The classical liberal injunction that economics must be separated from politics can never be fully achieved, or even, some would say, approximated.

This is reflected in academic debate, where there is disagreement between economists and political scientists in discussing the role and nature of international trade. Roughly speaking, the economist argues that the effects of the market mechanism of supply and demand are the prime determinants of the pattern of international trade, as with any other economic transaction. Keeping this premise in mind, the economist will primarily engage in examining 'actor behaviour', that is assessing state trade policies and foreign economic relations from the perspective of the maximisation of economic gains.[2] Susan Strange, among others, has questioned this assertion. She argues that economists are not really the right breed of academic fully to understand the structure and dynamics of international trade. '[A]nything that upsets or goes against economic theory is apt to be referred to as an "exogenous factor",' she says, 'especially shocking to economists unprepared by nature to expect power factors to intervene, whether from governments or operators in the market.'[3]

Political scientists bring a different perspective to the debate, by examining not only 'actor behaviour' but also 'systemic management'.[4] This 'systemic management' is a necessary element in examining international trade, where the efficient allocation of resources according to market principles may, and often does, clash with the maintenance of external sovereignty and internal unity, security, political and cultural autonomy, and other concerns of states coexisting in an anarchical setting. According to this argument, international trade is inherently politicised, as it occurs within the framework of a system of states in which the actions of the primary units – states – are governed by factors that include both political and economic considerations.

As with the international monetary system, discussed in the previous chapter, there exists an inherent tension between domestic policy and internationalism in international trade. This is primarily the result of the anarchical framework, as mentioned above. But the roots of this tension can also be traced through the different theoretical approaches espoused by liberals and free traders, economic nationalists and protectionists. These differences in theoretical approach were examined in detail in Chapters 2 and 3, but it is worthwhile summarising the differences for the purpose of discussing the desire to manage and regulate the international trading order.

Proponents of free trade are the intellectual heirs of Smith and Ricardo, who proposed their respective theories of absolute and comparative advantage. These theories evolved over time and were modified by neo-classical economists to take into account industrial and technological change in the modern world. Out of this evolution emerged 'factor endowment theories', which explain how a nation's comparative advantage is the result of the most efficient utilisation of a combination of factors of production, including not only natural resources, capital and labour, but also technology and management techniques.[5] Competition, the maximisation of efficiency, and the allocation of resources through the market are the fundamental principles underpinning these theories, which stress the potential mutual gains to be had by all participants in the system. In the short-term, not everyone will gain from a free-trade system. In the long-term, the operation of the market mechanism will encourage each participant to specialise in what they can produce at comparatively lower cost, and hence all will make gains through trade. The position of free traders and economic liberals is thus characterised as 'internationalist'. It plays down the role of nation-states and concentrates on the dynamics and effectiveness of transnational economic processes.

Economic nationalists, or protectionists (economic nationalists are not always protectionist, though this is their inclination), on the other hand, stress state interests and the interests of the producer as well as of the consumer. Trade, from this perspective, is not simply about efficiency and the unfettered operation of the market mechanism, but also about protecting the national interest. Autonomy, identity, national solidarity and independence are just as important goals as wealth and prosperity. Hamilton, Fichte and List, in their own respective ways, were the progenitors of protectionism, giving it its nationalist quality. That is not to say that all economic nationalists or protectionists do not lend credence to the utility and effectiveness of free trade. Some argue that relative self-sufficiency, or autarky, is an imperative of a modern state wishing to defend the interest of the nation and its citizens. Others lend credence to the utility of free trade in the long-term, but argue that to be able to participate in a highly competitive, interdependent world on an equitable footing, without sacrificing the national interest, protectionist policies may be short-term prerequisites. Protectionism in these terms is a means to an end in the search for security and the maximisation of power. One of the most acute economic nationalist criticisms of systems of free trade – especially that of the nineteenth century dominated by Great Britain – is that only the 'economic top dog' can actually pursue such a policy.[6]

The post-Second World War international trading system had to tackle this tension between nationalism and internationalism, between defending the narrow national interest and promoting the interest of the wider international system. Simultaneously, it was acknowledged that quite often the system requires a dominant actor to underpin the whole edifice. As with the Bretton Woods monetary arrangements, these tensions in international trade arrangements were resolved by the method and practices of 'embedded liberalism'. Multilateral institutions and codes of behaviour were created to promote the freeing up of trade in what can loosely be termed 'internationalism', while at the same time state interests were accommodated and a large degree of domestic autonomy permitted in what can loosely be termed 'nationalism'. The existing state-based system is in many ways fragmented, yet attempts are made to build a consensus and institutions to manage the system as a whole. As with the IMF, this was very much the case with GATT.

The Origins, Aims and Structures of GATT

During the Second World War, it became increasingly apparent that, as with international monetary affairs, international trade and commercial affairs would also have to be regulated in the post-war period. Two primary factors provided the motivation for the creation of an international institution to deal with international trade and commercial matters. Firstly, there was a general consensus among the developed countries not to repeat the errors made in the 1930s. During this period, states of all political persuasions too easily resorted to protectionist measures in response to difficulties at home. The growth in tariff barriers among the major economic actors in the system did little to ease the tensions being generated in the international system as a consequence of the rise of Fascism and Nazism, and the inability of the principal League of Nations powers to find a way to revise the peace established at Versailles. Secondly, there was a general fear in the US that, come the end of the war, the American economy would be vulnerable to recession, as it had been after the First World War. This would of course have a detrimental effect on the international system as a whole, let alone crippling the US economy.

These two potential problems, it was agreed, could be overcome through an international commitment to the principle of free trade, with reciprocal tariff guarantees and reductions, which would be regulated by an international trade organisation, or at least a multi-lateral convention on trade policy. This emerging conviction of wanting to avoid past pitfalls in international commerce though the establishment of an organisation or multilateral convention was reinforced by a zealous US commitment to replace previous trading arrangements with an open, liberal international trading order. As the senior partner in the war effort, and as the progressively dominant international economic actor, the US had it in its grasp to further this agenda.

The key problem facing the main architects of this envisaged order, the British and the Americans, was how to accommodate both the promotion of full employment domestically and the goal of free trade internationally. When negotiations began between, primarily, the US and Great Britain, as early as 1943, three broad areas of agreement were recognised. It was agreed that quantitative restrictions (quotas) on imports should be abolished; that the progressive reduction of tariffs should be a central plank of the system; and that an international agency managing an 'international code of trade behaviour' should be created.

From the outset, these negotiations were mired in differences between the US and Great Britain that at times became quite acrimonious. Even though the two negotiating parties were keen quickly to establish the framework for a broadly liberal international trading order, they found it difficult to relinquish trade practices that were of benefit to their respective domestic economies and spheres of influence. Britain proved extremely reluctant to abolish the imperial preference system, established at the Ottawa Conference in 1932, which gave it favourable access to the resources and markets of the dominions, an issue of historical and cultural solidarity and political status, as well as an issue of economic benefit. The US, on its part, wished to keep in place a series of tariff barriers that had been erected during the inter-war period and had greatly benefited the US economy.[7] Negotiations continued apace, and despite much dispute each side made enough concessions, largely by accepting to reduce tariffs, to enable a general agreement on tariffs and trade to be signed in October 1947. Twenty-three states were represented in

Geneva at the final negotiations of what became known as GATT, an agreement that was initially viewed as a short-term measure pending the creation of a fully fledged international organisation. This sister institution to the IMF, charged with regulating and managing the international trading system, was to be known as the International Trade Organisation (ITO). Between November 1947 and March 1948, a conference was convened in Havana to draw up its charter.

That the ITO never materialised was due to a serious divergence in the positions of the negotiating states, especially on the issues of multilateralism and discrimination. Negotiations also foundered on the demands of a surprisingly strong lobby of what have become known as less developed countries, consisting primarily of Latin American states and some former colonies of Great Britain and France. They feared the consequences of overly swift and extensive trade liberalisation, as proposed by the US, a fear shared by numerous European states in the aftermath of the war, and whose backing they received.

Consequently, what emerged was an agreement shot through with compromises. Even though it amassed 53 signatories, American congressional ratification was not forthcoming. The vast majority of states followed this example by not ratifying the convention themselves, and thus the ITO remained stillborn. By default, GATT, which was meant to be an interim measure, became the official organ through which the new trading order would be managed.

GATT was certainly not the envisaged international organisation by which international trade matters would be managed. It was a treaty and not an institution. More precisely, it was a treaty that provided for only a modest secretariat to monitor the fulfilment of its provisions. All signatories would participate in future negotiations, the so called GATT 'rounds' of talks, of which there have been eight, culminating in the Uruguay Round (1986–93). The goal of GATT was to create a multilateral and freer system of trade without the complete abandonment of national controls over trade barriers. It was intended to provide the framework through which international co-operation and domestic autonomy in commercial matters could co-exist. GATT was to work in close tandem with the IMF, whose system of fixed exchange rates would provide the required monetary stability for the commercial system to flourish. Speculation and politically motivated currency devaluations would not come into to play because of the

IMF, and thus could not interfere with the freer flow of trade that would be of mutual benefit to all participants in the long-term.

GATT comprised two main components: the general code of trade practice and norms of behaviour, and a specific list and schedule of tariffs covering hundreds of thousands of goods. The three main principles of GATT were: non-discrimination through the most-favoured nation principle, which stipulated that any concessions on tariffs on particular goods from a particular state would have to be extended to all signatories; reciprocity, which stipulated that if a state reduced its tariffs on another state's goods, this must automatically be reciprocated by the second state; transparency, which stipulated that all NTBs, such as quantitative restrictions and quality controls, should be replaced by the uniform measure of tariffs, which are much easier to monitor and ultimately, therefore, to reduce.

The centrality of tariffs to GATT is evident in the three principles outlined above. The idea was to promote the reduction of tariffs and the fair treatment of fellow signatories of GATT in an open and accountable way. But what is a tariff and what does it do? A tariff is a duty or custom (essentially a tax), levied on an import or paid on an export. One purpose served by tariffs is to generate revenue for the state without direct taxation of citizens. This was especially true of past periods, when direct taxation was not widespread or revenues were difficult to collect, and it still features as a central source of government revenue at the turn of the twenty-first century in countries like Russia. Another purpose served is in protecting and promoting domestic manufactures by making foreign imports artificially expensive and thus pricing them out of the market. This can be done either to protect an emerging or 'infant industry', or simply to defend a particular sector – automobile manufacture, shipbuilding, steelmaking – which may be a large employer.

As expected, tariff reductions proved to be the first aim of GATT, and by the mid-1960s good progress had been made. There were two reasons for this. Until the 'Kennedy Round' (1963–67), tariff reduction negotiations were conducted on an item-by-item basis. Initially this process concentrated on hundreds of 'unimportant' goods on which agreement was relatively easy among the signatories. When this list of goods was exhausted, and talks moved onto so-called 'vital goods', the process came to a standstill. The second, more important, reason for GATT's initial success concerns US domination of, or hegemony over, the international trading order. A booming and prosperous US economy in the 1950s and 1960s created liquidity and credit vital for the rehabilitation and development of the post-war international economy. This in turn oiled the wheels of commerce and led to an impressive growth in the volume of international trade. It is estimated that between 1948 and 1960, the average annual rate of growth in the value of exports of the non-communist world was 6 per cent, and between 1960 and 1973 nearly 9 per cent. These startling figures were largely considered attributable to GATT, and its success in reducing tariffs. Not surprisingly, states were eager to pursue further the process of tariff reduction. Whether it was or was not the chief factor in the growth of trade, it seemed to be bearing fruit. With the relative decline of the US economy in the late 1960s and early 1970s, however, the system started to grind to a halt.

This particular era in GATT's history raises two important theoretical questions. The first concerns the basic premise that trade liberalisation leads to increased prosperity. The evidence suggests that GATT talks in the 1960s were successful in that this period of tariff reduction corresponded with a period of impressive economic growth and wealth creation in the international system. In practice, according to this argument, it was the steady reduction in tariff rates that produced this remarkable international economic boom, as the average tariff rate fell from 25 per cent in 1950 to 13 per cent by 1970. This assertion has been challenged on the basis that in fact it was the power and prosperity of the dominant US economy that enabled trade liberalisation to occur. In funding a system that, in the process of recovery from the war, had a greater hunger for capital, the US created a situation ripe for trade liberalisation and hence reduction in tariffs. The system was able not only to absorb credit and capital investment, but also, as a consequence, to produce enough goods to 'soak up the purchasing power' evident in the system. Therefore, the reduction in tariffs resulted from the prosperity of the system, it is argued, and not vice versa.[8]

Linked to this is the second question, which again centres on the role of the US in the international trading order. Proponents of GATT would argue that its multilateral nature was a fundamental contributing factor to the smooth operation of the system, and the successful reductions in tariff barriers leading to freer trade. The counter-argument suggests that just as with the 'Pax Britannica', which underwrote the free-trade system in the nineteenth century, a 'Pax Americana' emerged post-1945, providing the international economic system with the necessary degree of stability for it to flourish. In this theory of 'hegemonic stability' it is argued that without a hegemon, or dominant leading actor, the system has little chance of success.[9] A stable and increasingly wealthy world economy, based on co-operation in a relatively peaceful environment, is primarily reliant on a political framework dominated by a powerful state, which underpins and provides leadership to the whole structure. Without this hegemonic actor, the system would lack both the means to achieve relative stability and the direction to pursue further co-operation. Open competition, reliance on the market mechanism, and even multilateralism cannot, in themselves, provide the framework for a prosperous world economy. According to 'hegemonic stability theory' (HST), in an anarchic international system the temptation to 'free ride' – to pay lip-service to rules but break them when it suits the national interest to do so – is great. The clever pursuit of this strategy can generate large gains, while others pay the costs. According to HST, a single powerful state is needed to make sure that, as a general rule, this does not happen.

This argument is partially discredited with the continuing existence of GATT and the emergence of the WTO, despite the relative decline in the power and status of the hegemon (a notion, incidentally, that does not go unchallenged). Nevertheless, the multilateral trading order did receive a big shock to the system in the 1970s and early 1980s, a period coincidental with the relative decline of the US economy and its ability to play the role of hegemon. A combination of events resulted in the temporary cessation in the tariff reductions achieved by GATT and a concomitant rise in the use of protectionist measures across the system, particularly NTBs. The termination of the adjustable peg, fixed exchange rate system established at Bretton Woods, and the floating of exchange rates in 1973, undermined the stability of the trading order. This exposed the unwillingness of the US to continue playing the leading role in the system. But it also pointed to its inability to do so in the face of the growing competitive challenge from the burgeoning economies of the EEC states and Japan, which heralded the relative decline of US economic power. The situation was further exacerbated by the OPEC-inspired oil crisis of 1973–4, all of these events culminating in a period of dormancy in the process of trade liberalisation. It was only in 1986 that a new set of GATT negotiations commenced, the so-called Uruguay Round, whose rocky journey culminated in the creation of the WTO.

Problems of and Challenges to GATT

Apart from the landmark creation of the WTO, the Uruguay Round also dealt with a series of structural inadequacies that had plagued GATT since its inception, and had provoked strong criticism. The majority of these inadequacies revolved around 'sectoral trade', some of which had not been included in the GATT framework. The two most important instances of this were the sectors of textiles and agriculture.

Since 1974, textiles had been governed by the Multi-fibre Agreement, which fixed quotas for textile and clothing exports, primarily from developing to developed countries. Even though officially recognised by GATT, this agreement contravened a corner-stone principle of GATT, that of non-discrimination, by allowing states to impose highly discriminatory quotas on scores of goods emanating from other GATT states. The specific repercussions of this agreement were felt by the developing countries, which bore the brunt of this discriminatory practice. This was especially damaging as comparative advantage in the production of textiles had shifted to the developing world, and the textile industry had become a crucial source of much needed foreign exchange. In one instance, in 1985, the US, Great Britain and France imposed quotas on shirts imported from Bangladesh, arguing that the immense growth of this sector in Bangladesh posed a serious threat to domestic manufacturers. In fact, in the previous year the Bangladeshi share of the shirt trade from the developing world to the developed world amounted to only 0.25 per cent.[10] This highly dubious discriminatory policy had a massive impact on the Bangladeshi economy, where 50 per cent of the country's shirt factories were closed and over 150,000 jobs were lost, but only a minor impact on the 'Northern' textile producers and consumers of Bangladeshi shirts. Discriminatory policies of this kind flouted the fundamental principle of non-discrimination and threatened the whole aim of promoting freer trade by the removal of protectionist measures. The general implication of this type of practice was the diminution of confidence in GATT and its international code of behaviour.

Agriculture was another area omitted from GATT on American insistence, under pressure from the powerful US farmers' lobby. This omission allowed the use of subsidies and price-support mechanisms within domestic economies to continue unchecked, thus enabling the price of imports to be undercut and rendered uncompetitive. It was also a manifestation of economic nationalism in a different form, in that, arguably, the US wanted to restrict agricultural imports in the name of food self-sufficiency and non-reliance on external sources for a basic commodity of great social, political and strategic significance.

The EEC also took advantage of the omission of agriculture from GATT by establishing the Common Agricultural Policy (CAP) in 1962. The objectives of the CAP were three-fold; firstly, to eradicate periodic food shortages and fluctuations in the supply and price of such a socially and politically important commodity; secondly, to ensure the economic survival of a vast agrarian and farming population that existed in a number of member states such as France; thirdly, to provide this population with a comparable income to other sectors of the European economy. In order to achieve these objectives, the EEC put into place a whole range of highly discriminatory practices. Farmers and dairy producers were offered a series of subsidies, price-support mechanisms, and other incentives to over-produce, and if desired export to foreign markets at more than competitive prices. In addition, a stiff levy was introduced to minimise imports from non-members. The CAP proved to be such a major enterprise within the EEC that it soon accounted for over 60 per cent of the total budget. The CAP discriminated in favour of the European farmer, and food producer in general, and rendered a highly lucrative market out of bounds for non-member exporters of agricultural products and foodstuffs.

While mainly directed at the domestic market and a domestic political constituency, as in the case of the CAP, discriminatory practices such as subsidies also have important international implications. They often lead to over-production and hence an excess supply of particular goods that cannot be sold domestically. As these goods are subsidised, and hence underpriced, they can be sold cheaply on foreign markets, undermining local production of similar goods. While GATT challenged the 'dumping' of products through Article VI, compensation sought through the provisions of GATT proved a lengthy and extremely expensive procedure that few developing countries could afford. These practices raised questions of equality within GATT, and furthered the argument that a multilateral trading order based on the principle of free trade favoured developed countries at the expense of developing ones.

Discrimination in the field of agriculture and foodstuffs took an additional form. Countries in the developed world would quite often set different tariff levels for refined and unrefined forms of products imported from the developing world. The 'raw' product would be liable to a much lower tariff rate than the refined version ready for sale to the consumer. For example, the EEC would levy a 2 per cent duty on unrefined palm oil imported from Malaysia. Palm oil would then be refined within the Community and sold on as margarine at a much higher price, thus turning a good profit for the producer and a raw deal for the consumer. If Malaysian palm oil producers refined their own product into margarine and attempted to export it to the EEC, it would be liable to a 25 per cent tariff rate. The producer would thus be saddled with both the cost of processing the unrefined product and the tariff, making the total burden in effect very much higher. This made the export of the refined product uncompetitive, and in effect allowed the developed world access to cheap raw materials that they could refine and make tremendous profits from. This situation is replicated in the vast Western markets for coffee and tea, where the exporters of these goods receive only 20 per cent of the price at which the refined product is sold. These types of practices in the agricultural sector amply demonstrated some of the serious structural inadequacies evident in GATT.

A third method by which the transparency and reciprocity of GATT has been undermined is through the existence of NTBs such as the imposition of luxury taxes on certain imported goods, domestic health and safety regulations that are frequently changed, and VERs. While these do not contravene the 'letter' of GATT 'law', they do infringe the underlying principles and spirit of the agreement, creating tension in the system and retaliatory actions between the signatory states.

Recent Revisions in GATT and the Creation of the WTO

The most important development at the conclusion of the Uruguay Round was the creation of the World Trade Organisation (WTO). The WTO manages and regulates the international trading system based on the principles of GATT, with which it co-exists. It has been endowed with binding powers of arbitration and the authority to impose massive fines on miscreant members. On joining the WTO, signatories have to accept GATT and a series of other agreements governing not only trade in manufactured goods but also trade in services, intellectual property rights, and rules for the settlement of disputes in any of these areas. The WTO carries out a wide range of tasks, and supplies an administrative capacity for the international trading regime through its General Council and permanent secretariat. It provides a framework for further trade negotiations and the implementation of any resulting trade agreements. It also provides a permanent forum in which trade issues can be discussed and the general economic policies of members harmonised. In reality, and perhaps paradoxically, the international trading order now has the institution that it attempted to create in the late 1940s.

The Uruguay Round also took up the mantle of restarting the tariff reduction process that had been stymied for so long because of the conditions of the international economy outlined earlier. The aim was to pursue a general reduction in tariffs of between 30–50 per cent of current levels. One of its great successes was the incorporation of the agricultural sector into GATT. The agreement stipulated that within 10 years of ratification, import controls, price support mechanisms and subsidies would all be converted into tariffs, adding more transparency to the system. In turn, the levels of these tariffs would have to be drastically reduced within this 10-year period. This will not only put an end to discriminatory practices, resulting in freer trade and more open competition, but will also bring agriculture into the mainstream of international trade, an especially important goal given that agriculture amounts to some 10 per cent of total international trade. Discriminatory practices in the field of textiles have also been curtailed. The Multi-fibre Agreement is to be phased out by 2005, and all trade in textiles and clothing now fall under the remit of GATT.

Within the Uruguay Round, members of GATT also negotiated two novel agreements in international trade in the fields of intellectual property rights and trade-related investment. The former covers copyright, trademarks and patents, and takes a strong position on the trade of counterfeit goods in an effort to curtail it. It covers a wide range of products, including computer software, designer clothing and pharmaceuticals, as well as pesticides and seeds. In what has been termed the 'nationalisation of science and nature', patents on seeds vital to the reproduction of crops have been claimed by a small proportion of the developed world, with some 70 per cent of the international seed trade in the control of less than a dozen states. The Uruguay Round brought these issues onto the agenda and took a series of measures to add transparency and equity to this growing area of trade. Similarly, the Uruguay Round provided a framework for initial discussion on the problem of trade-related investment measures (TRIMs). Agreement was also reached on a series of measures to bring this field into line with the general principles of GATT. TRIMs refer to the variety of measures taken by governments to circumscribe the freedom of action of foreign companies operating on their soil, for example restricting the proportion of capital that a foreign company can own in a home-based company. It is estimated that by the year 2002 the Uruguay Round agreements could add up to approximately US$250 billion to world trade, over 1 per cent of world GDP.

These changes, the result of an arduous seven-year-long negotiation process, have generally been welcomed by both the developed and developing worlds. The negotiation process was so drawn-out because of traditional clashes between the developing and developed states over the extent to which markets should be opened up, and the pace at which these reforms would be implemented. The agreement to include textiles and agriculture into GATT ate up a lot of negotiating time, as did the issues of intellectual property rights and trade invest-ment measures. Ultimately, the whole round of talks almost collapsed because of a major disagreement between developed countries, namely the US and EU, on whether agriculture should be brought into the agreement at all. This disagreement prolonged the negotiations for at least a year, if not more, and came close to destroying the whole round. The dispute was finally settled according to principles laid down by the Blair House Agreement of 1992, and the round was successfully concluded in 1993.

Despite the general acceptance of the success of the Uruguay Round, there is still stern criticism and opposition from those who believe that these agreements still discriminate against the developing world, and that they do not take seriously enough new issues of public concern, such as the well-being of the environment. It is also still to be seen how quickly the signatory states will be able to put tariff reductions back on track, and how the WTO will cope with recalcitrant states deemed to have contravened its rules and regulations.

Concluding Remarks

Ultimately, while the WTO and its reforms may be portrayed as a 'great leap forward' in the management of the international trading system, we are still faced with the same conundrum of attempting to manage the international system on the basis of multilateral agreement and negotiation, while simultaneously allowing states a large degree of domestic autonomy. The 'liberalism from above' manifest in the creation of an international institution to encourage, manage and regulate international trade has still to overcome the existence of 'illiberalism from below', in the form of sovereign states defending their perceived national interests through a range of explicit and implicit protectionist measures.

Notes on Chapter 6

1 Victoria Curzon Price, 'The Decay of GATT: Does Multilateralism Have a Future?' in Andrew Shonfield (ed.), *International Economic Relations of the Western World: 1959–71* (London, Oxford University Press for the Royal Institute of International Affairs, 1976), 139.

2 Benjamin J. Cohen, 'The Political Economy of International Trade', *International Organization* 44, 2 (1990), 264–5. Cohen argues that the study of 'actor behaviour' is not limited to economists as it is one of two fundamental questions tackled by 'International Political Economy'. What he does suggest is that economists focus on two narrow issues within the context of 'actor behaviour', namely, 'endogenous trade policy' and 'strategic trade policy'.

3 Susan Strange, *States and Markets: An Introduction to International Political Economy* (London, Pinter, 1988), 35.

4   Cohen, 'The Political Economy of International Trade', 264. By 'systemic management', Cohen literally means the management of the international economic and trading system through co-operative means of dealing with conflicts of interest.
5   The Heckscher–Ohlin Theory being the prime example.
6   See Chapter 3 for a detailed account of the economic nationalist school.
7   The Smoot-Hawley Tariff of 1930 was the main example. This all but closed off the US market to foreign trade.
8   Susan Strange, 'Protectionism and World Politics', *International Organization* 39, 2, (1985), 240–1.
9   The initial idea that a liberal international economic system requires a hegemon to function in an orderly and productive manner can be found in Charles Kindleberger, *The World in Depression 1929–1939* (Harmondsworth, Pelican, 1987). His concept of 'hegemonic stability', and the subsequent debates about 'hegemonic decline', has spawned a vast literature.
10 Kevin Watkins, 'GATT and the Third World: Fixing the Rules', *Race and Class* 34, 1, (1992), 26–7.

Select Bibliography

Conybeare, John, *Trade Wars: The Theory and Practice of International Commercial Rivalry* (New York, NY, Columbia University Press, 1987).

Curzon, Gerard and Victoria, 'The Management of Trade Relations in GATT', in Andrew Shonfield (ed.), *International Economic Relations of the Western World* (London, Oxford University Press for the Royal Institute of International Affairs, 1976). First class, concise overview.

Dam, Kenneth, *The GATT* (Chicago, IL, Chicago University Press, 1970). The origins, structure and evolution of GATT. A must on the early years.

Hoekman, Bernard and Michael Kostecki, *The Political Economy of the Multilateral Trading System: From GATT to WTO* (Oxford, Oxford University Press, 1995). The transition in the international trading system laid bare. A useful work combining description and careful analysis.

Krasner, Stephen, 'State Power and the Structure of International Trade', *World Politics* 28 (1976). Analysis of the pattern of international trade by leading realist theorist.

Keohane, Robert O., *After Hegemony: Cooperation and Discord in the World Political Economy* (Princeton, NJ, Princeton University Press, 1984). Renowned study of international economic co-operation. An early statement of what became 'neo-liberal institutionalism'.

Krueger, Anne (ed.), *The WTO as an International Organisation* (Chicago, IL, University of Chicago Press, 1998). Revealing guide to long-awaited international trade organisation. Highly useful reference work.

Milner, Helen, *Resisting Protectionism: Global Industries and the Politics of International Trade* (Princeton, NJ, Princeton University Press, 1988). Eminently readable defence of the role of the firm in promoting freer trade.

Rosencrance, Richard, *The Rise of the Trading State: Commerce and Conquest in the Modern World* (New York, NY, Basic Books, 1986). Eloquent study of the interplay between economic interdependence and the territorial state. Valuable work.

CHAPTER 7

The International Economic Order and the Challenge from the South

The Preamble to the UN General Assembly Declaration on the Establishment of a New International Economic Order (NIEO) of 1974 succinctly summarises the main contentions and presuppositions of the campaign that later was to bear that name. It asserts that: there is a 'widening gap between the developed and the developing countries'; this is an 'injustice'; 'the developing countries, which constitute 70 per cent of the world's population, account for only 30 per cent of the world's income'; it is 'impossible to achieve an even and balanced development under the existing international economic order'; the gap between rich and poor continues to widen 'in a system...established at a time when most developing countries did not exist as independent states'; and that this system continues to 'perpetuate injustice and inequality'.

The Significance of the Southern Challenge

The campaign for a NIEO began in the early 1970s and came to an end, in the face of stiff Western resistance, in the early 1980s. It constituted the high watermark of the attempt by newly independent states, along with a few older states (notably from Latin American), to transform the post-war liberal international economic order. This attempt also became known as the 'Southern challenge', since its proponents came mainly from the Southern hemisphere.

The Southern challenge is important in a number of respects. Firstly, the very basis of the international economic order was questioned. The validity of the principles of non-discrimination and reciprocity in trade were contested, as was the goal of free trade, as was the system of weighted voting within international financial institutions.[1] In a sense the NIEO was a call for greater international democracy.

Secondly, this challenge succeeded in putting the issue of world poverty, and especially the question of where responsibility lies for dealing with it, firmly on the international agenda. The answer to this question was, and is, far from obvious. Does responsibility lie with the poverty-stricken countries themselves? Does it lie with the rich countries of the North? Or does it lie with – for some a fiction, for others a reality – the 'international community'? This question goes to the heart of the North–South debate and remains one of the most fundamental questions in world politics.

In this connection it is important to note that one of the most radical demands of the NIEO was for 'full compensation' for past wrongs and present injustices. It was repeatedly demanded that compensation should be paid to all peoples who had suffered from, or who were still suffering from, 'colonialism and alien domination'.

Thirdly, the NIEO starkly illustrated the kinds of problems with which a much expanded international society of states would be faced in the future. Prior to 1945, the international society comprised a relatively small, homogeneous group of mainly European states, or states comprised primarily of peoples of European origin. But with the onset of decolonisation in the 1940s and 1950s, and the rapid acceleration of its pace in the 1960s, it was dramatically transformed into a much larger society with a much more heterogeneous membership. The exclusive European society of states of the eighteenth and nineteenth centuries gave way to the inclusive worldwide international society of the twentieth.[2] Given the vastly changed composition of this society, it was not long before its traditional economic and political bases began to be questioned. One of these bases was the rules and institutions of the post-war liberal international economic order. In brief, expansion and increased heterogeneity inevitably led to challenges to the 'rules of the game', including those of the international economic game.

Institutional Origins

The institutional origins of the NIEO can be traced back to the Bruce Report of 1946, the UN specialised agencies, the Non-aligned Movement, the United Nations Conference on Trade and Development (UNCTAD), and the Group of 77.

The Bruce Report on the future of the League of Nations laid great stress on the need for greater co-operation in the economic and social fields. In the wake of this, the UN Charter contained in its Preamble a commitment 'to employ international machinery for the economic and social advancement of all peoples'. The specialised agencies were created for this purpose, and the Economic and Social Council was established as a 'principal organ' of the UN. Significantly, it was placed under the auspices of the General Assembly. These developments ensured that economic and social matters would be given much more attention by international institutions than had been the case in the past. Moreover, they represented a move in the direction of solving major economic and social problems through 'international machinery', rather than leaving them to the market.

Two further developments gave newly independent and 'developing' states a firm institutional platform upon which their campaign could be launched. The creation of the Non-aligned Movement at the Bandung Conference in 1955 demonstrated that such diverse leaders as Nehru, Sukarno, Tito and Nasser, and such disparate countries as India, Indonesia, Yugoslavia and Egypt, could co-operate on matters of common concern. Secondly, in 1963 UNCTAD was established. Its membership consisted of four groups: African and Asian states; Western industrialised states plus Japan; Latin American states; and the COMECON countries. All of these groups were represented on the executive body of UNCTAD – the Trade and Development Board – but importantly, most seats were given to the first and third groups. These states soon combined to form the 'Group of 77', so called because it originally had 77 members.

In sharp contrast to the Bretton Woods institutions, therefore, UNCTAD was dominated from the outset by a coalition of developing countries possessing a permanent voting majority (despite the fact that well over half of its budget came from the third group of states). UNCTAD was an important institutional advance from the point of view of developing states for two further reasons: firstly, it provided a forum in which dialogue between North and South could take place, but one, unlike others, in which the leading role for setting the agenda rested with the South; secondly, it was established as a permanent institution, with a secretariat empowered to undertake research and supply information relevant to Third, as opposed to First, World needs.

Political Origins

A number of explicitly political factors also contributed to the emergence of the NIEO. As a result of the massive wave of decolonisation in the 1950s and 1960s, newly independent countries soon constituted a majority in the General Assembly. Not surprisingly, they soon began to use this organ as a vehicle for the pursuit of their interests. The OPEC oil embargo of 1973 further boosted developing countries' confidence. With the oil weapon, it was felt, the 'disenfranchised' South at last had a weapon that could be used to prise real concessions out of the 'selfish' North (meaning, in practice, the West). It is no coincidence that the three General Assembly resolutions calling for a NIEO followed hard on the heels of the OPEC embargo. It is also no coincidence that shortly afterwards plans were drawn up in UNCTAD for the creation of similar commodity cartels. Optimism abounded at the prospect of replicating OPEC's success with copper, tin and rubber. Finally, it is significant that the height of the campaign for a NIEO coincided with the period of détente between the superpowers. In this more relaxed political atmosphere, the US showed greater willingness to engage in constructive dialogue and accommodate Third World demands. The US agreed, for example, to increase OPEC representation at the IMF, to grant easier access for developing countries to World Bank loans, and dropped longstanding opposition to the convening of a Third Conference on the Law of the Sea.[3] The EEC agreed, in 1975, to set up the Stabex scheme of compensatory finance for its primary-producing former colonial trading partners in Africa, the Caribbean and the Pacific. Western countries also agreed in principle to contribute to the Common Fund of UNCTAD's Integrated Programme for Commodities.[4]

In the latter part of the 1970s, however, several events conspired against this conciliatory mood. The Soviet Union and Cuba stepped up their involvement in Angola, Mozambique and the Horn of Africa. The Shah of Iran, a key American ally in the Middle East, was overthrown, plunging the region into uncertainty and provoking a general rise in oil prices and widespread fears of inflation. The US became increasingly suspicious of Soviet intentions in the field of arms control. Anxiety over Soviet designs in the economically and strategically important Persian Gulf was dramatically heightened in 1979 when the Soviet Union invaded Afghanistan.

All these things contributed to a much firmer line being taken in Washington on foreign policy. The term 'North–South' had been coined precisely for the purpose of conveying the message that relations between the industrialised North and the industrialising South had replaced the 'East–West' superpower conflict as the principal division – the chief source of tension – within international society. These events demonstrated that this was not the case. The election of free-market conservative governments in London and Washington led to a further toughening and tightening of policy. Rhetoric from the leading Western states became much more aggressively individualistic and libertarian. The collectivist and redistributionist NIEO rapidly became a prime target of this rhetoric.

Intellectual Origins

Any analysis of the origins of the NIEO would be incomplete without mention of its intellectual origins. In broad terms it was inspired by two closely related egalitarian political doctrines: reformist socialism and Keynesianism. These doctrines place considerable emphasis on the need for management and regulation of the marketplace, including: the regulation of the supply and price of essential raw materials; the achievement of high and stable levels of employment; the re-distribution of wealth from those who benefit most from the system to those who benefit least; and the notion of 'positive' as opposed to 'negative' liberty (the freedom to enjoy such things as decent housing, a good education and a decent diet, as well as freedom from such things as arbitrary arrest, detention without charge, 'cruel and unusual punishment'). They also emphasise the need for centralised mechanisms for the performance of these tasks. Echoes of this philosophy can be seen in many NIEO demands, particularly for:

non-reciprocal transfers of technology; the idea of a global development fund financed by a system of international progressive taxation; the demand for 'real' sovereign equality, meaning, according to some interpretations, 'one state, one vote' in international organisations;[5] and the demand that resources of the seabed should be declared part of the 'common heritage of mankind' (the implication being that the benefits derived from the exploitation of these resources must be 'shared equitably by all states', without regard to the market principle that level of benefit should be proportional to the level of investment or financial risk).

But the NIEO was more immediately informed by some of the more moderate forms of dependency theory, as advocated, for example, by Professor Raul Prebisch, the Secretary General of the Economic Commission for Latin America (ECLA). Prebisch's argument was based on the economic experience, as he saw it, of Latin America since its incorporation into the world economy in the late nineteenth century. During this period, Latin America took on the role of supplier of raw materials and foodstuffs to the industrial countries, importing the manufactured goods of the industrial countries in return. According to classical liberalism, such a division of labour, based on the principle of comparative advantage, was rational. Both parties would benefit and resources would be used to maximum effect. Prebisch argued, however, that because of adverse terms of trade this was not so. In fact, Latin American countries found themselves having to export more and more commodities in order to import the same amount of manufactures. They increasingly had to run in order to stand still.

His explanation for this perverse state of affairs was two-fold. Firstly, he argued that the income elasticity of demand for commodities was less than one: in other words, any increase in the income of consumers led to an increase in the consumption of commodities, but not to the same degree. As people get richer, they spend a smaller and smaller proportion of their income on commodities. By the same token, the income elasticity of demand for manufactures was greater than one: as people get richer, they spend a greater and greater proportion of their income on manufactured goods. Thus the income elasticity of demand for the bulk of Latin American exports was less than one, whereas the income elasticity of demand for the bulk of Latin American imports was more than one. This imbalance in the income elasticities of demand between the industrial centre and the primary-producing periphery resulted in a steady improvement of the terms of trade of the former and a steady decline in the terms of trade for the latter. Hence the chronic balance-of-payments problems that Latin American countries found themselves running into.

Secondly, Prebisch argued that rising wage levels in the industrial centre and stagnant wages levels in the periphery had the effect of pushing up prices in the former and depressing them in the latter. Since the late nineteenth century, productivity increases in the centre had been matched by increases in wages. This was largely a result of the growth of the power and influence of trade unions and designated working-class or 'labour' political parties. In response to this, manufactures increased in price, aided and abetted by the growth of monopoly and the consequent diminution of free competition (see Chapter 2). In the periphery, however, increases in productivity were manifested purely in increases in profits for the large landowners. This was due to the availability of a large pool of labour and weak trade-union organisation. Prebisch observed that throughout its history of incorporation into the world economic system, the wages of the mass of workers in Latin America had barely risen above subsistence level. There was no tendency, therefore, for prices to increase.

By way of empirical demonstration, Prebisch and his ECLA colleagues claimed that whenever the links with the world economic system were broken, during the world depression of the 1930s, for example, or during the Second World War, the economies of Latin America experienced a spurt in their industrial growth. This spurt came to an end as soon as the crisis in question ended, and the role of Latin America in the international division of labour resumed. The conclusion was drawn that the only way for Latin America to achieve rapid industrial growth would be to break some of its links with the outside world and deliberately encourage industrialisation through a policy of import substitution.[6]

This policy, import substitution industrialisation (ISI), was adopted by all the main Latin American states by the late 1950s. It involved a range of restrictive and redistributionist measures, including the imposition of tariffs, currency manipulation, income redistribution (to boost demand for domestically produced manufactures), land reform (to reduce the power of the old, exporting oligarchies, and move away from reliance on one or two 'cash crops' towards greater diversity of agricultural production) and commodity agreements aimed at raising and stabilising export earnings.

By the mid-1960s, however, it was clear that this new strategy of industrialisation was failing. The drive for rapid industrialisation led to increased demand for imports of raw materials, spare parts and capital goods. But the diversification of agriculture to the detriment of traditional cash crops, meant that insufficient foreign exchange was being generated to pay for these increased imports. In addition, in the short-run, ISI did not reduce demand for aggregate imports but merely shifted their composition away from consumer goods towards capital and other goods needed to increase the country's productive capacity. The implication of this was considerable, and wholly unforeseen. Any interruption in the flow of imports (for example because of a balance-of-payments crisis) now had profound consequences not only for the level of consumption, but also for the development plans and stability of the entire economy.

There were other problems. The shift from labour-intensive to capital-intensive methods of production led to increased unemployment and a consequent fall in purchasing power and consumer demand for the very goods being produced. The scale of the plant imported, from steel mills to automobile factories, was in many instances too big for domestic demand. As a consequence, they often ran at less than full capacity, thus wasting resources. A further significant development was that many multinational corporations (MNCs), in order to side-step the various protectionist measures directed against them, began to establish production units in the developing countries themselves. The view of the ECLA was that there was nothing intrinsically wrong with this: that is, there was nothing intrinsically wrong with what became known as 'foreign direct investment'. Anything that increased the productive capacity of the nation was good. But these MNCs specialised in the production of relatively expensive, high value-added consumer goods: cars, hi-fis, sports equipment and branded drinks rather than the trucks, buses and machine tools needed for general economic development. Modern advertising techniques ensured that demand for these goods remained high, despite government attempts to encourage, as they saw it, more wholesome patterns of production and consumption.[7]

The failure of ISI led many to see the need for more radical steps if Latin American and other Third World countries were to free themselves from their dependent position in the world economic system. The diagnosis of Prebisch and the ECLA was broadly accepted, but by the late 1960s many felt that their remedies did not go far enough. For some, the only way forward was a complete break with the world system. Third World countries, they said, should only trade among themselves, and strive for a high degree of self-reliance. For others, the way forward was to campaign for a complete over-haul of the existing international system: its rules, principles and institutions. Third World states could not 'go it alone', but neither could they achieve their developmental goals in a system heavily loaded against them.

In 1964, Prebisch became the first Director General of the newly established UNCTAD. In the wake of his earlier analysis, and in the light of the failure of ISI, he immediately used his position to argue for reforms of the international economic system. The principal task was to find an acceptable means of offsetting the deterioration of the terms of trade from which so many developing countries suffered. He argued, *inter alia*, for international commodity agreements to prevent the prices of commodities falling below a certain level; for compensatory finance arrangements to assist those who suffered from sudden shifts in the terms of trade; and for the abrogation of the most-favoured nation clause of GATT, which prevented developing states from discriminating against the manufactured exports of developed countries and receiving preferential treatment for their own exports. Only by such means, Prebisch insisted, could the exchange of commodities and manufactures take place on an 'equitable' basis and the economic hopes of developing countries have any chance of being realised. His ideas were immensely influential on both the philosophy and the content of NIEO.

Conflicting Interpretations

The NIEO – its emergence, significance and implications – has been interpreted from a number of contrasting ideological standpoints. Radical observers, such as Teresa Hayter and André Gunder Frank, have interpreted it as a forlorn and ultimately futile attempt by 'under-developed' countries to break out of the international economic straightjacket of dependency and domination. Their failure to do so, so the argument runs, proves the thesis that the grip of the 'centre' on the 'periphery' is so great that nothing short of revolution will radically alter periphery prospects. The centre, they further claim, was able to tighten its grip and thereby maintain its dominance by successfully co-opting a small but significant group of OPEC and newly industrialised states.

Not all radicals have been sympathetic to the NIEO. Bill Warren, writing from a classical Marxist viewpoint, has attacked dependency theory, of which the NIEO, as we have seen, was partly an expression, for being 'bourgeois nationalistic'. In Warren's view, dependency theorists put so much stress on the state, and its power vis-a-vis other states, that they failed to notice that capitalism *is* performing its historic task of developing the productive forces of backward economies. In playing the bourgeois game of national power and prestige they elevated superficial subjective factors above long-term objective factors. The inevitable consequence was that the historic task of capital was being temporarily obstructed, and the historical juncture at which economic and social conditions would be ripe for the establishment of socialism postponed.

Some of the most carefully reasoned critiques of 'NIEO ideology' have come from the pens of free-market liberals. Peter Bauer and Basil Yamey of the London School of Economics wrote a series of powerful articles arguing that this ideology frustrated the growth of those virtues – thrift, diligence, prudence, trust, respect for law and order – necessary for the creation of a stable and prosperous market economy. They dismissed utterly the suggestion that poverty was a product of exogenous factors.[8]

Other liberals, not so uncompromising in their faith in the market, have been more sympathetic. The Brandt Report – produced in 1979 by a distinguished international team of 'elder statesmen' under the chairmanship of former West German Chancellor Willy Brandt – asserted that redistribution of wealth from North to South was not only a matter of moral duty but also of common interest. It contended that the poor performance of Northern economies in the 1970s was a direct product of lack of development in the South. Along the lines of Hobson's prescriptions for dealing with the problem of underconsumption, the report advocated a transfer of resources, particularly through increased investment, in order to make developing countries more productive and increase their purchasing power.

This, in turn, would enable them to purchase the goods of the recession-hit industries of the North. A virtuous circle of development, trade and growth would thereby be created.[9]

Certain realist thinkers, such as the American political scientist Robert Tucker, contended that the rhetoric of the NIEO was a disguise for the pursuit of less noble objectives. He pointed out that liberal supporters of the campaign for a NIEO in the West – the 'new political sensibility' – conceived redistribution in terms of individuals and on the basis of notions of shared humanity. Their starting point was that everyone should be guaranteed a minimum economic standard. But Third World elites – the 'new egalitarians' – saw redistribution not in terms of individuals but in terms of states. Not for nothing was one of the principal documents of the NIEO entitled the Charter on Economic Rights and Duties of States.

In Tucker's view, there was no guarantee that wealth redistributed to Third World states would find its way into the pockets of Third World individuals. Indeed, these elites were playing the age-old game of acquiring power and prestige. Intellectuals of the new political sensibility assumed that demands for greater global equality would lead to the transformation of the international system. Global institutions would be created to manage increased interdependence and enhance collective well-being. But in Tucker's view, Third World elites were not interested in transforming or over-turning the hierarchical international system, but simply in improving their position within it.[10] Moreover, the logic of their demands was not greater order, as the new political sensibility supposed, but greater disorder. Third World elites, he maintained, would inevitably use their new-found wealth to increase the might of their states – perhaps, ultimately, through the acquisition of nuclear weapons.

Tucker's book is an eloquent testimony to the power of critical thinking and a damning indictment of the logic and implications of the NIEO. But it did not go unchallenged. It was pointed out, for example, that the distinction between state equality and individual equality is not nearly as clear in practice as Tucker assumed. The state remains by far the most important instrument through which groups and individuals seek goals of many kinds: wealth, security, justice, freedom and dignity. If the state is seen as the chief instrument for the achievement of these goals, why not the goal of individual equality? Similarly, Third World nationalists struggling against

colonial domination saw the achievement of statehood and independence as a precondition for the achievement of the freedom and
dignity of individual men and women. If statehood is the precondition
for the achievement of individual freedom, is not meaningful
statehood (as opposed to merely 'formal' or 'quasi' statehood) the
precondition for the achievement of meaningful individual equality?[11]

The fact is that the conservative assumption of Tucker and the
radical assumption of the 'new egalitarianism' are both incomplete.
Changes in the distribution of wealth among states do not automatically lead to increased equality within them. But neither do they
automatically preclude it. The result depends on the particular
regime and society in question, the variety of which defies the
attempts of sociologists and political scientists simply to classify them
for the purposes of general analysis. Tucker's 'new egalitarianism'
and 'new political sensibility' are founded on generalisations no less
sweeping than Frank's or Wallerstein's 'centre' and 'periphery'.

The Impact of the NIEO

At this point it might be asked, how successful was the campaign for
a NIEO? How many of the demands were actually met? The
answers are 'not very' and 'not many'. The demand for 'control' of
the activities of MNCs was partially met with the drawing up of a UN
Code of Practice. A commitment was given that the discriminatory
Multi-fibre Agreements would be renegotiated. But it was not until
the GATT agreement of 1994 that the Northern industrial countries
legally bound themselves to phase out these agreements (and then
over a period of ten years). The demand for preferential treatment
in trade matters was partially met through Part IV (1965) of GATT
and concessions granted by the EEC in the Yaoundé and Lomé
Conventions.[12] The demand for redistribution of wealth was to some
extent met by increases in the availability of 'softer' IMF and World
Bank loans.

Against these modest concessions must be placed Western rejection
of: full implementation of the Integrated Programme for Commodities;
the 'common heritage of mankind' principle; compensation for past
exploitation; much greater 'democracy' in international economic
institutions; and large-scale debt relief. In addition, of the many rich

industrial countries that committed themselves to raising the proportion of their national income devoted to foreign aid to 0.7 per cent
during the First UN Development Decade (1960s), only Sweden
was successful. Not even Sweden succeeded in reaching the target of
1 per cent set during the Second Development Decade (1970s).

It should also be noted that during the Uruguay Round of
GATT talks of the late 1980s and early 1990s negotiations over
issues of particular importance to the South constituted no more than
a sideshow. The main negotiations were between the three dominant
economic powers: the US, the EU and Japan. The US was largely
successful in getting agreement on tough new rules on intellectual
property: on patents, copyright and trademarks. It was also successful
in getting tough new rules on trade in services. But concessions on
textiles and agriculture – areas of particular importance for developing
countries, and where industrial countries, despite their free-trade
pretensions, heavily protect their markets – were far less substantial.

Accounting for Failure

A number of explanations have been put forward to account for the
failure of the NIEO. First, it has been suggested that the pro-NIEO
arguments were, quite simply, intellectually untenable. States will
never agree to such radical steps, it has been argued, unless they can be
sure that the benefits accruing to them will far outweigh the costs. The
supporting arguments of NIEO were insufficiently coherent to generate the required level of assurance. Second, it has been contended
that to the extent to which international economic relations are
characterised by a mercantilist struggle for power, the West was
bound to win since it has far more power than the South. Third, it
has been argued that the list of NIEO demands was too wide-ranging.
This list was not the end-product of a carefully worked out, coherent,
plan. On the contrary, it was a product of 'tit-for-tat' bargaining. In
technical terms, it was based on reciprocal interests rather than common
interests. The common interests shared by such a heterogeneous
grouping as the 'South' proved to be much more limited than was at
first thought. The final set of demands, therefore, had to accommodate
a variety of outlooks and interests: there had to be 'something in it
for everyone'. The price was a loss of coherence.

Perhaps the only issue on which the Southern camp was completely united was the 'transfer of technology'. Indeed, differences within the camp began to appear as early as 1975. By this time, three important sub-groups could be broadly identified: an Islamic group; a Latin American group; and an African and Asian group. Tensions arose over the unequal distribution of the payments made by OPEC to compensate developing states for the dramatic rise in oil prices following their oil embargo of 1973. The bulk of these payments went not to those states hardest hit, but to fellow Islamic states, especially those directly engaged in the struggle against Israel. Differences in the Non-aligned Movement made matters worse. A rift soon opened up between radical states, led by Libya and Cuba, and a more conservative grouping, led by Saudi Arabia and Egypt. The former saw the US and the West as the 'natural enemy' since they, after all, were the chief progenitors and agents of capitalist imperialism. The latter were not hostile to the US, nor to capitalism, and tended to see socialist and other radical states as more of a threat to their security and well-being than such abstract behemoths as 'capitalist imperialism'.

With hindsight, it seems more and more likely that 'Southern solidarity' was more apparent than real. The standard characterisation of the international economic hierarchy during the Cold War into First, Second, and Third Worlds tended to obscure more than it revealed. Today there is talk of many 'worlds': a 'first world' composed of the economic, financial and technological superpowers of the US, the EU and Japan; a 'second world' composed of the economically advanced countries of the rest of the Organisation for Economic Co-operation and Development (OECD); a 'third world' composed of the rapidly developing newly industrialised countries of East and Southeast Asia (the four 'Tigers': Korea, Taiwan, Hong Kong and Singapore); a 'fourth world' comprised of the 'old NICs' (the large semi-industrialised Latin American countries: Argentina, Brazil, Uruguay and Chile); a 'fifth world' of the 'near NICs' in South East Asia (the 'Tiger Cubs': Malaysia, Thailand, Indonesia; perhaps China and India, too); a 'sixth world' consisting of the 'transitional economies' of Eastern Europe and the former Soviet Union; a 'seventh world' consisting of the few remaining remnants of 'world communism' (Cuba, North Korea, Vietnam and, more contentiously, China); and an 'eighth world' consisting primarily of sub-Saharan African countries that continue to suffer negative growth rates and whose populations continue to be plagued by periodic famine, malnutrition, high infant mortality, low life expectancy, illiteracy and many other ills associated with extreme poverty.

Finally, the NIEO was to a considerable degree overtaken by events. In a very short space of time, the diplomatic climate within which negotiations had to be conducted changed drastically for the worse. The new environment of the 1980s – recession at home and renewed Cold War abroad – was not at all conducive to an amicable settlement of the issues.

Notes on Chapter 7

1   Voting power in international financial institutions is a function of financial contribution. The more a member state contributes to the annual budget of an institution the more votes it receives on its governing council. Thus of the 181 members of the IBRD (part of what is now known as the 'World Bank Group' along with the International Development Association [IDA], the International Financial Corporation [IFA], the Multilateral Investment Guarantee Agency [MIGA] and the International Centre for Settlement of Investment Disputes [ICSID]) France and Britain each have 4.33 per cent of the vote, Germany 4.52 per cent, Japan 7.91 per cent, and the US 16.49 per cent. The two most populous countries in the world, China and India, each have 2.8 per cent of the vote, the same as the rather more sparsely populated but financially rich Saudi Arabia. See www.worldbank.com.

2   See Hedley Bull and Adam Watson (eds), *The Expansion of International Society* (Oxford, Clarendon Press, 1984).

3   The US, along with its chief Western allies, was opposed to certain items on the proposed agenda for the conference, notably on extending territorial waters from 3 to 12 miles, on the codification of state practice on exclusive economic zones, and on the development of a 'regime' based on the 'common heritage of mankind' principle for the exploitation of the resources of the deep seabed. The conference was eventually convened in 1973. After protracted negotiations, a UN Convention on the Law of the Sea was drafted in 1982. It did not, however, receive the requisite number of ratifications to enter

into force until 1994. A number of Western countries, including Britain, Germany and the US, are still opposed to some of its key provisions (especially in Part XI relating to the exploitation of the deep seabed). See Peter Malanczuk, *Akehurst's Modern Introduction to International Law*, 7th revised ed., (London, Routledge, 1997), 173–97.

4   This was part of the Lomé package of trade and aid measures designed to assist development in former dependent territories. Its object was to stabilise the export earnings of a range of commodities. See Marjorie Lister, *The European Community and the Developing World* (Aldershot, Avebury, 1988).

5   Some states decried the West for hypocritically professing democracy while jealously guarding their voting privileges in such bodies as the UN Security Council (where Britain, France, China, Russia and the US hold a veto), the IMF (where voting power is determined by level of financial contribution), and the World Bank (ditto). The UN General Assembly is one of the few permanent bodies where decisions (more accurately 'recommendations', since they are not binding under international law) are made on the basis of 'one state, one vote', i.e. regardless of size, wealth or power.

6   See Ian Roxborough, *Theories of Underdevelopment* (London, Macmillan, 1979), 27–9.

7   Ibid., 32–5.

8   See P.T. Bauer and B.S. Yamey, 'Against the New Economic Order', *Commentary* (April 1977); P.T. Bauer, 'Western Guilt and Third World Poverty', *Commentary* (January 1976); P.T. Bauer, *Dissent on Development: Studies and Debates on Development Economics* (Cambridge, MA, Harvard University Press, 1976); P.T. Bauer, *Equality, the Third World, and Economic Delusion* (Cambridge, MA, Harvard University Press, 1981).

9   Independent Commission on International Development Issues (Brandt Commission), *North–South: A Programme for Survival* (London, Pan, 1980).

10 This is also, broadly, the thesis of Charles Jones, *The North–South Dialogue: A Brief History* (London, Pinter, 1983).

11 See Fouad Ajami, 'The Global Logic of the Neoconservatives', *World Politics* 30 (1978), 451–68; Robert H. Jackson, *Quasi-States: Sovereignty, International Relations and the Third World* (Cambridge, Cambridge University Press, 1990). 'Meaningful statehood' would involve, at a minimum, the ability to provide a high degree of law

and order, the ability to defend the state against (most) external threats and internal subversion, a basic education for all citizens, a basic system of public health, and the ability to provide all citizens with a basic level of social and economic security. The command of international respect, which itself may be a factor in 'meaningful statehood', is increasingly contingent on the achievement of these goals. For an interesting recent analysis of the notion of the 'legitimate state', see Agostinho Zacarias, *Security and the State in Southern Africa* (London, I.B. Tauris, 1999).

12 The Yaoundé Convention between 18 African states and the EEC was signed in 1969. The Lomé Convention between 46 African, Caribbean and Pacific (ACP) states and the EEC was signed in 1975. There have been three subsequent Lomé conventions (1979, 1984 and 1989). Lomé IV provides for 12 billion ECUs of development assistance (mainly in grants), and gives ACP states tariff-free access for virtually all of their exports into the EU market.

Select Bibliography

Augelli, Enrico, and Murphy, Craig, *America's Quest for Supremacy and the Third World: A Gramscian Analysis* (London, Pinter, 1988). Radical analysis of American 'hegemony'.

Bhagwati, J. and J.G. Ruggie, *Power, Passions and Purpose: Prospects for North–South Negotiations* (London, MIT Press, 1984). Astute analysis from leading developmental economist and the political scientist who invented the term 'embedded liberalism'. Examines emergence of 'regimes' to govern international economic relationships in the absence of a strong and willing hegemon.

Brett, E.A., *The World Economy since the War: The Politics of Uneven Development* (London, Macmillan, 1985). Excellent account of the evolution of the post-war world economy from a broadly Marxist perspective. In contrast to conventional studies, the North–South relationship is treated as central.

Donelan, Michael, 'A Community of Mankind', in James Mayall (ed.), *The Community of States* (London, George Allen and Unwin, 1983). Subtle analysis of the concept that underlay much NIEO thinking.

Hayter, Teresa, *The Creation of World Poverty: An Alternative to the Brandt Report* (London, Pluto Press, 1981). Thought-provoking and often trenchant. No-holds-barred attack on liberal capitalism. Prescriptions for change in final chapter less compelling than the main body of the work.

Jones, Charles, *The North–South Dialogue: A Brief History* (London, Pinter, 1983). Blow-by-blow empirical account. The most detailed analysis of its kind in the field. Highly useful.

Johnson, D.H.N., 'The New International Economic Order', *Year Book of World Affairs* 37 (London, London Institute for International Affairs, 1983). Concise and lucid examination of the legal aspects of the Southern challenge.

Krasner, Stephen, *Structural Conflict* (Berkeley, CA, University of California Press, 1985). Much celebrated realist critique.

Murphy, Craig, *The Emergence of the NIEO Ideology* (Boulder, CO, Westview, 1984). Valuable counterpoint to Krasner and Tucker from leading left-liberal thinker.

Marchand, Marianne, 'The Political Economy of North–South Relations', in Richard Stubbs and Geoffrey R.D. Underhill, *Political Economy and the Changing Global Order* (London, Macmillan, 1994).

Prebisch, Raul, *Towards a Dynamic Development Policy for Latin America* (New York, NY, UN, 1963). Detailed analysis and programme for change from economist at the centre of the North–South debate.

Shaw, Timothy, 'Beyond any New World Order: The South in the 21st Century', *Third World Quarterly* 15, 1 (1994). Valuable *tour d'horizon* of the political and economic challenges currently facing the developing world.

Tucker, Robert, *The Inequality of Nations* (New York, NY, Basic Books, 1977). Bold and eloquent critique from realist perspective. A semi-classic.

UNCTAD, *Towards a New Trade Policy for Development: A Report by the Secretary General of UNCTAD* (New York, NY, UN, 1964). Early report which did much to set the agenda of the North–South debate.

PART III

ISSUES
AND
TRENDS

CHAPTER 8

Economic Aid

Foreign aid is a notoriously complex policy issue. It takes a variety of forms and emanates from a host of sources. Its purpose and efficacy is a matter of great controversy. It can include the transfer of funds, credits, goods, technical assistance and knowledge. It is usually civilian in nature, but can, according to some definitions, take the form of military assistance. Aid policies are pursued by governments as well as by international organisations, private voluntary organisations and charities, and use public funds as well as the donations of private individuals.

In the examination of the economic factor in international relations, of most relevance is the extension of official foreign economic aid. In assessing the role and impact of economic aid one needs to: define and explain the concept of economic aid; describe the emergence of aid as policy and place it in its historical context; examine the various critiques of aid; and identify new patterns in aid policy.

Definitions

Economic aid can be defined as a transfer of resources from the government and public agencies of one state, or those of a group of states, to the government and public agencies of other states for any purpose other than the fulfilment of an obligation. Such a transfer of resources can only be considered to be aid if it 'involves no element of mutuality, bargain or *quid pro quo*'.[1] Aid is a government-to-government exchange of public economic resources, not commercial flows of loans and credits,[2] and comes in two forms: bilateral, from one state to another; or multilateral, from one or more states or international institutions to a state or group of states. Aid can be 'tied' to the purchase of certain products from the donor state, or 'untied'. Most bilateral aid is tied. Quite often foreign aid is double-tied, in that not only does a portion have to be spent on goods and services from the donor state, but also on specific projects within the recipient state. Tied and double-tied aid is common in the case of bilateral aid. Hence there is much merit in the received wisdom that multilateral aid is fairer to the developmental needs of recipients, in that they have greater leeway in the use of the funds and how they are apportioned.

Nevertheless, economic aid, as a form of economic statecraft, is difficult to precisely define, and its impact is difficult to calculate. In characterising economic aid as a form of statecraft, the implication is that aid is a means to an end, and by definition this end is for the most part political rather than economic (or humanitarian). Economics, in this case, is an instrument of politics. It is the utilisation of economic resources as a tool designed to influence the internal or external behaviour of other states and thus achieve political ends. Unlike the other main instrument of economic statecraft, economic sanctions, economic aid is intended to influence or change the behaviour of the target by offering an inducement rather than imposing a penalty.

Consequently, economic aid is not purely, or even mostly, a form of 'international do-gooding'. It is not simply a manifestation of altruism on the part of the wealthier, more developed countries in the international system towards those less well off. At times, economic aid does have ends that are not strictly speaking political. The extension of humanitarian assistance, emergency relief and the meeting of basic human needs is one such instance. There is, therefore, a clear moral dimension to the extension of economic aid. But, as will be shown, this does not detract from the central argument that by giving economic aid, states are implicitly or explicitly attempting to influence other states. A further argument suggests that aid is a spur to the generic development and growth of the international economy, and in this respect is primarily intended to achieve economic rather than political ends. Even if there is a strong economic rationale for the extension of economic aid, this too does not detract from the basic argument that, for the most part, the intended ends of aid are political. But these arguments do lead to the conclusion that any examination of aid policy must take into account the existence of a complex interplay between its political, economic and moral dimensions.

The rationale behind the extension of foreign aid can be broken down into four basic components. In the first component, economic aid is given for political and strategic considerations. During the Cold War, for example, both the US and the USSR spent billions of dollars and roubles either to entice regimes into their respective spheres of influence or to cement the friendship of existing 'allies'. This was especially true of their relations with states in the developing world, which were more susceptible to economic inducements, but not exclusively so if one bears in mind the important example of the Marshall Plan, which involved the US and the states of Western Europe. In another example, the oil-rich Arab Gulf states poured vast amounts of money into the coffers of Iraq during the 1980s. By doing so, they wished to cement Saddam Hussein's friendship and to guarantee that he could continue to prosecute the war against militantly Islamic Iran, which was considered a threat to the stability of the Persian Gulf.

In the second component, aid is utilised for the purpose of promoting international economic development. In the aftermath to the Second World War, aid was extended to increase the number of states participating in the liberal international trading order. Greater participation in the free-trade system would generate, it was felt, greater volumes of trade, a 'broader' market, and hence greater prosperity in the world as a whole. This was a particular hallmark of much US thinking on foreign aid to the developing world until the 1960s.

The third component is the provision of aid for humanitarian and moral purposes. Aid has been extended in the form of emergency relief operations to alleviate suffering in the wake of natural disasters and famines.[3] Significantly, this is the only kind of aid that is normally wholly untied to the purchase of specific products or engagement in specific projects. Aid has been provided with the intention of alleviating poverty on the basis of 'shared humanity', according to which it is the duty of the better off to help the less well off. Guilt has also proved a weighty motivation for the extension of economic aid. In parts of the developed world, aid is considered a way of making good a wrong, such as past colonial exploitation. Former imperial states such as Great Britain and France have long used economic aid packages to smooth the transition of former imperial possessions to full statehood and participation in the international system, feeling a sense of moral duty and responsibility towards former subjects.

The fourth component encompasses conditions of the post-Cold-War period, in which aid has become a tool for the pursuit of a wide variety of other goals. These include the fight against corruption, the development of 'good governance', the promotion of human rights, and the development of democratic institutions and practices in the less developed world and the post-communist transition states. The 'structural adjustment' policies of the IMF are also a more contemporary phenomenon, in which both Western economic and political values are strongly recommended to recipient states in the form of reform packages upon which the aid is conditional.

The Emergence of Aid Policy

Between 1950 and 1990, it is estimated that some US$700 billion was spent on economic aid. Initially, in the immediate post-war period, aid was viewed as an inadequate means to alleviate the ills wrought on the international economy by the war. In fact there was a widely held view that not only would aid packages fail to cure the imbalances in the system but in fact could lead to permanent imbalances. This was partly the reason why in the negotiations for the Havana Charter and the creation of GATT the developed states were extremely reluctant to heed the demands of the less developed states for preferential treatment. Latin American states, and representatives from several current and former British and French colonies, were insistent that attention be paid to the needs of less developed states, an issue which in the longer term would lead to the creation of an agenda for economic development. This issue was indeed left off the agenda, but any negative preconceptions of economic aid were swiftly swept aside with the success of the Marshall Plan for the reconstruction of Western Europe.

Between 1948 and 1952, the US spent US$17 billion on the Marshall Plan for Western Europe in what proved to be a highly successful aid policy. Since it stimulated recovery and development in Europe, it was thought that it was a policy that could be applied more broadly. The Marshall Plan encapsulated both economic and strategic goals. On the one hand, it was designed to reconstruct and stimulate the Western European economies, thus enabling the re-establishment of lucrative and long-standing trade links with the US, as well as providing fertile fields for US investment and markets for US goods. On the other hand, it also evolved into a stark anti-communist measure intended to safeguard the democracies of Western Europe from the perceived Soviet threat by providing a secure economic footing for pluralist political systems. Poverty and economic instability were considered to provide a fertile breeding-ground for political extremism. This was the lesson drawn from the experience of Germany in the 1920s. Only by tackling these twin evils could the ever present 'enemy within' be effectively contained.

Following the enactment of the Marshall Plan and its initial success, aid was incorporated as official US policy, as 'Point Four' of President Truman's 1949 inaugural address. It is worth reproducing this point to show the importance attached to economic aid by the Truman administration, and the official rationale behind this new departure in policy:

> We must embark on a bold new programme for making the benefits of our scientific advance and technical progress available for the improvement and growth of under-developed areas. I believe we should make available to peace loving peoples the benefits of our store of technical knowledge in order to help them realise their aspirations for a better life. And in co-operation with other nations, we should foster capital investment in areas needing development.

This presidential pledge was swiftly translated into policy through the Act for International Development in 1950. Coming so soon after the Marshall Plan, this was an indication of the seriousness of the US intentions to pursue the use of economic resources as instruments of its foreign policy in the post-war world. At the heart of this policy lay the premise that economic backwardness was partially attributable to an insufficiency of physical and capital resources, skilled labour and the economic infrastructure. This, it was believed, could be remedied through the extension of aid in the form of capital, commodities and industrial goods, and technical assistance. This would provide a spur to sustainable economic growth, which if maintained would lead to higher living standards and mutual benefits for all. The US, the largest aid provider at the time, operated on the basis of three fundamental assumptions about foreign aid: firstly, that external aid should only be a catalyst and spur for economic growth, not a substitute for it; secondly, that public funding should only be provided as a stimulus for private capital. Thirdly, that even though trade was considered the primary engine of economic growth, aid could assist in providing the economic platform that would allow under-developed states to gain entry into the system of free trade, thus stimulating further growth.

These assumptions, predominant in the late 1940s and early 1950s, dovetail neatly with the principles that informed the creation, contemporaneously, of the Bretton Woods system of international monetary and trade management. Aid as a spur to the economic development of under-developed countries, it was felt, would ultimately enable them to participate in the liberal international monetary and trading order. In turn this would make for a larger international economic system in which there would be more players, larger markets, a higher volume of goods being traded and capital circulating, and hence greater and greater gains for all. This was at the heart of the economic rationale for the extension of foreign aid.

However, this assertion omits two factors that lead to the emergence of different interpretations of the purposes and uses of aid: the historical context of the evolution of aid policy post-1945; and the theoretical implications of economic aid as a policy of mutual benefit to donor and recipient.

The Historical Context

It is indicative of the swiftly changing uses, in the minds of US policy-makers, to which aid could be put that the Act for International Development was replaced by the Mutual Security Act within one year of coming into force. This second act stipulated that aid would only be supplied if, in its application, it strengthened the security of the US. The onset of superpower rivalry in the form of the Cold War quickly distorted the initial premises on which the extension of foreign aid was based. From the early 1950s it became evident that economic aid was simply another weapon in the US armoury with which to pursue its anti-communist foreign-policy goals. The promotion of economic development, and by extension the strengthening and expansion of the international monetary and trading order, was not the primary consideration behind US aid policy. In fact, aid became an instrument of foreign policy whose ends could be defined as almost exclusively political. By supplying economic aid to countries in the developing world in order to win their friendship and to stop them from succumbing to pressure from the communist bloc, the US was defending its own security interests. As one scholar has suggested, US aid in this period was neither 'foreign' nor 'aid', in that its only intention was to promote the national interest of the US itself.[4]

It is clear that the politicisation of economic aid in the context of the Cold War started with the landmark aid package, the Marshall Plan. While the plan had more than one goal, the growth in the dispensation of US aid in the 1950s and 1960s became very much a function of the Cold War. The almost exclusive aim became to influence states that, in political or strategic terms, were important to the security concerns of the US. As President Kennedy made clear in 1961, 'foreign aid is a method by which the US maintains a position of influence and control around the world and sustains a good many countries which would definitely collapse or pass into the communist bloc'.[5]

Some allies of the US, such as Great Britain and France, dispensed aid for reasons other than Cold War geopolitical and strategic concerns, principally in relation to their post-colonial obligations.[6] Other states such as Sweden, pursued an aid policy on the moral grounds of helping the less well off. Nevertheless, the vast bulk of aid from the 'North' to the 'South', including that from the USSR, during the Cold War was extended with superpower rivalry in mind. An analysis of the geographical areas to which the US extended aid packages, especially in the 1960s, provides clear evidence of this assertion. The vast bulk of these packages were destined for countries in South East Asia, the Middle East and Latin America. South Vietnam, South Korea and Iran, were prime beneficiaries in the first two regions mentioned. Countries in Latin America, such as El Salvador, Brazil and Argentina, were aided through the Alliance of Progress, which aimed to generate a commitment to democracy, but also served the function of furthering the anti-communist goals of the US. These were the regions in which US interests were most at stake and which, it was felt, had to be defended against Soviet influence at all costs.

Therefore, the Cold War coloured the way economic aid developed as a tool of foreign policy. It was in this era that the first aid initiatives were taken and the first conclusions drawn regarding its utility. What was initially viewed as the use of an economic instrument of foreign policy to achieve primarily economic ends, with possible political spin-offs, transmuted into a policy of employing the same instrument to achieve primarily political ends. Economic aid was dispensed in the political and security interests of the donor state with possible spin-off benefits for the recipient state. 'Let us remember,' said Richard Nixon in 1968, 'that the main purpose of American aid is not to help other nations but to help ourselves'.[7]

Critiques of Aid

There are those who argue that foreign economic aid is inherently political, irrespective of the historical or systemic context in which it operates. The most forthright argument asserts that since state aid consists of public funds raised by taxation it is by nature a political activity. James Mayall argues that since foreign aid is a government-to-government transaction, it is unavoidably a political action. In addition, since aid predominantly involves a reciprocation of benefits in the form of donor influence over recipients, either bilaterally or multilaterally, it is by implication inherently political.[8] Irrespective of the stated objective of the aid policy, it is this attempt to influence, either implicitly or explicitly, which renders it a political action.

For the most part, any benefits that accrue to the recipient state as a result of an economic aid package will be economic. By comparison, benefits accruing to the donor state are not necessarily tangible or quantifiable. Influence, respect, friendship and elevated status on the international stage are all foreign-policy goals that can be achieved through aid policy, yet there may not be visible or tangible evidence of this. For instance, the cynic would argue that the Nordic states, and primarily Sweden, who place great emphasis on the moral and humanitarian goals of their distinctive and extensive aid policies, expect to reap benefits from these policies. They extol the virtues of the unilateral nature of the policies, and couch them in terms of altruism from which they expect no benefit at all. In fact, they are unconscious reflections of national policy based on a particular interpretation of national interest at a particular time. Benefits will be had from these seemingly altruistic aid policies in the form of enhanced status and respect in international affairs. This, in turn, allows them to view the international arena from the moral high ground, and to act with more authority within it. In this way, Swedish aid policy is not a denial of realism but a subtle manifestation of it. The Swedish state is using the most effective means available to it to enhance its power and prestige.

An even more extreme view is that aid is a form of bribery in which the donor state offers resources and demands something morally shady in return. This could take the form of rights to military base facilities, or the promise of a supporting vote in the UN Security Council. In effect, the donor state is seen to be extracting favours through financial inducements. Foreign aid could also take the form of extortion or blackmail in this extreme view, a donor state threatening to withhold or not renew a promised or existing aid package if the recipient state does not carry out its wishes. This has certainly been the case in US relations with both Greece and Turkey, to which it extended vast amounts of aid, in the form of military assistance throughout the Cold War period. The relationship between Greece and Turkey has been a rocky one, characterised by a series of disputes over territorial and maritime claims in the Aegean, the question of divided Cyprus, and the status of certain ethnic and religious minorities. Both countries are NATO members, and hence allies of the US. Whenever there was a heightening of tension between Greece and Turkey, the US would quite often step in as a powerful mediator, and more often than not threaten to cut off military assistance to either or both of these countries unless they mended their ways.

A more subtle analogy is often made between the extension of aid and the convention of exchanging of gifts. In the latter, one automatically assumes that when making a gift it will be reciprocated in one way or another at a later date, that there will be some kind of *quid pro quo*. This analogy suggests that the same could be true of aid. The donor does not demand anything in return, but there is an expectation that the favour will be returned by the recipient state at some future date. Thus expectations and not conditions can be the vital element of mutual benefit in aid policy. Two neighbouring countries, country A and country B sign an aid agreement in which

A grants B US$10 billion unconditionally, in that there are no explicit clauses in the agreement stating the donor's demands. There is the expectation, nonetheless, on the part of A that B will not launch a full-scale military attack on A. This expectation is implicit, there is a *quid pro quo* in the mind of the donor and hence a mutual benefit to be had.

A concrete example of this could be extrapolated from Japanese aid policies in the 1980s and 1990s. In the late 1980s, Japan surpassed the US as the world's largest provider of foreign economic aid, and its share of the funds of the Development Assistance Council of the OECD jumped to 18 per cent. The stated objectives of Japan's aid programmes are primarily to assist in the economic development of less developed countries, while over 75 per cent of its aid packages are extended to countries in the Asian-Pacific region. Within this region, one of the recipients of Japanese economic assistance is the People's Republic of China. While the development of the Chinese economy is in the interest of Japan because of its market potential, Japanese leaders have a secondary objective in mind. China could be termed a developing economy, although it cannot be categorised alongside the African and poorer Pacific recipients of Japanese aid. China, nonetheless, is a potential military threat with its vast military and nuclear capability. In this sense Japanese aid serves the dual purpose of facilitating the creation of a lucrative Chinese market from which it can reap benefits, but also ensuring that China will not find any value in physically threatening Japan or its broader interests in the Asian-Pacific area.

The moral dimension of economic aid policies has captured the imagination of the broader public, especially with respect to the humanitarian issue of the richest in the world helping the poorest, or alleviating basic human needs in time of emergency. The potency of these moral considerations, among the public at large in parts of the developed world, was clearly shown by the Western reaction to the drought and famine in Ethiopia in the late 1980s. Individuals and private organisations took it upon themselves to raise vast sums of money to provide food aid and other forms of assistance to confront the problems arising in the Horn of Africa. Out of these public concerns arose phenomena such as the Live Aid and Band Aid projects. These were extremely successful, but also attracted the equally successful involvement of a wide range of charities and voluntary organisations such as Oxfam, Save the Children Fund, War on Want and many others. On the back of the accomplishments of individuals and charities, governments followed and funds continued to flow.

The argument that aid is intrinsically politicised as it is a government-to-government exchange, and implicitly an act involving potential mutual benefits, has contributed to the rejection, by extreme neo-liberals, of aid as an effective means of eradicating poverty and promoting economic growth. Some criticise the moral or humanitarian grounds for the extension of government-to-government aid. According to one of its most vehement critics, 'the moral obligation to help less fortunate people rests on individuals and cannot be discharged by entities such as governments'.[9] It is argued that governments have no right to use public funds in the pursuit of what they feel is a moral obligation to aid less fortunate countries. The transfer of resources from rich to poor should be allowed to happen 'naturally' through the mechanism of the market, or through the beneficent acts of individual men and women channelling funds through charities and non-governmental organisations. Any moral duty to relieve need is a question of individual conscience and not a matter for public authorities. Charity is a beautiful virtue, but it is an individual human virtue, not one that applies to large corporate bodies such as states. In addition, opponents of the moral argument for economic aid have claimed that aid policy is a system whereby poor people in rich countries subsidise rich people in poor countries. The recipients, they say, of the bulk of aid funds are wealthy Third World elites. The ultimate source of these funds is the hard-pressed Western taxpayer. They further contend that not only do recipient governments consistently misappropriate aid packages, they also use them to increase their power and role in society. This exacerbates matters, since it is the overweening and self-serving power of elites that creates the problem of economic stagnation in the first place. According to this neo-liberal view, anything that strengthens the power and role of governments, especially in the economic sphere, is a palpable economic and social wrong.

Neo-liberal economists also attack the economic rationale of aid. They attempt to debunk the idea that foreign aid can spawn efficient, growth-oriented economies that can then participate in the international economy in an effective, competitive manner. They argue that economic aid restricts the inflow and deployment of private capital, as there is a steady flow of (and increasing addiction to) public funds from abroad. Economic aid also encourages the adoption of inappropriate models of development borrowed from advanced economies. The race to develop heavy and other capital-intensive industries (including the mechanisation of agriculture) in the 1960s is a case in point. They conclude, citing the example of the newly industrialised countries of South East Asia, that domestic economic success and international competitiveness stem from factors other than the provision of economic aid from the developed world. However, if one considers the level of favourable discrimination that states such as South Korea and Taiwan enjoyed from the West, and from the US in particular, during the Cold War, this conclusion is not entirely convincing. In addition, it has to some extent been superseded by the crisis in the South-east Asian economies of the late 1990s. These economies have not proven to be as stable, dynamic, and self-sustaining as was once supposed. To hold them out as models of pure private enterprise and market-led growth, therefore, is not entirely credible.[10]

In the sphere of economics, the most basic argument queries the validity of economic aid as policy by posing the question, did the North receive aid in its period of development? The position questions the fundamental assumption of aid as a spur to economic growth, and asserts that where the political and social conditions allow it, capital will flow, commercial activity will increase, and hence development will take place. Aid cannot ameliorate political conditions that are unfavourable to economic growth and development.

These extreme liberal views have their counterparts at the other end of the political spectrum. Radical thinkers, most notably Teresa Hayter, argue that aid is a form of imperialism in which the transfer of resources from the developed to the developing world is simply a means by which the former seeks to maintain its dominance over the latter. It is a policy designed to keep the developing world in a position of dependency. One way in which this occurs is through the strengthening of links between the developed donor states and elites in the developing world. This, in turn, furthers the process of exploitation within the recipient states as their elites reap the biggest benefits from the aid programmes, and strengthen their political hold over, and ability to exploit, the rest of the population. There is very little 'trickling down' of the aid funds from the recipient government and its supportive elites to more deserving social classes who could make the best economic use of it; very little generation of new business and new industry. In fact, the redistribution process simply does not actually occur. Hayter cites a study conducted in Brazil, one of the world's biggest recipients of World Bank aid in the 1960s and 1970s, to corroborate this argument. In the period between 1960 and 1977, when the aid programme to Brazil was at its height, the share of GNP of the poorest 50 per cent of the population fell from 17 per cent to 12 per cent, while the share of GNP of the richest 1 per cent of the population rose from 12 to 18 per cent.[11] While such statistics are notoriously unreliable, and the evidence may be self-serving, it does give a flavour of the arguments and figures that are put forward to support this type of case.

From this ideological perspective, even food aid is viewed to be counter-productive to the mass of the population of recipient states, and is criticised as being a political weapon of the developed world. In providing food aid – or to give it, it is said, its real name, dumping cheap produce on developing markets – donors are merely perpetuating the dependence of the developing world on the developed world for food, and undermining both domestic producers and attempts to create food self-sufficiency. Donor states are therefore using the provision of fundamental humanitarian needs, in this instance food, to create and maintain markets in the developing world to the detriment of local farmers and producers, and to the benefit of their own domestic producers and suppliers.

New Patterns of Aid Policy

In the post-Cold-War era, two further forms of economic aid have come to the fore and have provoked much debate. The first is that of structural adjustment policies, which, even though a long-standing tool especially of aid from multilateral institutions such as the IMF and the World Bank, have became more prevalent since the 1990s. Structural adjustment programmes attach specific conditions to aid, which go far beyond attempting to induce change in one particular sphere of the recipient's domestic or external behaviour. Adjustments have to be made in a range of policy areas that have increasingly come to reflect the principles and values of Western liberal democracies, and their economic systems. It is today standard practice for recipients of aid from OECD countries to be required to: reduce the size of the public sector; place the public finances under strict control; introduce various counter-inflationary measures such as reductions in public sector wage growth; liberalise trade policy; reform fiscal policy in the interests of free enterprise; privatise commercially viable public enterprises; and instigate institutional reform in both the economic and political spheres in the interests of transparency, pluralism and accountability.

The second form of post-Cold-War aid also emphasises the conditions upon which funds will be released, but primarily concentrates on political issues that need to be addressed. The three main areas of focus in this second form are usually the promotion of human rights, 'good governance' and democratisation. As with structural adjustment programmes, this form of aid conditionality reflects the powerful position of the Western industrialised world in the international system. Western states contend that their political and economic systems, and the values upon which they are based, have proved their worth and are universally valid, hence they should be adopted throughout the international system. Their unassailable economic standing in the international system means that these values can be imposed through economic aid packages. Nevertheless, institutions such as the EU promote aid conditionality for other reasons as well. The EU likes to portray itself as a 'civilian power' that uses foreign policy tools other than coercion or force in order to achieve progressive change. This is especially the case with regard to transition economies in the post-communist world and states aspiring to EU membership. Inevitably, both these forms of aid have come under heavy criticism and have sometimes been characterised as new ways of perpetuating the 'neo-imperialism' of the North in economic and political terms over the developing and transitional worlds.

Concluding Remarks

Economic aid has been a prominent tool of foreign policy for over 50 years. Despite its longevity, there is still no consensus on its proper function, its effectiveness and its moral validity in the modern international system. The motivation for extending economic aid by political leaders is always questioned, and results of aid are largely unquantifiable. Yet, in the post-Cold-War world, aid is still seen as a vital element in the toolbox of foreign policy, a testament to its versatility and the ability to serve more than one purpose. Indeed, as this chapter has shown, the three dimensions of aid – economic, political and moral – are always at work. Both in motivation and in effect, aid policies are always an admixture of these three elements.

Notes on Chapter 8

1   David Baldwin, *Economic Statecraft* (Princeton, NJ, Princeton University Press, 1985), 292.
2   Cited ibid., 292.
3   The authors accept the argument that famines are rarely 'natural disasters'. Usually they are a consequence of war or bad economic policy. See Amartya Sen, *Poverty and Famines: An Essay on Entitlement and Deprivation* (Oxford, Clarendon Press, 1981).
4   Baldwin, *Economic Statecraft*, 291.
5   Teresa Hayter, *Aid as Imperialism* (London, Verso, 1983), 5.
6   It should be noted that in the 1920s the view that the primary objective of British colonial policy should be to promote systematically the social, economic and political well-being of dependent peoples, and prepare them for self-government was one held by only a small minority of predominantly left-wing thinkers. By the mid-1940s, however, it had become government policy. Under the Colonial Development and Welfare Act of 1940, a substantial sum of money was made available, for the first time, for colonial development. The Colonial Development Act of 1945 further strengthened Britain's commitment to the economic, social and political advancement of her subject peoples, though it fell short of providing a clear commitment to their future independence. No official 'considered long-term assessment' was ever made of the likely course of decolonisation. See Paul Kennedy, *The Realities Behind Diplomacy: Background Influences on British External Policy 1865–1980* (London, Fontana, 1985), 332–7. See also Penelope Hetherington, *British Paternalism and Africa, 1920–1940* (London, Frank Cass, 1978); Ronald Robinson, 'The Moral Disarmament of African Empire 1919-1947', *Journal of Imperial and Commonwealth History* 8, 1 (1979).

7   Teresa Hayter, *The Creation of World Poverty: An Alternative to the Brandt Report* (London, Pluto Press, 1981), 83–4.

8   James Mayall, 'Some Reflections on Professor Bauer's Case Against Aid', *Millennium: Journal of International Studies* 2, 3 (1973).

9   P.T. Bauer, 'The Case Against Aid', *Millennium: Journal of International Studies* 2, 2 (1973), 9.

10   In this connection, one should also note the extensive role of the Ministry of International Trade and Industry (MITI) in fostering economic development in Japan. See Chalmers Johnson, *MITI and the Japanese Miracle: The Growth of Industrial Policy, 1925–1975* (Stanford, CA, Stanford University Press, 1982).

11   Hayter, *The Creation of World Poverty*, 93.

Select Bibliography

Berger, Peter, *Pyramids of Sacrifice* (London, Allen Lane, 1976). Subtle analysis of the socio-economic implications of aid distribution strategies.

Boone, Peter, *Politics and the Effectiveness of Economic Aid* (London, London School of Economics/Centre for Economic Performance, 1995). Concise examination of the utility of competing methods of determining the efficacy of economic aid. Concludes that economic criteria have little value in isolation from political considerations.

Browne, Stephen, *Foreign Aid in Practice* (London, Pinter, 1990). Foreign economic assistance and the 'real world'. Informative work of reference.

Burnell, Peter, *Foreign Aid in a Changing World* (Buckingham, Open University Press, 1997). Old questions recast in the context of the post-Cold-War world. Does aid assist in economic development? What is the relevance of technical assistance? Helpful reworking of old themes.

Cassen, Robert (et al.), *Does Aid Work?* (Oxford, Clarendon Press, 1986). Detached and objective analysis of the effects of economic aid on economic development and the alleviation of poverty.

Lumsdaine, David, *Moral Vision in International Politics: The Foreign Aid Regime, 1949–1989* (Princeton, NJ, Princeton University Press, 1993). Novel and brave exposition of aid as altruism. Emphasis on the rise of moral concerns in international relations. Robust and readable.

Packenham, Robert, *Liberal America and the Third World: Political Development Ideas in Foreign Aid and Social Science* (Princeton, NJ, Princeton University Press, 1973). Definitive account of the history of foreign aid. Highly informative on changing strategies and goals.

Riddell, Roger, *Foreign Aid Reconsidered* (Baltimore, MD, Johns Hopkins University Press, 1987). Did much to rekindle interest in economic aid following a period when little was being said on the subject.

Svensson, Jakob, *When is Foreign Aid Policy Credible? Aid Dependence and Conditionality* (Washington, DC, World Bank Policy Research Department, 1997). Highly informative work on the complex subject of 'conditionality' and the vexed question of aid 'legitimacy'.

Walters, Robert, *American and Soviet Aid: A Comparative Analysis* (Pittsburgh, PA, University of Pittsburgh Press, 1970). Revealing and subtle analysis of superpower strategies. Aid as influence is the underlying theme.

CHAPTER 9

Economic Sanctions

The use of economic sanctions as a tool of foreign policy has become a ubiquitous feature of international society. Post-1990, the UN Security Council has imposed mandatory economic sanctions on no less than 12 states, while there are nearly 40 other instances of sanctions imposed by states, either unilaterally or multilaterally. If the means of achieving foreign policy goals,[1] or the goals of the 'international community', are viewed as a continuum, then economic sanctions are conveniently located at a mid-point between inactivity and the use of force. But this is not the only reason why there has been such rapid growth in the popularity of economic sanctions as a form of statecraft. In assessing this growth in popularity four areas need to be addressed: firstly, the definition of economic sanctions; secondly, the objectives of economic sanctions; thirdly, the types of measures that can be employed and how they are selected; fourthly, the efficacy of economic sanctions and how this can be measured. Even though economic sanctions have become a favoured instrument of decision-makers in today's world, they have a long history. During the twentieth century there were three broad reasons for the increase in profile and use of economic sanctions.

Firstly, throughout the century there was an increased sensitivity to the use of force as a legitimate and appropriate method of resolving disputes between states. In the aftermath of both world wars, alternatives to force were sought as a means of resolving disputes, upholding international law, and imposing the will of the international community on recalcitrant states. The cessation of hostilities after two world wars gave issue to the foundation of two new international organisations, the League of Nations and the UN. It was hoped that these bodies would provide a focal point for a new more co-operative system of international relations. The architects of the League and the UN enshrined the use of economic sanctions in Article 16 of the Covenant and Chapter VII of the Charter. This codification of economic sanctions in the two most important treaties of the twentieth century enhanced the notion that resort to their use was a legitimate means of enforcing international law and preferable to the use of armed force.

Secondly, the emergence of the nuclear age, in conjunction with the onset of the Cold War, reinforced the sensitivity of states to the use of force. In the longer term the advent of nuclear weapons and policies of nuclear deterrence produced a strategic stalemate. The fear of a nuclear holocaust resulting from a direct military exchange between the Cold War protagonists produced an intrinsic limitation on the use of force between them. Yet the combination of this military stalemate and the dread of a nuclear holocaust made it vitally important to understand the capabilities and limitations of alternatives to military force. The use of economic sanctions was explored as a means by which states caught in the Cold War deadlock could attempt to influence the policies of rival states without fear of escalation. On another level, since a more forceful policy could not be initiated, economic sanctions were increasingly seen as a means whereby symbolic or punitive action could be taken by the international community against a recalcitrant state. However, despite the perceived utility of economic sanctions as a form of statecraft during the Cold War, the UN only imposed mandatory sanctions on two occasions between 1945 and 1990, against Rhodesia in 1966 and Iraq in 1990, as the superpower stalemate dominated the workings of the Security Council.

Thirdly, the growth in the importance attached to global economic activity, and the increase in economic interaction among states, which has come to be known as interdependence, has strengthened the case for the use of economic sanctions as an instrument of statecraft. As states have become increasingly sensitive and vulnerable to each others' actions through heightened levels of mutual economic dependence, economic tools of foreign policy – such as economic sanctions – are progressively considered more effective in achieving goals abroad. In addition, in an era in which the use of military force is seen as a last resort, and highly disruptive to lucrative patterns of international commerce, greater value has been attached to sanctions as a means of influence internationally. This is much in line with liberal thought, which asserts that war is both irrational and anachronistic, and that it impedes the development of a harmony of interests through trade and commerce, in which growing prosperity leads to more peace. Within the parameters of this rational, commercial world economic sanctions provide a more modern, and to some acceptable, instrument of foreign policy.

Definitions

Defining economic sanctions is not the simple task that it may at first appear. They are generally held to be the imposition of economic penalties in an attempt to change the political behaviour of a 'target' state. They are thus political acts inasmuch as they utilise economic instruments of foreign policy to bring about a change in the internal or external policies of a state, or to undermine the authority and stability of its government. Their use is based on the assumption that there exists either a direct or an indirect relationship between economic activity and political behaviour, and that the authority and behaviour of a regime rests partly on economic foundations. Even though economic sanctions may be conceived as a substitute for force, they are, nonetheless, coercive in intent and as a form of statecraft move beyond persuasion towards compulsion. They may be seen as an indication of the willingness on the part of the target state to use force, and thus can be interpreted as a prelude to war. But the imposition of economic sanctions does not necessarily lead to a resort to arms. In essence, according to this generally held view, economic sanctions are a non-military form of coercion in which economic measures are employed to achieve political ends by inflicting hardship.

The problem with this definition is that, as we shall see, economic sanctions are often imposed despite there being no serious expectation on the part of the 'sender' state that the behaviour of the target state will be thereby significantly changed. They are sometimes imposed for the secondary objective of appeasing domestic public opinion; of demonstrating to this or that domestic audience that 'something is being done'. Similarly, they are sometimes imposed for the tertiary reason of defending international norms, of demonstrating to the world that the sender state takes certain norms seriously and will not stand idly by when faced with their breach. For this reason, economic sanctions are best seen as economic penalties imposed as a declared consequence of a target state's failure to observe international standards or comply with international obligations.[2] The beauty of this definition is that it does not presume the real objective of the action taken, focusing instead on what is sometimes called the 'declaratory intent' of the sender. The downside of the definition is that it does not capture those rare instances, such as when the US applied economic pressure on Britain and France in opposition to their seizure of the Suez Canal in 1956, generally regarded as acts of economic sanction, but where the target state is not openly accused of 'failing to observe international standards' or breaching 'international obligations'.

The history of economic sanctions in the twentieth century suggests that they are a form of peaceful coercion. They provided an alternative to military force in an era when war was increasingly seen as irrational or immoral and certainly ever more dangerous with the proliferation of nuclear weapons. Economic sanctions were progressively seen to be more in line with attempts to create and manage a prosperous and orderly international monetary and trading system through the structures of Bretton Woods. Furthermore, the codification of economic sanctions in international treaties and agreements signified their acceptance as legitimate policy instruments in the defence and enforcement of international rights. But, as we shall see, they are also a means of placating domestic public opinion, demonstrating displeasure and meting out punishment to rogue or pariah states acting against accepted international norms. So what, more precisely, are the objectives of economic sanctions?

The Objectives of Economic Sanctions

If conceived of as non-military forms of coercion, in which economic measures are employed to achieve political ends by inflicting hardship on the target state, then the goals of economic sanctions can be quite clearly identified. The state imposing sanctions will have one or more of the following three general objectives.

The first is to destabilise a government that, while not necessarily contravening any norms of international behaviour or violating international law, is proving to be a thorn in the side of one or more members of the international system. A good example of this is to be found in the unilateral imposition of economic sanctions by the US on Cuba. Castro's revolution created a regime in Cuba that was seen as unacceptable to the US. In the context of the East–West conflict, Castro imposed a political system alien and hostile to the US in its own 'backyard', and which also went against the interests of US business. The regime was also deemed to be subversive to the regional interests of the US in Latin America, through its attempts to spread its revolutionary ideology and assist revolutionary movements elsewhere in the region. In this instance, Cuban policy was also in breach of international law through its subversive actions, and the Castro regime was frequently accused of supporting terrorism and engaging in espionage. While Castro's Cuba provided more than a symbolic threat to US pre-eminence in Latin America, the real threat emanated from Castro's backer, the USSR. Washington deemed the Cuban threat important enough to impose economic sanctions, but not important enough to risk overthrowing the regime by military means (with the one exception of the Bay of Pigs fiasco). It was only during the Cuban Missile Crisis in 1962, when the Soviet threat came to the fore through the installation of nuclear missiles capable of reaching the US mainland, that Washington took stronger measures, imposing an air and naval blockade. The general US objective was to destabilise an unfriendly and disagreeable regime through the employment of an accepted means of coercion designed to induce economic havoc.

The second objective is to coerce a government into changing a particular aspect of its domestic policy, deemed by certain actors to go against the basic rules, norms and principles of international society. A good example of this case is the imposition of economic sanctions against South Africa in opposition to the long instituted policy of apartheid. South Africa swam against the tide of growing international concern for the maintenance of basic human rights by upholding a strict racist system of discrimination against, and segregation of, the state's black population. On the back of mounting hostility among the black African states, and a groundswell of public outrage in the West, a series of economic sanctions were imposed on South Africa. The aim was not only to ostracise that state from the broader international system, and show the international community's displeasure, but also to compel the government of South Africa to abandon its policy. The South African government, invoking Article 2(7) of the UN Charter, argued that it had a sovereign right to rule as it wished within its own borders. Those opposed to apartheid, however, argued that freedom from racial discrimination had become a peremptory rule of international law, that is a law from which no derogation was permitted regardless of circumstance. They also pointed to a growing body of international law on human rights, which suggested that the absolute principle of non-intervention was no longer deemed acceptable. If not a duty, states certainly had a right to intervene in the domestic affairs of another state if there was reasonable evidence that massive and systematic violations of human rights were occurring.

The third objective is to force a government into changing a specific element of its foreign policy that violates international law. A clear-cut example of this was the decision by the international community to impose mandatory economic sanctions on Iraq, in response to Saddam Hussein's invasion of Kuwait.

This is not the only way of classifying the objectives of economic sanctions. The most widely cited typology is that of James Barber.[3] According to Barber, there are primary, secondary and tertiary objectives involved in the imposition of sanctions. Interestingly, although the efficacy of sanctions are usually judged in relation to their primary objectives, Barber maintains that secondary and tertiary objectives are often more important. Primary objectives are usually the formal, public, 'official' objectives. The real motivating factors are often secondary and tertiary.

Primary objectives are usually clearly defined and have a clear-cut goal: to change the behaviour or reverse the actions of the target state either internally or externally. At this level, it is the behaviour and attitude of the target state that determine what policy will be pursued in attempting to coerce it into changing its behaviour. There are many examples that illustrate the use of economic sanctions to meet clearly defined primary objectives. In the case of Rhodesia in the 1960s, sanctions were imposed by the UK to force the government of Ian Smith into reversing its unilateral declaration of independence. Earlier, in 1935, Britain and France, among others, imposed economic sanctions against Italy in response to the latter's flagrant violation of the Covenant of the League of Nations in invading a fellow member of the League, Abyssinia. The objective here was to force Italy to end its invasion and withdraw its troops, thus complying with its obligations in the Covenant and under international law. In a third case already referred to, the UN imposed economic sanctions on Iraq in 1990 to force it out of Kuwait whose sovereignty it had flagrantly violated.

At this level, the instigating states are communicating a clear message to the target state and attempting to invoke a change of policy through inflicting economic hardship. But Barber goes on to argue that implicit in the employment of economic sanctions is not only a desire to force change on the part of the target state but also to meet secondary goals, which concern the expectations, motivations and status of the initiating state rather than the behaviour of the target. With respect to the Rhodesian and Abyssinian examples, it was clear that Great Britain and its allies were not going to risk war to meet their stated primary objectives. In the case of Rhodesia, the magnitude of the dispute and the distance between the parties did not warrant, or make feasible, prosecution of a war. In the case of Abyssinia, neither Great Britain nor France were ready or willing to engage Mussolini's Italy in a full-blown armed conflict. This would not only be costly in terms of men and material, but it also might have the undesired effect of pushing him further into the arms of Hitler. In both instances, while the initiators' primary objectives were the reversal of a specific policy, the secondary objectives concerned the appease-ment of domestic public demand for action. In both instances, Great Britain, a so-called great power, could not sit by idly watching the flouting of its national interests or of international law. The case of Kuwait is similar, despite the fact that the use of force was not ruled out, and was ultimately pursued. International public opinion demanded that immediate action be taken against Saddam Hussein and his regime. The imposition of sanctions enabled the UN to satisfy this demand, thus precluding the need to take precipitous military action and preserving its international prestige.

Secondary objectives, therefore, involve decisions concerning the status and actions of the initiator state, which go beyond changing the behaviour of the target. Such decisions could result in purely symbolic acts: to demonstrate to public opinion, for example, that 'something is being done'; or to demonstrate to 'world opinion' that the initiator state is serious about international law, honours its obligations, and is prepared to take tough action in their defence.

At the third level of this *schema*, that of tertiary objectives, it is neither the behaviour of the target state nor which of the initiator state which is under consideration. Tertiary objectives refer to the broader international sphere, in which sanctions are imposed to further the maintenance of international order or for the defence of a particular code of international conduct. These objectives could range from underlining the immorality of the use of force as an instrument of policy, to demonstrating the utility of an international organisation, to sending a message to other states contemplating such unruly, unlawful behaviour.

In our three cases highlighted above, we can see that there were tertiary, as well as primary and secondary, considerations at play. In the Rhodesian case, the United Kingdom wished to demonstrate its solidarity with the African members of the Commonwealth (who vehemently opposed the actions of the Smith regime in Rhodesia). It also wanted to underline the notion that there are more acceptable, civilised ways of resolving disputes than through the use of force. In fact, these two tertiary objectives were linked. Britain wished to show its newly independent Commonwealth cousins that the bad old days of imperial arrogance and bullying were over. She was now not only prepared to listen to her former dominions but to demonstrate that the threat or use of force was no longer an acceptable way of doing Commonwealth business. In the Abyssinian case, a tertiary objective was the demonstration of the utility of the League of Nations as an organisation able to resolve international disputes peacefully. Similarly, it could be said that tertiary objectives were in evidence in the case of the Gulf. The withdrawal of Iraq from Kuwait and the placating of public opinion were the foremost objectives. Yet beyond that lurked the goal of underlining the prohibition of the use of force as an instrument of national policy, other than in self-defence. The promotion of the UN as a central guarantor for the maintenance of international peace and security in the post-Cold-War world was a further tertiary objective.

In the examples given above, which illustrate different types of objectives for imposing sanctions, there had, for the most part, been a clear violation of international law. In these instances, the primary objectives of the initiating states were clear and involved the rectification of a wrong committed against the international legal order. However, things are not always so clear-cut. Sometimes states impose economic sanctions when they feel themselves to be a victim of an act of wrong-doing, with respect to which there may not exist a general consensus in the international system, and the illegality of which is far from certain. The *fatwa* issued against the British author Salman Rushdie, condemning him for anti-Islamic sentiment in his novel *Satanic Verses* is one such case. Great Britain imposed economic sanctions on Iran even though a religious authority and not the government of Iran issued the *fatwa*, and that it involved no clear contravention of international law. Similarly, in 1992, Greece imposed sanctions and then a blockade on the newly independent state of Macedonia, for appropriating the name 'Macedonia', which the Greeks claimed belonged to their cultural heritage. State interests were at stake, and it could be argued that the name issue betrayed certain territorial ambitions against Greece. Yet no law had been broken, nor had an international consensus been reached on the unacceptability of Macedonian actions. In both instances it was the expectation of wrong-doing, not actual wrong-doing in terms of current international law, that led to the imposition of economic sanctions. These sanctions were both an economic penalty to force change and a public proclamation that wrong-doing, actual or potential, would not be tolerated.

It should be noted, however, that while such proclamations can be 'a public expression of the community's moral disapproval of [an] act', they can also be punitive in intent.[4] In this instance, the sender state is attempting to scold the target state morally. Sometimes sanctions are imposed simply to punish a state: according to Nossal, such sanctions are not just about anger or retribution but are purposeful actions conducted for specific reasons to hurt or injure a state 'guilty' of wrong-doing. Sanctions as punishment is not a form of sadism. They have a definable end, which is to harm the interests of the target state and not to let its wrong-doing, or evidence of it, go unpunished. In 1981–2, for example, the Polish leader, General Jaruzelski, declared martial law in order to counteract the growing power of the trade union Solidarity movement. In response, the US, and more reluctantly its European allies, imposed a range of economic sanctions, including the halting of the trans-Siberian gas pipeline project, which was being built largely by Western companies and financed by Western credits. No one in Washington seriously thought that such a measure would force General Jaruzelski to rescind his declaration. The object was simply to punish his regime and his overlords in Moscow for their abject oppression of democracy.

While economic sanctions provide a foreign policy instrument that, some say, is preferable both morally and practically to the use of armed force, and emphasises the importance of the economic element in international relations, they can be portrayed as simply another exhibition of the workings of power politics. It is no great surprise, according to this view, that the vast bulk of sanctioning activity is conducted by rich, powerful states against relatively poor, weak ones. The US imposes economic sanctions far more frequently than any other power. Sanctions are thus not a more moral form of state-craft, but a weapon of the rich and the powerful. They are no less a product of the cool calculation of national interest than any other foreign policy measure.

More importantly, one could argue that economic sanctions are useless in their own right as a form of influence, and only work as a prelude to war. To illustrate, one can look to the Argentinian invasion of the Falkland Islands and Great Britain's subsequent reaction. In light of the three-fold typology of primary, secondary and tertiary objectives, Britain's imposition of economic sanctions were intended to: compel Argentina to withdraw; mollify domestic opinion and mobilise it against the Argentinian invasion (and perhaps to win a second term in office for the incumbent Prime Minister, Margaret Thatcher); and demonstrate to other dictatorships around the world that Britain does not tolerate such flagrant breaches of international law. A more cynical line would suggest that the imposition of eco-nomic sanctions was merely a charade. The true aim of this imposition was to buy time as a prelude to the use of force. British armed forces had to be mustered and sail some 8000 miles to the Falklands. This would be a lengthy process. In the interim period between the Argentinian invasion and the British resort to arms, the imposition of economic sanctions provided evidence of British displeasure and its intent to right a wrong-doing.

In other instances, sanctions are imposed because a state has no other instrument of foreign policy at its disposal. Sanctions, to paraphrase Winston Churchill, are the worst of all measures except for all the others. In 1980, for example, the US imposed economic sanctions on the USSR following the latter's invasion of Afghanistan. Initially, the US verbally condemned the invasion but could not risk military action for fear of nuclear war. But it felt obliged to take further practical measures to highlight its disapproval of Soviet policy, which it argued had breached international law by violating the territorial integrity of a sovereign state. In the context of the superpower conflict, the imposition of economic sanctions was the only remotely credible US policy alternative.

In fact the US has a long history of frequent resort to economic sanctions for foreign policy objectives. Woodrow Wilson, so influential at Versailles and in the establishment of the League of Nations, was a great champion of sanctions. True to his liberal convictions, he saw them as an 'economic weapon', a 'peaceful, silent [and] deadly remedy'. Wilson's promotion of sanctions as a 'peaceful weapon' that would obviate the necessity to use force in foreign affairs left a powerful legacy. This legacy, in tandem with the vast extent of US commitments abroad, especially after 1945, the strength of the American economy, and a general disinclination to risk the lives of American soldiers, largely accounts for the frequent US use of economic sanctions. Wilson's legacy is much in tune with the liberal streak that colours much of American political life, and which at times has played a major role in shaping the foreign policy agenda of the US. President Carter, in office from 1976 to 1980, relentlessly pursued states deemed to be gross violators of human rights, and attempted to compel change in these states through the employment of economic sanctions. During his term in office, the US imposed, or maintained, sanctions against 10 states, including the Soviet Union, to coerce improvement in their human rights record. Force was not considered the most appropriate or viable instrument in the pursuit a foreign policy goal steeped in the deep liberal tradition of respect for individual rights and freedoms, so close to the heart of the American political experience.

As leader of the Western world during the Cold War, and the sole remaining superpower following the collapse of the Soviet Union, the US developed more international commitments and obligations than any other state. These commitments and obligations to friend and foe alike could not always be dealt with through more traditional diplomatic means of dialogue and negotiation. Neither was recourse to force a practicable option in most cases.

The US has sometimes imposed economic penalties on friendly states and allies in order to get them to reconsider an inconvenient or disagreeable policy. In the late 1940s, the Netherlands was on the receiving end of economic pressure applied by the US to push it into granting independence to Indonesia, a Dutch colonial possession. Similarly, during the Suez Crisis in 1956, the US sought a withdrawal of French and British troops from the Canal Zone through the imposition of economic penalties. In both cases, the objectives of US policy were driven by a desire to limit the influence of former empires and colonial powers and drive forward the process of decolonisation. That the target states were friend and allies did not deter the US from pursuing its interests. But the nature of the relationship with these states meant that use of force was ruled out. Economic sanctions were thus the toughest measure that could be taken.

Rival states, or those unfriendly to American interests, have often been the target of US sanctions for a variety of reasons. As mentioned, Poland, then a member of the communist bloc, was targeted with sanctions in 1981 following the declaration of martial law and oppression of the Solidarity movement. The USSR was punished through economic sanctions for its downing of the Korean airliner, KAL 007, in 1983. But much of the rationale behind the use of sanctions by the US has been issue-based. International terrorism has been a frequent cause for recourse to sanctions. Libya, Syria and Iraq were all accused of sponsoring terrorist organisations and activities, and were subjected to economic sanctions at various times in the 1970s, 1980s and 1990s. State-sponsored terrorism both threatened US interests in the Middle East and endangered the lives of US citizens, who were often the targets of attacks. They also, it was argued, constituted a serious breach of international law. Yet the US was not always able to pinpoint the sources of these attacks, or track down their perpetrators, so economic penalties against those considered to be their chief sponsors proved a viable policy option.

The proliferation of nuclear technology and weapons testing has resulted in a variety of states being targeted with economic sanctions. India, Pakistan, South Africa and France have all suffered sanctions as a result either of their acquisition of nuclear technology, development of nuclear capabilities, or the testing of nuclear devices. The proliferation and testing of these technologies could arguably be seen as a threat to international stability, and in American eyes it is a distinct challenge to the pre-eminence of the US in the nuclear field.

As the states involved in these activities have not always heeded diplomatic entreaties and cannot be coerced through armed force, economic sanctions were imposed to show displeasure, maintain an agreed international code of conduct, and protect US interests.

With respect to India and Pakistan, US policy was driven by a complex mixture of commercial and strategic interests. Concerned with the burgeoning nuclear programmes in both countries' in the early 1970s, the US pursued the imposition of export controls on India and Pakistan in 1974. India had recently tested its first nuclear weapon. Pakistan was considered not to be meeting agreed international safety standards in the development of its nuclear programme. The imposed export controls targeted technology and materials vital for the pursuit of both countries nuclear programmes. This was a direct indication of strategic concerns. The proliferation of nuclear technology and its military application on the Indian sub-continent threatened an already unstable strategic balance in the area, and could easily lead to a major catastrophe if war erupted between India and Pakistan. More importantly, US strategic interests could also be harmed by the emergence of nuclear states in the region, which could challenge the authority of the US in its broader superpower relationship with the USSR, and China. While strategic concerns were paramount there was also an important secondary consideration for US policy-makers. Commercially, US business was losing out to Western competitors in the sale of nuclear technology to states such as India and Pakistan. Canada had provided the nuclear reactor from which India had developed the fissile material needed to build and test its first nuclear weapon. France and Belgium were involved in deep negotiations with the government of South Korea for the delivery of raw material and technology vital to the development of its nuclear programme. As such, the US believed it was also losing out in the commercial stakes. The imposition of export controls on nuclear technology, which the US pressed allies like Canada to agree to on India and Pakistan, served the dual purpose of meeting strategic interests by curtailing the development of nuclear technologies with potential military applications, and serving short-term US commercial concerns.

US use of sanctions is often driven by a belief in the strength of the American economy, and its centrality to the international economy. Its enormous agricultural productivity, especially in vital foodstuffs such as grains, its technological capability and capacity for innovation, and its powerful role in the world of commerce and finance, enable US governments to employ the economic weapon in lieu of the other tools of foreign policy. Grain embargoes against the USSR were a common feature of the Cold War era, as were the boycotts of technology transfers to the Eastern Bloc to forestall economic development and the evolution of military capabilities. The freezing of Iranian financial assets during the American hostage crisis of 1979 was another such case, as has been the threat of boycotts against EU products during and after the trying Uruguay Round of GATT talks. Such is the faith in the power of the US economy that successive US administrations have found themselves employing sanctions as a vital weapon in their foreign-policy armoury. The existence of interests worldwide, the variety of its commitments, its global reach, the strength of its economy, its political inheritance, and its international status, collectively account for the disproportionate prominence of economic sanctions in US foreign policy.

In general, therefore, in a complex foreign-policy environment, economic sanctions may be the least undesirable of a highly undesirable set of alternatives. To the layman it may not be easy to identify or disentangle the objectives that the initiating state is attempting to achieve. For the policy-maker, the intended end is usually multifaceted, and not always consonant with publicly stated objectives.

Selection and Implementation of Measures

In selecting the specific measures to be imposed on the target state, the initiator can choose from two broad categories. The sanctions employed can be in the form of a general embargo suspending all trade (with the possible exception of basic humanitarian needs such as food and medication) and financial transactions, freezing the target state's foreign assets and severing transport links. Or they can be more selective measures covering particular commodities and/or financial services seen as vital to the target state's economy. As Robert Pape says, 'trade may be suspended completely or tariffs merely raised slightly, financial flows may be wholly or partially blocked or assets seized; the entire opposing economy may be targeted or just one critical sector'.[5]

The policy-maker has to select his or her measures from a wide menu of choice. She or he must gauge the expected impact of the measures to be employed and calculate their chance of success in meeting intended objectives. This in itself is an inexact science, which becomes more complicated when examined in the light of the existence of multiple objectives, as outlined above. Thus, the initiator must take into account a variety of factors when faced with the task of selecting the most appropriate measures. It is important for the initiator to, *inter alia*: pinpoint the objectives; assess the general sensitivity of the target to economic pressure; locate precisely the areas of the target state's economic life that are most vulnerable; calculate the speed with which sanctions can be imposed and the duration for which they will have to remain in place; estimate the likely reaction of the target state; and, ultimately, evaluate the cost of the sanctions to itself.[6] If the goal is merely symbolic, the task is rendered easier and none of the practical and economic considerations come into play.

Bearing in mind these considerations, initiators are left with the conundrum of 'how much is enough and at what cost?' When primary objectives are being pursued, such as the eviction of Iraq from Kuwait, harsh, blanket measures will be employed to put as much pressure on the target regime as possible. Even so, there is always the fear that the tenacious pursuit of primary objectives through harsh, blanket measures could, in due course, compromise the end the sanctioning state wishes to achieve. For example, severe sanctions could be imposed on a state with the objective of undermining or overthrowing an unfriendly or repressive regime. But if the measures are successful, they may actually cause a level of dislocation, if not destruction, which will live long after the target regime has been overthrown. In this instance the post-sanction regime, consisting of those same elements in society that the sanctioning state wished to assist, could itself be faced with the very economic difficulties which led to its predecessor's downfall. US efforts to undermine the Sandinista regime in Nicaragua in the 1980s led very much to this kind of outcome.

There is always the added possibility that a sustained, long-term, policy of harsh economic sanctions could have the reverse effect of that intended. Severe economic penalties, extended over a lengthy period, may actually solidify popular support around a particular regime that the sender state is attempting to undermine or overthrow because of its actions abroad. A 'siege mentality' often emerges, in which the population of the target state develops a feeling of victimhood, and identifies with and rallies around the governing regime, not because it has made a rational assessment of its policies, but because it gets caught up in a wave of nationalist fervour. This was very much the case in the Yugoslav wars in the 1990s. The international community imposed severe and extensive sanctions on Serbia, holding the Milosevic regime responsible for the conflicts in Bosnia–Herzegovina and Kosovo. One of the goals of these measures was to turn the Serbians against their leadership, and perhaps incite forceful opposition to the prosecution of these wars in the former Yugoslavia. In fact the sanctions had the reverse effect. Economic deprivation and international isolation drove the people of Serbia into closer support of the Milosevic regime, not because they felt in tune with his domestic policies, or necessarily supported his foreign policies, but because he represented the interests of the Serbian nation, which was now under attack. There can be an explicit nationalist reaction to the imposition of sanctions within the target state that can totally undercut the intended objectives.

If secondary and tertiary objectives, such as placating domestic opinion or taking a public stand against wrong-doing, are higher up the agenda, then less harsh and perhaps selective measures will be employed. On this occasion, what is at stake is not so much the behaviour of the target state but attitudes towards the initiator. The economic costs to the initiator will have to be closely calculated and compared to the desired end.

The conventional view is that initiating states will bear only so much economic dislocation in their own economies before they desist. But as David Baldwin argues, to calculate whether sanctions are excessively costly it is important to compare their costs with the expected costs of alternative policies, including the use of force.[7] In this argument, the costs of lost business and income to the imposing state can never exceed the cost of the ultimate coercive alternative to economic sanctions, war. Prosecuting a war (especially by liberal democracies), incurs not only financial costs, but also the potential weakening of domestic institutions, damage to the image of the state, grave risks to the popularity of a government, a fall in morale, and most fundamentally of all, loss of life. Consequently, it is argued that states are willing to tolerate a remarkably high degree of economic hardship and injury, since such material costs will always be preferable to the political and moral dangers of going to war.

Economic sanctions are imposed either unilaterally, as in the case of Great Britain and Rhodesia, or multilaterally, as in the case of the Arab states against Israel. In the first instance, the initiator must have a sufficiently powerful economy and control over commodities or services vital to the economy of the target state for sanctions to have any effect. In the second instance, it is generally agreed that without universality of application, sanctions have very little chance of achieving primary objectives. If not applied universally, the vulnerability of the target state to external economic pressure is drastically reduced, as it will always be able to find willing trading partners, be they private enterprises or states. During the years of illegal white minority rule in Rhodesia, the fellow white minority government in South Africa provided a vital economic lifeline. Rhodesia was totally surrounded by boycotting states, with the single exception of South Africa. The latter not only supplied the former with oil and arms, but also acted as a conduit for her exports. Significantly, one of the most important factors in the retreat of the Smith regime in 1979 was not the mounting human and physical cost of the guerrilla war, or the constant pitch of international condemnation, but the sudden withdrawal of South African support.

Measuring the Effectiveness of Sanctions

The conventional way of measuring the effectiveness of economic sanctions is by assessing whether the target state complies with the initiator's demands after economic sanctions have been threatened or imposed.[8] If the target state changes its behaviour in the particular policy area demanded by the initiating state or states, then sanctions can be said to have succeeded. It will be noted here that this methodology presupposes, somewhat crudely, that the only worthwhile objectives are primary objectives.

If sanctions are imposed and the target state complies with the initiator's demands, then certain economic indicators can be examined to ascertain what economic damage the selected measures have inflicted on the target's economy. These indicators could include direct and indirect costs, such as price rises in specified sectors of the economy, or general disruptive trends, such as rising inflation and unemployment. One could also assess forgone economic potential, especially the loss of export earnings, and the implications of this loss for the wider economy. A recent study contends that, 'the most important measure of the intensity of economic sanctions is aggregate gross national product loss over time.'[9] In other words, the cumulative decline in the national income of the target state is the best indicator of whether sanctions have been effective or not (and to what degree). This type of measurement of success, which rests exclusively on economic criteria, is not universally accepted.

Economic sanctions may succeed not only because of the tangible economic damage caused, but due to the political, diplomatic, psychological and military pressures that accompany them. This is a vitally important point. Sanctions are not simply about economic costs, but about other forms of power relations. The effectiveness of sanctions cannot be determined by a simple cost/benefit analysis. Many studies of the efficacy of economic sanctions start from the assumption of a direct relationship between economic pain and political compliance. When such compliance is lacking the conclusion frequently drawn is that 'economic sanctions don't work'. Johan Galtung has called this the 'naive theory' of economic sanctions. It should never be assumed, he says, that damage inflicted on an economy, and hardship on a society, will inevitably lead to political change. Instead, a whole range of factors, not least psychological and socio-political, have to be taken into account when assessing the efficacy of economic sanctions.

To put it otherwise, there is a distinction to be made between methods of assessment relying on the 'property concept' and those relying on the 'relational concept'. The 'property concept' refers to the tangible effects that sanctions have on a country's industry, trade and commerce. Concrete evidence culled from the examination of indicators relating to these economic activities is the surest way of determining whether real damage has been done to the economic fabric of the target. In turn, it is this real damage that determines whether or not the target state will comply with the initiator's demands.

The 'relational concept', on the other hand, additionally takes into account non-tangible effects. According to this 'relational' approach, the effectiveness of sanctions can only be assessed and understood in terms of a combination of tangible economic effects and intangible socio-psychological effects relating to perceived loss of influence, prestige and status.[10] Such an approach is especially relevant when considering the reaction of the target state to the *threat* of economic sanctions. When in place, sanctions can have identifiable and quantifiable economic consequences. When merely threatened, the consequences, if any, are inevitably intangible and unquantifiable. If the threat of sanctions is enough to force the target state into compliance, then the potential economic costs to that state have to be considered in conjunction with other non-economic factors in determining the reasons for it. As mentioned above, the diplomatic and military pressures that often accompany the threat of sanctions, as well as considerations of international image and status, can be enough to tip the balance in favour of compliance.

Concluding Remarks

The history of the use of economic sanctions suggests that these measures came into vogue in the twentieth century as a result of moral considerations and the rise of the perceived effectiveness of economic instruments of foreign policy in an interdependent world. Although their efficacy is often doubted, at heart they are extremely versatile tools of political power employed by states in the pursuit of a variety of objectives both domestic and international. As one analyst has recently argued, 'International relations theorists have always appreciated the power of the sword, but disagree about the importance, utility and definition of economic power...If economic sanctions are a potent tool of diplomacy, then world politics can be made less violent than it was in the past.'[11]

Notes on Chapter 9

1   Sometimes called 'means of pressure'. For an excellent account see F.S. Northedge, *The International Political System* (London, Faber and Faber, 1976), 225–49.
2   Margaret Doxey, *International Sanctions in Contemporary Perspective* (London, Macmillan, 1987), 4.
3   James Barber, 'Economic Sanctions as a Policy Instrument', *International Affairs* 55, 3 (1979).

4   Kim Richard Nossal, 'International Sanctions as International Punishment', *International Organization* 43, 2 (1989), 306.

5   Robert A. Pape, 'Why Economic Sanctions Do Not Work', *International Security* 22, 2 (1997), 93.

6   Doxey, *International Sanctions*, 98.

7   David A. Baldwin, *Economic Statecraft* (Princeton, NJ, Princeton University Press, 1985), 40.

8   Pape, 'Why Economic Sanctions Do Not Work', 97.

9   Ibid., 94.

10 Baldwin, *Economic Statecraft*, 22–4.

11 Daniel D. Drezner, *The Sanctions Paradox: Economic Statecraft and International Relations* (Cambridge, Cambridge University Press, 1999), 8.

Select Bibliography

Cortright, David, George Lopez et al., *The Sanctions Decade: Assessing UN Strategies in the 1990s* (Boulder, CO, Lynne Rienner, 2000). Useful work analysing the recent rise to prominence of economic sanctions in the UN policy toolbox. Concise and coherent.

Doxey, Margaret, *Economic Sanctions and International Enforcement* (London, Macmillan for the Royal Institute of International Affairs, 1980). Renowned scholar of economic sanctions mixes analysis and description to excellent effect. Comprehensive in coverage. A landmark work.

Doxey, Margaret, 'Sanctions against the Soviet Union: The Afghan Experience', *Yearbook of World Affairs* Vol. 37 (London, Institute of World Affairs, 1983). Detailed and judicious study of the difficulties of applying sanctions in a complex international, regional and 'intra-alliance' setting. Convincingly establishes the paramount importance of US domestic factors.

Doxey, Margaret, 'Sanctions in an Unstable International Environment: Lessons from the Gulf Conflict', *Diplomacy and Statecraft* 2, 3 (1991). Critical analysis of the first phase of economic sanctions against Iraq, emphasising the importance of 'burden-sharing'.

Drezner, Daniel N., *The Sanctions Paradox: Economic Statecraft and International Relations* (Cambridge, Cambridge University Press, 1999). Unorthodox study pioneering game theory and employing statistical analysis in balancing the sanctions 'equation'. Highly prescriptive.

Galtung, Johan, 'On the Effects of International Economic Sanctions', *World Politics* 9, 3, (1967). Enduring, powerful critique of the effects of sanctions on targets. Still highly relevant.

Haass, Richard N. (ed.), *Economic Sanctions and American Diplomacy* (New York, Council on Foreign Relations, 1998). Where do sanctions figure in American diplomacy and statecraft? An insider's guide from a prominent policy-maker.

Hufbauer, Gary C., Jeffrey J. Schott and Kimberley A. Elliot, *Economic Sanctions Reconsidered: History and Current Policy* (Washington, DC, Institute for International Economics, 1990). Benchmark empirical study of sanctions in theory and practice. Much lauded, hence also much attacked by academics and policy-makers.

Lenway, Stefanie A., 'Between War and Commerce: Economic Sanctions as a Tool of Statecraft', *International Organization* 42, 2, (1988). Review article. Potent re-evaluation of the role of economic statecraft in foreign policy.

Lindsay, James, 'Trade Sanctions as Policy Instruments: A Re-examination', *International Studies Quarterly* 30, 2, (1986).

Losman, Donald, *International Economic Sanctions: The Cases of Cuba, Israel and Rhodesia* (Albuquerque, NM, University of New Mexico Press, 1979). Detailed analysis of three important case studies.

Yeats, Charles, *Morality and Economic Sanctions* (Nottingham, Grove Books, 1990). Bucks the trend by examining the moral rather than material dimensions of economic sanctions.

CHAPTER 10

Regionalism

The subject of regionalism has generated much excitement since the end of the Cold War, both with regard to its theoretical and policy dimensions. The reasons for this are readily explained by two developments in the international arena. First is the rapid proliferation in the number of groupings referred to as regional trade arrangements (RTAs). This includes longer-established institutions such as the EU, but also NAFTA and the Asia-Pacific Economic Co-operation forum (APEC) among many others. As these groupings sprout up in every part of the world, they impinge on international trade issues and global institutions such as the WTO. As they incrementally have a greater impact on the shape and operation of the international system, this makes them worthy of increased study. This impact is even more significant if viewed in conjunction with the importance increasingly attached to economic matters in the aftermath to the Cold War. Policy-makers' attention, therefore, is immediately attracted by any regional arrangement, or set of arrangements, that may have a substantial impact on international trade and hence the stability and health of the international economy as a whole.

The second reason for the growth in interest in regionalism complements the first, and is primarily theoretical in its origins. Debates concerning the development and impact of regionalism and regional groupings on the international system evolved out of the analysis of the emerging EEC in the 1950s and 1960s, and have continued apace ever since. Today, the emergence of powerful trading blocs and the general perceived rise in the importance of international economics generate intense debate on the actual nature of these blocs, how they evolve, and what impact they have on international order and the shape of the international system. Do these trading blocs, such as the EU and NAFTA, amount to new types of 'power groups' or 'power blocs'? Does the relationship between them amount to a new form of balance of power in the international system, replacing the moribund rivalries and alignments of the Cold War? What is being examined is whether these new RTAs have come to dominate the international system in the same way that the super-powers and their allies did for the second half of the twentieth century.

Within this broader question there also exists a strand of theorising that examines the concept of 'economic security'. If, as is generally assumed, the distinction between 'high' and 'low' politics is becoming blurred, if not reversed, there arises the issue of whether economic security is becoming more important than the more traditional forms of military security based on defence and defensive alliances. Can a state, or group of states, predicate its security from external threats on a stable and prosperous economy? How vulnerable are states to economic forms of warfare that could result from an outbreak of hostile rivalry between the most powerful of these new trading blocs?

A further theoretical question raised by the growth of regionalism is its relationship with 'globalisation'. There is an overwhelming inclination towards, if not fascination with the extremely broad trend loosely termed globalisation and thus there is considerable debate as to how regionalism and globalisation co-exist, both in theory and in practice. Is regionalism, for example, a fragmentary process disruptive to further globalisation? Or does it constitute a stepping stone on the path of globalisation, especially in the field of trade? Are regional economic groupings building blocks in or stumbling blocks to the process of globalisation?

Any discussion of regionalism is therefore multi-dimensional and incorporates debates on the increasingly blurred dividing line between high and low politics in the international sphere. It also involves concerns with the evolution in the nature of state security and of potentially dramatic changes in the global economic system. But the issue of regionalism generates multi-dimensional discussion primarily because there are multiple definitions of the term. As a phenomenon it takes a variety of forms. It differs from arrangement to arrangement. It thus has varied effects on the global trading order and its political management.

Definitions

The term regionalism is commonly used to describe any number of arrangements and groupings that are simply 'less than global'. Andrew Hurrell provides us with a five-fold typology with which we can examine the phenomenon.[1] Firstly, there is regionalisation, which is often referred to as 'soft' or 'informal' regionalism. This relates to autonomous economic processes – and not conscious state policies – that lead to economic interdependence or integration in a particular area, often with immense social implications. The extremely close human and economic links that have evolved between Mexico and California constitutes a particularly good example of this phenomenon.[2] Secondly, there is regional awareness and identity. This involves shared perceptions of belonging to a particular community shaped by certain common values, history and a common cultural heritage. Many people in Southeastern Europe, that is the Balkans, share this awareness and identity. It is often a product not of consciousness of what they have in common, but how they differ from 'outsiders'. Thirdly there is regional inter-state co-operation. This could be defined as a regime or formal organisation between a group of states. Mercosur, the common market of the 'Southern Cone' states of Brazil, Argentina, Uruguay and Paraguay, provides a good example. Fourthly comes state-promoted integration. This is when states consciously make policy to promote the reduction of trade barriers, and barriers to the free movement of capital and labour. This in turn leads to the foundation of a centralised authority that regulates all the relevant issues at a day-to-day level. The EU is the prime example of this phenomenon. Fifthly, there is regional cohesion. This could be the result of any combination of the above categories, and is typified by the region playing the defining role in relations between states in the area and forming the organising basis for coordinated policy in the area.

This is a broad typology that goes beyond the discussion of economic regionalism, which is the main concern of this chapter. It is important, however, to register the various different types of regionalism. It should not be assumed that economic factors provide the only motivation or that economic regionalism is the only significant type.

It has been asserted that regionalism is 'a single space which has been judged suitable for the attainment of a range of tasks [at an] intermediate level of competence' – that is at a level between the state and the global system.[3] In this more functional characterisation of economic regionalism, the space and tasks referred to are intended to maximise efficiency and thus have 'utilitarian value'. This immediately focuses attention on economic regionalism, especially the growth of regional trade arrangements, which is its main facet. Economic regionalism can be defined as an attempt to promote freer trade, and greater capital and labour mobility, on a restricted geographical basis, between states that constitute a formal arrangement that intercedes between the state and the global level. In the context of Paul Taylor's characterisation, the 'space' he refers to is delimited by the territorial boundaries and economies of the participating states, while 'tasks' refer to a broad range of issues, including the promotion of free trade. The space does not necessarily have to be contiguous, as in the example of the US–Israeli Free Trade Area. And the task can go beyond freeing up trade into promoting broader economic integration, if not union, as in the case of the EU.

A more detailed definition of economic regionalism is provided by Andrew Walter. He suggests that it is 'the design and implementation of a set of preferential policies within a regional grouping of countries aimed at the encouragement of the exchange of goods and/or factors between members of the group'.[4] Two assumptions made by Taylor and Walter have to be questioned. In both instances the authors seem to assume that economic regionalism inevitably promotes freer trade. But we have to examine the impact of regionalism on multi-lateralism, assess whether its inherent discriminatory practices against non-participating states are malign or benign, and consider the prospect of regional arrangements replacing the power alignments of previous eras as a source of conflict in the international system. Similarly, both authors are in agreement that economic regional arrangements are the product of conscious state policy, and we have to consider the possibility that such arrangements have emerged largely spontaneously, as the result of 'natural economic forces'.

Practical Forms and Types of Economic Regional Arrangements

Using the characterisation and definition cited above, there are five identifiable forms that economic regional arrangements can take.[5] It must be emphasised, that all five conform to the rules and regulations of GATT and the WTO, notwithstanding certain extremely ambiguous restrictions. Article 24 of GATT states that '[T]he provisions of the Agreement shall not prevent, as between the territories of contracting parties, the formation of a customs union or a free trade area or the adoption of an interim agreement for the formulation of a customs union or free trade area'.

Firstly, economic regional agreements can be struck to promote sectoral co-operation or integration. In this case, two or more states agree to co-operation between or integration of specific sectors of their economies, or strike such a bargain in relation to a specified good or series of goods. This type of agreement can take the form of a free trade area or a customs union in the areas specified. The best example of this is the European Coal and Steel Community founded by France, the Federal Republic of Germany, Italy and the Benelux states in 1951. This agreement allowed free trade in coal and steel within the Community, and was regulated by a supranational High Authority, which if necessary could control prices and production.

Secondly, economic regional arrangements can take the form of free-trade areas through which the contracting states agree to eliminate quantitative trade restrictions and tariffs against each others' products. In this type of arrangement, while there is an agreed code of behaviour covering all contracting states, there is no agreed behaviour or policy towards third parties; each of the contracting states can pursue whatever commercial policy they wish with respect to non-signatories. In free-trade areas there is very little, if any, institutionalisation of the agreements above and beyond state-to-state relations, and there is certainly no inherent tendency towards integration. Two good examples of free-trade area are the European Free Trade Area (EFTA) created in 1958 by seven European states that were not included in the Treaty of Rome, and NAFTA, comprising the US, Canada and Mexico.

Thirdly, economic regional arrangements can take the form of a customs union in which the contracting parties not only form a free-trade area governing commercial relations between them, but also commence treating non-members uniformly in commercial matters. A customs union entails the imposition of a common external tariff barrier against non-members and could also lead to a certain degree of institutionalisation, as occurred with the EEC created in the

1950s and 1960s. Mercosur is another case of a customs union that treats non-members uniformly.

Fourthly, economic regional arrangements can take the form of a common or single market. This structure builds on the customs union in that not only does it create a unified market for the free trade of goods among the participants, but also creates a free labour market, freedom of movement, a single market in financial services, and adds a common external tariff barrier. In this instance there is also a high level of coordination and co-operation in a wide-ranging field of policy, resulting in the increasing integration of the economies of the states involved. Some argue that a concomitant of this is a high degree of central authority and institutionalisation. A single market requires a single set of authorities to police it. The Single European Act of 1987, an important development in the evolution of the European Community, provides a good example of this process of integration and centralisation.

Lastly, there is a fifth type of arrangement, an extreme case, that of economic and monetary union. In this case all aspects of the economies of the participating states are regulated by the same rules and authorities, including the creation of a common currency. The EU post-1999 is the clearest example of this case, although certain member states – notably Britain and Denmark – have shown reluctance to participate fully.

It is no coincidence that much reference is made to the EU and its antecedents in illustrating the types of functional regionalism possible. It is this institution that has developed furthest in the continuum between regional co-operation and full regional integration. It is this institution that has generated the most excitement and controversy, whether in policy or academic circles. There are two fundamental areas of interest for scholars and policy-makers emanating from the evolution of the EU: firstly, the applicability of the methods of European integration to other parts of the world, and the possibility of the 50 years of peace, ostensibly created by the European experiment, being replicated elsewhere; secondly, and by way of contrast, the reaction to the progressive construction of a set of discriminatory practices, which has led some outsiders to view Europe as a 'fortress', an inward-looking group of states increasingly removed from and hostile to the outside world. But we must not be limited to the European model in our examination of economic regionalism, since by the late 1990s it was estimated that there were nearly 110 RTAs in the world. More importantly, the volume of trade within regional groupings was said to account for over 50 per cent of world trade. Thus while the European model provides rich pickings in theoretical and policy-related material, the phenomenon of economic regionalism is much broader and has a wider impact than one highly sophisticated example.

The Nature and Role of RTAs

To understand the origins of practical forms of economic regionalism, and assess their impact on the international economic and political system, we have to go beyond the typologies and definitions set out above. The assumption that regionalism has primarily taken the form of a plethora of RTAs leads to the conclusion that regionalism is at heart driven by economic concerns. States pursue regional arrangements primarily because of the economic gains to be had from increased economies of scale and the generation of larger volumes of trade through regional trade liberalisation.

There is, however, a highly political element in the founding and evolution of regional economic arrangements. Indeed, the relationship between political and economic factors is a crucial one, especially with regard to the impact of these types of arrangements on the international system. In attempting to unravel this relationship, a number of preliminary questions have to be asked and distinctions made.

Firstly, is economic regionalism a descriptive or prescriptive term? Is it a term that has been coined to describe various arrangements? Or is it a method of organisation that is prescribed to promote prosperity and diminish conflict in the international system? Or is it both? If it is the former, then it is a 'catch all' term used to describe a wide range of activities and is of limited value. If it is the latter, then it takes on a narrower and more valuable analytical and policy-related role. The same question can be asked in a slightly different way. Should economic regionalism be viewed simply as an evolved state of affairs in a particular part of the international system, with its associated economic and political ramifications? Or should it be viewed as a consciously pursued economic and political project aimed at achieving specific goals within the international system?

Secondly, is the development of economic regionalism market-led or institutionally driven.[6] If market-led, economic regionalism is likely to be a largely autonomous economic process driven by commercial and financial interactions. These interactions take place in increasingly larger volumes leading to high levels of economic interdependence among the participants, and could result in the form-alisation of the process in a loose regional arrangement, such as APEC, which does not impose any obligations on the participants. If institutionally driven, economic regionalism is governed by policy that forces the pace of co-operation, and perhaps integration, and is consciously designed and executed for economic and political reasons. In this case, there could be a great degree of formalisation and institutionalisation of the arrangement, including the potential ceding of what are seen as sovereign rights to a supranational authority. NAFTA is an example of a consciously designed RTA that is limited in scope and institutionalisation. The EU, at the other extreme, is highly centralised and institutionalised in its push towards complete economic integration.

Thirdly, are economic regional arrangements 'open' in character, or 'closed'?[7] Open RTAs are not exclusive in their membership, and are less discriminatory in their practices towards non-members. They are viewed as contributing more to the general liberalisation of international trade and the freeing of markets. Generally speaking, loose free-trade areas, such as EFTA, fall into this category. Closed regional arrangements, on the other hand, apply strict rules of member-ship, are highly exclusive, and adopt a discriminatory stance towards the outside world. Those who describe the EU as Fortress Europe see it very much in these terms. Closed regional arrangements can also be described as neo-mercantilist enterprises, which cause trade diversion and close off markets to extra-regional competitors.

Fourthly, and related to the previous question, are RTAs trade liberalising or trade diverting?[8] If categorised as trade liberalising, then economic regional arrangements are totally compatible with the rule-based, multilateral international trading system governed by the GATT agreements and the WTO. They are, in fact, furthering the aims of this international trading system by freeing up trade in an ever increasing number of sectors in the economy, albeit on a restricted geographical basis. If seen as diverting trade, and even being integrationary in ambition, then these regional arrangements are less compatible with the rules and aims of GATT and the WTO. In fact, this particular form of organisation points to an agenda that moves radically away from furthering purely economic ends, such as trade liberalisation, and into the realm of attempting to achieve other objectives that are primarily political. Here, economic co-operation or integration are seen as a means to an end rather than an end in itself, in that the prosperity and stability that may ensue as the result of economic regionalism is intended to be the platform upon which political ends can be achieved. At the heart of the tension between 'Euro-enthusiastic' nations such as Germany and France, and 'Euro-sceptic' nations such as Britain and Denmark, is the fact that whereas the former see economic integration as a means to a wider political end – the submerging of national identities and sovereignties under a single, federal European unit – the latter see economic integration as a means to a wider economic end – greater prosperity. They see 'Europe', in other words, as predominantly an economic enterprise.

The argument about ends throws into sharp relief the essential relationship between economics and politics in the examination of economic regionalism. Are open, trade-liberalising regional arrangements primarily using economic means to achieve economic ends such as growth and prosperity? And in more closed regional arrangements, are economics used to achieve more grandly conceived political ends? These are two questions of paramount importance that we will take a closer look at.

Interpretations

The pessimist would argue that the growth of regional economic organisations, and primarily the 'big three' (the EU, NAFTA and APEC), is an indication that states increasingly prefer this type of arrangement as a method of pursuing their narrow self-interest. According to the pessimist, RTAs are vehicles for the creation of more exclusive and larger self-sufficient units based on protected economies which discriminate against outsiders. They are the embodiment of a new, grander form of mercantilism. They harbour highly vested group interests, and are governed not by narrow nationalism, which was the guiding light of previous attempts at autarky and self-sufficiency, but by a new form of nationalism based on regional identity, and primarily defined by the existence of other communities and identities outside the area. The logic of this argument implies that these commercial blocs will become ever larger and more powerful, with the result that the international trading system will become divided into relatively few units pursuing conflictual policies. This will not only hinder the workings of the liberal international trading order, which is based on the premise of the progressive liberation of international commercial flows, but will also transmute into a struggle between competing power blocs. In essence, this is a metaphor for a new form of balance of power in which states are banding together in ever larger groups in order to ward off potentially hostile 'others'.

This new balance of power becomes increasingly threatening, in this pessimistic outlook, if viewed in conjunction with the development of institutions such as the EU, which are primarily using economic means to achieve political ends. The origins of the EU are not to be found solely in the idea that a customs union, a free-trade area, a single market or economic and monetary union will have immense economic benefits, leading to stability, growth and prosperity. These ideas have to be considered in tandem with the idea that the EEC/EU was, and is, an attempt to establish a security community, both to guarantee peace and security among long standing rivals, and to ward off external threats from those who do not share the same culture and values. Ultimately, the 'constitution' of the EU, the Treaty of Rome, is interpreted as having the goal of political union that is the creation of a superstate based on premises that go far beyond those of an RTA. If the international system is viewed as a zero-sum game, then these increasingly large regional groupings will take on the more traditional characteristics of states, engaging not only in competitive relations with other groupings, but perhaps also in conflictual ones. These may take the guise of economic warfare, but could quite readily spill over into something more violent in the protection of not national, but rather regional or supranational, interests.

In the same vein, regionalism can be seen as the natural response of weaker states to the more powerful, or a response of 'satellites' to a regional hegemon or 'metropole'. For instance, Mercosur can be seen as the response of a group of Latin American states to the challenge posed by the economic hegemony of the US. This, it is argued, is a crude form of a balance of power that may manifest itself in economic terms but bears all the hallmarks of a more traditional method of conducting international affairs. Alternatively, RTAs could be viewed as hegemons in their own right. NAFTA has been characterised as a 'rule constrained hegemonic order in which acceptance of US objectives is traded for access to US markets'.[9]

Thus, according to this view of regionalism the emphasis is not only on the potentially disruptive nature of these arrangements on international order, but also on the possibility that despite using economic measures these groupings are gradually being drawn into playing a game of power politics. NAFTA, APEC and the EU are no longer economic regions, governed by agreements, that participate in the established multilateral international trading order, but rather units that as they become more integrated, increasingly begin to compete with one another, and not only in the economic field but also in the political.

A more optimistic, if not liberal, outlook of regionalism places greater emphasis on the economic aspects of these arrangements, and concludes that these can only be beneficial to international order. This view holds that as the numbers of free-trade associations (FTAs) and RTAs grows there is an ever increasing process of trade liberalisation in the world economy. This in turn requires increasing codification of the norms and rules governing international trade, thus increasing their transparency in line with the multilateral trading order already in existence. In this outlook, economic regionalism also serves the function of eroding the power of the state and breaking down economic nationalism and mercantilism. This, in turn, can lead to a wider acceptance of interdependence. As interdependence grows, co-operation or even integration between states – sometimes referred to as functional interdependence – may be necessary to manage the complex sets of relations that have emerged. As a result of this more co-operative management of the relations between states, sources of conflict progressively diminish in the system, as more and more effective ways are found of controlling them. Borrowing from the classical liberal view, it is held that as regional clusters achieve greater levels of prosperity, so the likelihood of war is diminished. This view can be applied to the EEC/EU, yet it remains to be seen whether it will come about elsewhere in the world.

A third view argues that the emergence of increasingly powerful trading blocs is a phenomenon of the economies of the developed world, and is little more than a contemporary version of the vast economic gulf between 'North' and 'South'. Dependency between states has been replaced by hegemony through RTAs and FTAs. Thus the relationship between NAFTA and Mercosur in the Americas is not an equal one but one in which the core–periphery, or metropole–satellite, relationship is pursued by other means. It is also replicated globally with the dominance of the grouping of the EU, NAFTA and APEC. In essence, this line or argument states that while the method of organisation of regional agreements may be novel, at heart they basically reproduce the same types of global economic dependence and dominance that have been a constant feature of the twentieth century.

Regionalism and Globalisation

In conclusion, we have to consider the extent to which regionalism and globalisation are complementary or contradictory phenomena. As discussed in the next chapter, globalisation is a broad concept that means many things to many people. In the context of this discussion, globalisation will be limited to the idea of a 'global economy', in which economic unification is taking place and markets and TNCs are replacing the traditional predominance of the state.

On the one hand, regionalism is said to pose a threat to globalisation in that it promotes a process of fragmentation in the world economy through the erection of protectionist barriers, trade discrimination, exclusion of goods and services and the general fortress mentality it may entail. In this sense, regionalism clashes with globalisation, as it is a 'state-centric' project on a larger scale, while the latter is viewed as a process in which the power of the state is receding and the significance of national frontiers is progressively eroded. Furthermore, globalisation is seen as a universal process giving rise to universal issues that need to be managed by issue-based functional institutions many of which would work on a global scale. This of course clashes with the idea of regional arrangements that provide issue management within a particular geographical territory, with reference to the interests of specific states, and perhaps to the detriment of the interests of third parties.

On the other hand, regionalism is seen to have a complementary, if not symbiotic, relationship with globalisation on three different levels. Firstly, the discriminatory and exclusionary policies pursued by many regional trade arrangements make it necessary for TNCs to become insiders in other regions by linking up with domestic producers. This was very much the case in Japanese automobile manufacturers' links with their British counterparts and their setting up of production lines all over Britain in the 1980s and 1990s as a way of bypassing EU legislation. It as argued that these sorts of arrangements spur on the process of globalisation, as large international conglomerates are formed and become active in a range of markets. Secondly, as more and more regional groupings and RTAs spring up, this reduces the number of parties in negotiation over the management of the international economy. EU members, for instance, are represented by one official, the Trade Commissioner, at international trade talks, as was the case during the Uruguay Round. As there are fewer parties involved in talks, it should, in principle, be easier to reach consensus over further liberalisation of trade and thus enhance the process of globalisation. Thirdly, it could be argued that even though globalisation is eroding the authority of the state, global economic relations still need to be managed, and the only bodies able to perform this task in the absence of states is the newly emerging regional bodies.

There is a further strand of thought that goes as far as suggesting that globalisation leads to regionalism and not vice versa. For example, globalisation generates a marked increase in global competition for markets. These markets are increasingly viewed as regional rather than local, due to the economies of scale they afford. It is more efficient and profitable to target a regional market that shares the same patterns of consumer demand, rather than to always pinpoint individual states. If firms and states increasingly treat several states as a cohesive grouping, this could create the conditions for the emergence of an RTA. Some argue that this is happening with the economy of Central Europe. Poland, Hungary and the Czech Republic are increasingly being viewed as a coherent economic unit, and are targeted as such by firms.

In addition, it could be argued that issues of genuine global concern are few and far between, and in any case most effects will be seen on a regional level. It is more likely that states will share interests and respond to changing trends in the global economy on a regional level. International differences and disparities on the whole make it less likely that coherent policies can be formulated at the global level. There may be a widespread international concern with environmental degradation, or with the depletion of fish stocks, but it is more likely that these issues will be dealt with on a regional rather than a global scale. Such a response is likely to be more coherent and more effective.

Concluding Remarks

As with globalisation, regionalism is a very broad term that can be interpreted in a variety of different ways. This chapter has shown that there are many forms of regionalism and several competing interpretations of their economic and political significance. Whether economic regionalism is a trend which will continue to grow and result in ever larger and more competitive regional groupings is a question for much speculation. One thing is for sure: 'there are no natural regions ... [they] are socially constructed and hence politically contested', and hence they can be challenged and reconstituted.[10]

Notes on Chapter 10

1   Andrew Hurrell, 'Regionalism in Theoretical Perspective', in Louise Fawcett and Andrew Hurrell (eds), *Regionalism in World Politics: Regional Organization and International Order* (Oxford, Oxford University Press, 1995), 39–45.

2   Ibid., 40.

3   Paul Taylor, *International Organization in the Modern World: The Regional and Global Process* (London, Pinter, 1993), 7.

4   Andrew Walter, 'Regionalism, Globalization, and World Economic Order', in Fawcett and Hurrell (eds), *Regionalism in World Politics: Regional Organization and International Order*, 78.

5   See Richard Gibb, 'Regionalism in the World Economy', in Richard Gibb and Wieslaw Michalak (eds), *Continental Trading Blocs: The Growth of Regionalism in the World Economy* (Chichester, John Wiley and Sons, 1994), 23–7.

6   Vincent Cable and David Henderson (eds), *Trade Blocs?: The Future of Regional Integration* (London, Royal Institute of International Affairs, 1994), 5–6.

7   Ibid., 8–9.
8   Ibid., 9–10.
9   Andrew Hurrell, 'Explaining the Resurgence of Regionalism in World Politics', *Review of International Studies* 21, 4, (1995), 343.
10 Ibid., 333–4.

Select Bibliography

Anderson, Kym and Richard Blackhurst, *Regional Integration and the Global Trading System* (Hemel Hempstead, Harvester Wheatsheaf, 1993). GATT-sponsored collection examining resurgence of regionalism. Is regionalism compatible with GATT? Answers provided from a variety of viewpoints.

Bhagwati, Jagdish, *Regionalism and Multilateralism: An Overview* (New York, NY, Columbia University, 1992). Eminent scholar, powerful argument and highly readable work. A defence of multilateralism.

Coleman, William and Geoffrey Underhill (eds), *Regionalism and Global Economic Integration: Europe, Asia and the Americas* (London, Routledge, 1998).

Gamble, Andrew, and Anthony Payne (eds), *Regionalism and World Order* (Basingstoke, Macmillan, 1996). Support for a 'new regionalism', intervening between state and global governance. Useful expose of emerging theoretical and practical trends.

Lawrence, Robert, *Regionalism, Multilateralism and Deeper Integration* (Washington, DC, The Brookings Institution, 1995). Should national economies be further integrated? Excellent analysis of key cases.

Lawrence, Robert, 'Emerging Regional Arrangements: Building Blocks or Stumbling Blocks?' in Richard O'Brian (ed.), *Finance and the International Economy: 5, The AMEX Bank Review Prize Essays* (Oxford, Oxford University Press, 1991). Important article arguing that the forces propelling the current trend towards regionalism are fundamentally liberal, not protectionist as they were in the 1930s.

Mansfield, Edward and Helen Milner, *The Political Economy of Regionalism* (New York, NY, Columbia University Press, 1997). A revealing free-trade perspective on the implications of regionalism. Self-consciously 'IPE' in approach.

Ohmae, Kenichi, *The End of the Nation State: The Rise of Regional Economies* (London, Harper Collins, 1995). High priest of globalisation turns his attention to the rise of 'economic regions'. Self-referential, quirky and provocative.

Rosencrance, Richard, 'Regionalism in the Post-Cold War Era', *International Journal* 46, (1991).

Thurow, Lester, *Head to Head: The Coming Economic Battle among Japan, Europe and America* (London, Nicholas Brealey, 1992). Doom-laden scenarios of future economic conflicts among the primary economic blocs. Pop economics at its best.

Winters, Alan L., *Regionalism versus Multilateralism* (London, Centre for Economic Policy Research, 1996). Concise synopsis of potential clashes between regionalism and multilateralism. A useful introduction.

CHAPTER 11

Globalisation

Globalisation is a big and amorphous subject. Academic discussion of it takes place within and between many different disciplines, most notably Economics, Geography, Information Technology, International History, International Relations, Management Science and Sociology. The word 'globalisation' has a lot in common with words like 'imperialism' or 'sovereignty'. It is used in a variety of different ways, in a variety of different contexts, for a variety of different purposes. Within academic debates, one can identify a number of different concepts of globalisation at work. One can identify a number of different theories about its nature, how it emerged, its significance, the speed with which it is advancing, and its normative implications. But it is also a word of political rhetoric: a word used in actual political debates in order to rally support, win friends and confound enemies. Indeed, the qualities which make it so useful a word politically – its ambiguity and emotiveness – are precisely the qualities that make it so hazardous a word when it comes to serious analysis.

A Global Economy?

The term 'global economy' has entered into the vocabulary of politics with some force. In debates, both popular and specialist, it is increasingly used in preference to its older cousins 'international/world economy' and 'international/world economic system'. The clear implication is that the world has recently become more economically unified, perhaps to the extent that a single 'global' economic system

177

has emerged, replacing the more fragmented 'world' system of regimes that preceded it. This is because 'global' suggests one-ness or unity in a way that 'world' does not. We can say 'it's a diverse world', but we cannot say 'it's a diverse globe'. The former phrase is clear and comprehensible. The latter is awkward and borders on incoherence.

Is this change in nomenclature justified? Is the world economy now 'global'? It is true that a larger and larger share of world production is concentrated in the hands of a relatively small number of TNCs; that TNCs earn more and more of their revenues from foreign sales; that more and more of their manufacturing is done in foreign countries. It is also true that the scope of the mass media has increased enormously, aided by breathtaking advances in information technology. The spread of television and the development of satellite broadcasting means that everyone in the world can be exposed, often simultaneously, to the same images. States find it increasingly difficult to insulate their societies from these images and the ideas, values and tastes that go along with them. Moreover, ownership of the mass media – of the production of films, books, broadcasting, newspapers, magazines, audio-video cassettes, compact discs – is concentrated in a small number of very large TNCs. The rapid growth of electronic communication adds a further, potentially countervailing, dimension. The Internet not only enables the instantaneous transmission of complex information across the globe in an interactive and highly cost-effective way; it also holds out the prospect of a worldwide 'virtual' marketplace: a universally accessible and rapid medium for trading goods and services produced in and supplied from all corners of the world. The arrival of a worldwide virtual marketplace could do much, certainly in the short term, to undermine the oligopolistic position of many TNCs.

The international scope and nature of many of these activities is undeniable. But have they become global? It would be premature to describe trade as global. All states employ import controls, operate industrial and regional policies, manipulate interest rates, and seek to keep the exchange value of their currency within certain bounds for the purpose of favourably distorting the pattern of trade across frontiers. The expansion of 'e-commerce' might do much to undermine the capacity of states to influence the pattern of world trade. But at present the goods and services traded through this new medium account for only a tiny fraction of the total, and although the Internet enables consumers to bypass attempts by public authorities to limit, or promote, or raise revenue on, the purchase of certain products (for example recorded music, on-line publications, data products, airline tickets and hotel reservations), it should be noted that, in all but the most totalitarian countries, trade in such products has traditionally been liable to only limited state interference. Patterns of trade in most goods and services will continue for the foreseeable future to be influenced by states' fiscal, regional, industrial, import and export policies. In addition, it is perhaps no surprise that in recent years treasury and customs and excise departments in all leading countries have set up dedicated e-commerce divisions.

It would be similarly premature to describe production as global. In addition to the above measures, all states provide subsidies, offer tax incentives and gear their public procurement policies for the purpose of keeping and attracting certain kinds of industrial production within their frontiers. Labour is far from global. Freedom of movement is guaranteed within the EU. A citizen of one Member-State is entitled to live and sell his or her labour in any other Member-State. A high degree of labour mobility exists in certain sectors of the world economy (for example international finance and banking), and has long existed in certain professions (for example architecture, medicine and academia). But these footloose professionals are in the main highly specialised workers, and their numbers are relatively small. The vast majority of workers live all of their lives not only in their state of origin, but in the particular locality in which they were born.

It appears to be the case that only finance – the buying and selling of bonds, equities, derivatives, futures and currency – can be described as truly global, in the sense of being largely unimpeded by the desire of states and other public authorities to control its flow from one part of the world economy to another.

The notion of a genuinely global economy is not, therefore, well founded. International finance may operate on the assumption of a largely borderless world. So do some aspects of the media and communications industry. The general significance of national boundaries and the power and influence of public authorities may, indeed, be declining. But the vast majority of the world's economic activity takes place in a world in which the national boundary matters and the role of public authorities is often decisive. Declarations of the existence of a global economy are best seen, therefore, as declarations of intent, and a fine example of the tendency in politics, both in study and in practice, to 'couch optative propositions in the indicative mood'. At worst this makes them 'items in a political programme disguised as statements of fact'.[1] The most that can be said is that certain aspects of the world economy are globalising.

The Appeal of 'Globalisation'

The appeal of the notion of globalisation nonetheless remains broad. It has been enthusiastically embraced by many shades of political opinion, from the Marxist left to the libertarian right. For Marxists it represents confirmation of the truth of Marx's theory of capitalism. It is a source of much needed encouragement in the wake of the failure of the Soviet experiment and the collapse of communism. For state socialists it provides a useful explanation for the decline of the welfare state, or at least certain important aspects of it, the emasculation of the trade union movement, and the failure of redistributionist policies to create a fairer society in the 1960s and 1970s. For free-market liberals (also known as 'neo-liberals' or the 'New Right'), it represents the victory of the market, and the end of the illusion – the disastrous illusion – that the state can effectively direct economic activity. The enthusiasm shown by both the Marxist left and the libertarian right is particularly striking. Both, it should be noted, share the common ground of distrust of, or hatred for, or aesthetic aversion to, the state, the former because it sees the division of mankind into nation-states as artificial and a reflection of the interests of the bourgeoisie, the latter because it sees the division of the world into nation-states as economically irrational, and wishes to confine the state qua public authority to the job of 'holding the ring' (within which individuals and firms can freely compete in pursuit of their economic interests). Both of these doctrines look forward to the unification of the world: to the transcendence of the territorial state and the creation of a single community of mankind. The beauty of the notion of 'globalisation' is that it implies that this will come about auto-matically, perhaps even painlessly, through the inexorable unfolding of socio-economic processes.

The Globalisation of 'Globalisation'

Yet the broad appeal of the concept has been acquired at a price. The term rose to popularity during the mid-1980s, with the victory of 'Thatcherism' and 'Reaganomics', the deregulation of international financial markets, the spread of microchip technology, and the dawning of a new era, characterised by *glasnost* and *perestroika*, in the Soviet Union. The clear intention was to signal the emergence of new economic and technological forces that had the potential radically to transform the socio-economic, and ultimately the political, organisation of the world. But as the popularity of the concept spread, so its parameters grew. While early writers located the origins of globalisation in the microchip and communications revolution of the 1980s, in the current literature one finds the origins of globalisation traced back to a wide range of things: the growth of the European colonial empires; the nineteenth-century revolution in communications (the railway, the steamship, the telegraph); the Industrial Revolution; the rise of the nation-state; the advent of capitalism. The dawn of globalisation has even been traced back to the Crusades (and, more broadly, the attempt to create a universal Christian empire under a single Papal authority in the middle ages), the rise of Islam, and Imperial Rome. Globalisation, therefore, is a concept that needs to be handled with great care. While early authors had some very specific technological and economic developments in mind, more recent authors have used the term to mean any thing, process or phenomenon, that unifies: from conquering armies to the microchip revolution.

One other word of warning should be given. Academic debate about globalisation is afflicted with some terrifying jargon: 'distanciation', 'structuration', 'societalisation', 'securitisation', 'culturisation', 'dedifferentiation', 'desacralisation', 'disetatisation'. The ugliness of these words is in most cases not mitigated by their analytical utility. One also finds in the literature an alarmingly large amount of dense and convoluted prose. The following passage is by no means unrepresentative:

> ...as objects become more mobile they progressively dematerialise and are produced as symbols...cognitive symbols, symbols that represent information; and aesthetic signs, symbols that represent consumption. Their proliferation, in turn, promotes two kinds of

reflexivity. First it promotes a pattern of... 'reflexive accumulation', the individualised self-monitoring of production and of expertise and an accompanying increasing and widespread tendency to question authority and expertise. Second, it promotes an expressive reflexivity in which individuals constantly reference self-presentation in relation to a normatised set of possible meanings given in the increased flow of symbols – people monitor their own images and deliberately alter them.[2]

The author of this passage is undoubtedly knowledgeable. He may even have profound things to say. If he has, however, this is surely not the way to say them.

Theories of Globalisation: Liberalism

Theories of globalisation can be divided into two broad camps: liberal and Marxist. The liberal line of argument is well known. Firstly, liberals contend that markets (whether for finance, or for goods and services) are increasingly worldwide in scope and that the driving force behind this development is technological change and the utility-maximising decisions of private actors. Governments and states are bystanders in this process. They are increasingly powerless to do anything about it.

Secondly, they contend that the emergence of global markets tremendously increases economic efficiency. The wider the market, as Adam Smith pointed out, the larger the division of labour. The larger the division of labour, the greater the scope for reducing costs through the achievement of economies of scale. Thirdly, they contend that globalisation, in the long run, will bring about societal convergence around the twin pillars of the market and liberal democracy. A 'global civil society' founded upon liberal principles is in the making. The spread of knowledge, ideas and values becomes ever more easy, through the development of satellite broadcasting, faster and cheaper air travel, the fax, the Internet and so on. The very nature of these technologies makes this flow difficult to stem. Increased contact and communication between peoples and the worldwide diffusion of ideas will proceed, they further contend, at an ever accelerating pace. Simultaneously, states are being forced by the market to liberalise their economies. To attract foreign investment, and foster an economic environment conducive to innovation, enterprise and growth, states find themselves increasingly having to adopt open-market policies. (At present, however, the reduction of taxes and the opening-up of labour markets is only one side of the equation. The other side is the provision of subsidies, regional policies, training and education programmes, and other means to stimulate investment, 'artificially').

Hand-in-hand with the free flow of knowledge and ideas, and the spread of the market, is the growth of representative government and respect for human rights (especially the classic civil and political freedoms of Western political thought). As the open market spreads, merchants, businessmen, financiers and entrepreneurs become wealthier and more influential. Gradually they begin to use their influence to demand a greater say in their country's government. They also soon come to realise that the efficient conduct of business is impossible without freedom of movement, speech and conscience, the due process of law, and legal equality. As with the growth of the open market, the growth of what some call 'political globalisation' is dynamic. Once unleashed it has a logic of its own.

Finally, for some liberals – Kenichi Ohmae for example – globalisation is a kind of panacea: the final victory of the hidden hand, the consummation of God's Diplomacy, even 'the end of history'. Others, however, are more guarded. Globalisation, they say, is not an entirely benign process. Along with the spread of wealth, knowledge and individual freedom, comes environmental damage, economic dislocation, migration and potentially the political friction that inevitably results – as Rousseau maintained – from growing interdependence.[3] These problems cannot be left to sort themselves out. They need to be consciously monitored, and if not resolved, then certainly managed, and the worst of their effects mitigated. But another by-product of globalisation is the erosion of the power and authority of the state: the ability of the state to regulate what goes on 'within and across' its borders. Therefore, a conundrum arises as to how this vital management role is to be performed. The answer that these more guarded liberals give is the setting up of new 'global' institutions with wide-ranging power and authority, and the 'upgrading' of old international institutions such as the IMF, the World Bank and the International Atomic Energy Agency (IAEA). The scope and gravity of these problems is simply too big, they contend, for states and other actors to cope with individually. They must, therefore, act in concert. But this is difficult in the absence of some kind of coercive authority to guarantee compliance. The temptation to 'free-ride' and privilege the short over the long term is simply too strong. Therefore strong supranational institutions operating on a global scale are required.

Theories of Globalisation: Marxism

It could be argued that Marx was the first (and some would say still the most sophisticated) theorist of globalisation. The following passage is from a short book entitled *Manifesto of the Communist Party*:

> The need of a constantly expanding market for its products chases the bourgeoisie over the whole surface of the globe. It must nestle everywhere, settle everywhere, establish connections everywhere.
>
> The bourgeoisie has through its exploitation of the world market given a cosmopolitan character to production and consumption in every country. To the great chagrin of Reactionists, it has drawn from under the feet of industry the national ground on which it stood. All old-established national industries have been destroyed or are daily being destroyed. They are dislodged by new industries, whose introduction becomes a life and death question for all civilised nations, by industries that no longer work up indigenous raw material, but raw material drawn from the remotest zones; industries whose products are consumed, not only at home, but in every quarter of the globe. In place of the old wants, satisfied by the productions of the country, we find new wants, requiring for their satisfaction the products of distant lands and climes. In place of the old local and national seclusion and self-sufficiency, we have intercourse in every direction, universal inter-dependence of nations. And as in material, so also in intellectual production. The intellectual creations of individual nations become common property. National one-sidedness and narrow-mindedness become more and more impossible, and from the numerous national and local literatures, there arises a world literature.
>
> The bourgeoisie, by the rapid improvement of all instruments of production, by the immensely facilitated means of communication,

draws all, even the most barbarian, nations into civilisation. The cheap prices of its commodities are the heavy artillery with which it batters down all Chinese walls, with which it forces the barbarians' intensely obstinate hatred of foreigners to capitulate. It compels all nations, on pain of extinction, to adopt the bourgeois mode of production; it compels them to introduce what it calls civilisation into their midst, i.e., to become bourgeois themselves. In one word, it creates a world after its own image.[4]

This is a remarkably vivid statement of the main facets of what today is often described as 'globalisation'. Indeed, if one substitutes 'the market' or 'private enterprise' for 'the bourgeoisie', many liberals, paradoxically enough, would find little in it with which to disagree.

Inspired by Marx, some have drawn the conclusion that globalisation is not a post-1945, or a post-Bretton Woods, or a post-Cold-War phenomenon – though its pace has certainly increased during this time – but a phenomenon triggered by the growth of industrial capital.

Indeed, some observers (for example Meghnad Desai) have argued that the period 1930–80 should be seen not as the norm but as the exception. During this 50-year period, the state tried by various means – collectivisation, economic planning, self-sufficiency, Keynesian demand management, exchange controls, incomes policies, nationalisation, ISI – to control economic activity. But all these 'national' solutions failed. The 'natural' and 'internationalising' forces of the market or the historical forces of capitalism inevitably reasserted themselves, as Marx so presciently predicted.[5]

Modern Marxist-inspired theories of globalisation come in a number of different forms. Notable thinkers include, from the discipline of International Relations, Robert Cox, inspired by Habermas and the Frankfurt School of Critical Theorists, and Stephen Gill, inspired by the Italian Marxist writer Antonio Gramsci. Perhaps the two most acclaimed theorists of globalisation are from the discipline of Sociology: Anthony Giddens and Leslie Sklair. Giddens is best described as a 'post-Marxist'. His work is built on the insights of the three founding fathers of Sociology: Marx, Durkheim, and Weber. He is best known for his 'Third Way' an approach to society and politics that recommends a 'post-ideological' middle path between capitalism and socialism, private ownership of the means of production and public, the individual and the community, national citizenship and global responsibility. The application and adaptation of Marx's theory of capitalism to the circumstances of the post-Cold-War era is most striking in the thought of Leslie Sklair. For this reason, and for its clarity and simplicity, Sklair's 'sociology of the global system model' (GSM) will be taken as our principal example of the Marxist approach.

Sklair conceives globalisation in terms of the growth of 'transnational practices'. In particular, he identifies three key types of transnational practice: economic, political and cultural – ideological. Each of these types is characterised by a major institution: economic transnationalism is characterised by the TNC; political transnationalism by the 'transnational capitalist class' (TCC); and cultural–ideological transnationalism by the 'culture – ideology of consumerism'. The TCC is comprised of four groups: TNC executives and their local affiliates; 'globalising state bureaucrats'; 'capitalist-inspired politicians and professionals'; and 'consumerist elites' (merchants, retailers, the media).

Sklair makes three main contentions. His first is that we have reached the 'globalisation stage of world history'. This stage, he says, can only be properly understood in terms of the primacy of the economic power of the TNC, organised politically by the TCC. Particularly significant is the control by the TNC of the 'global mass media'. This is the principal means by which the 'culture–ideology of consumerism' is propagated.

Sklair's second contention is that conventional state-centric models of world politics (a category in which he contentiously includes dependency theory and world systems theory – on which, see Chapter 4) are increasingly unable to explain important developments in the social and economic world. When it is claimed that one country exploits another, does this mean, for instance, that poor North Americans exploit rich South Americans? The GSM disaggregates the state and directs attention to transnational capitalists, not whole countries. Similarly, when it is said that one country has graduated from the semi-periphery of the world economy to the core (say South Korea), or that another is about to be relegated from the core to the semi-periphery (as was said of Britain in the 1970s), does this mean that the economic well-being of all the people in the former has improved and the latter declined?

This, according to Sklair, would be a superficial conclusion. What in fact has happened is that the TCC (consisting of both

Korean and British nationals) has shifted its attention, and some of its operations, from one part of the world to another, and that the working classes have been weakened in one part of the world relative to another.

Sklair's third contention concerns the nature of the process of globalisation. For liberals, globalisation is largely a spontaneous phenomenon: the unintended consequence of millions of individuals and thousands of firms simply pursuing their economic interests as they see them. For Sklair, however, globalisation is something directed and contrived. In his view, the TCC has a mission: organising the conditions under which its interests, and the interests of the system, can be advanced locally, regionally and globally. Above all else, it is the TCC's job to spread the 'culture – ideology of consumerism' and thereby ensure a growing market in which TNCs can sell their products and maximise their profits.

But the effect of the 'culture – ideology of consumerism' is to increase the range of consumer expectations and aspirations without necessarily ensuring that the mass of consumers have the means by which to satisfy them. The result, according to Sklair, is indebtedness, alienation, crime, drug addiction and a wide variety of other ills of modern social life.

Problems with Liberalism

There are a number of problems with the liberal approach to global-isation. Firstly, many liberals contend that the process of globalisation is ineluctably eroding the power and authority of the state, but that this process, nonetheless, needs to be managed. If so, the question arises, by whom? The conventional answer, as pointed out, is the creation of new, authoritative, international institutions, global in scope.

There is, however, a problem with this answer. These are bodies set up, funded by, and accountable to states. If states are not to be in the driving seat in this regard, the question arises, who is? Liberals have yet to provide a convincing answer. Though many of them dis-like or distrust the state, it appears that they cannot do away with it quite as easily as they would like to.

Secondly, many liberals assume that globalisation is a uniform phenomenon: that its various themes and strands are in harmony. But a deep tension exists, certainly in the short run, between establishing the conditions for the success of globalisation and the spread of liberal values such as participation and representation. In order to achieve liberalisation – for example, as part of an IMF 'structural adjustment' programme – pressure is put on states to subdue 'populist' political parties and privatise (and thereby 'de-politicise') certain key sectors of the economy (for example, agriculture, banking, railways, ports, energy, telecommunications). Some argue, however, that 'de-politicise' is a euphemism for 'de-democratise', and that 'privatisation' in effect means 'de-democratisation'. Such measures, they say, involve the transfer of assets that previously belonged to the whole people (or at least to the 'nation') to a small, unaccountable group of capitalists and speculators. Structural adjustment and other austerity measures may make a country more economically efficient, but they rarely make it more democratic. In addition, the track-record in the civil and political field of corporatist states such as Singapore and South Korea suggest that if there is a political logic, as well as an economic logic, to global-isation, it is one that takes many years to unfold. Globalisation may well be the handmaiden of democracy but in several cases it has proven to be neither a particularly efficient nor an entirely loyal one.

Thirdly, liberals have acknowledged that the pace of global-isation is uneven but they have failed to analyse seriously the social and political implications of this fact. A number of recent liberal writers have pointed to the divide between a prosperous, stable and peaceful bloc of liberal states and, on the other hand, the instability, poverty and chaos that currently characterises much of the rest of the world; between a 'Grotian' core and a 'Hobbesian' periphery; between 'zones of peace' and 'zones of turmoil'.[6] Even if this divide is narrowed in the long run, the question remains, what happens in the short run? Is not the liberal globalising project likely, in many areas of the world, to be halted, even put into reverse? Many recent convulsions in world politics – from the campaign for a NIEO to the Iranian Revolution, from anti-IMF riots in Brazil and Mexico and anti-WTO riots in Seattle and Washington to the rise of Islamic revivalism, from the attempt by UNCTAD to control and limit the activities of TNCs to the massacre of Chinese democracy campaigners in Tiananmen Square – can be seen as part of a backlash against globalisation, and one that is unlikely to go away.

Fourthly, in their dislike and distrust of the state, and their enthusiasm for transnational relations, some liberals have pointed to the proliferation of non-state actors as evidence that a global civil society is in the making. But not all transnational actors are as benign or socially responsible as sometimes supposed. Along with the Red Cross, Oxfam, Amnesty International and Greenpeace must be counted the Mafia, international drug cartels, arms dealers and terrorist groups. Nor should it be supposed that such groups are representative or accountable. They are not necessarily more democratic than the state. Most, indeed, are not democratic at all. Therefore, the movement of the world in a transnational direction should not necessarily be hailed as a democratic advance. If the rise of the transnational actor betokens the arrival of a global civil society, it is one that currently takes a most rudimentary form.

Problems with Marxism

Similarly, there are a number of problems with the Marxist approach to globalisation, the GSM in particular.

Firstly, the term 'globalisation' is used interchangeably with 'transnationalism' and especially 'transnational linkages of capital'. A new and portentous-sounding term is introduced, therefore, but no extra meaning is conveyed. 'Globalisation', in a word, lacks specificity. Why, therefore, introduce a new term if ones currently in use have the same meaning?

Secondly, the GSM asserts the primacy of the power of the TNC. The only empirical evidence presented for this claim is the fact that over 60 countries in the world have a GNP of less than US$10 billion, whereas 135 TNCs have sales in excess of US$10 billion. The biggest TNCs, it is consequently said, 'have more economic power at their disposal than the majority of states'.

But this does not take into account the fact that TNCs are more constrained – by shareholders, by customers, by governments – from exercising this 'economic power' than states.

Moreover, turnover, profits and sales, do not directly translate into 'economic power'. Even the biggest TNCs are sometimes extremely vulnerable to public opinion, law suits, media speculation, industrial action, civil disturbances, changes in government policy, and market failure, as recent cases involving such giants as Exxon, BP, Union Carbide, Microsoft, BAT, Gallagher and Philip Morris amply demonstrate. To assert the primacy of the power of the TNC is at best premature.

Thirdly, the somewhat un-Marxist notion that the TCC has a 'mission' can be challenged. It implies a self-consciousness, a degree of organisation, and a degree of unity among the TCC that is nowhere demonstrated. TNCs sometimes co-operate, form rings and cartels, collaborate in joint projects, share 'set-up' costs for new products. More often than not, however, they are in competition with one another, often ferociously (witness the growth in recent years of mergers and acquisitions, in particular 'corporate raids'). Their interests conflict as much as they coincide. It may be in the interest of every TNC to keep its costs down, but it is not in the interest of any TNC for its rivals to have equal success in keeping their costs down.

Fourthly, according to Sklair, the effect of the 'culture–ideology of consumerism' is to increase the range of consumer expectations and aspirations without necessarily ensuring the income to buy. But if consumers do not have the necessary income to buy, how have TNCs managed to sell their goods in ever greater quantities? It is true that in recent decades there has been a huge increase in the developed world in consumer credit. But credit is not something entirely divorced from wealth and income. On the contrary, in general, and in the long run, 'unsound credit' is the exception rather than the rule. There seems to be, therefore, a contradiction in Sklair's argument. The implication is that the TCC is somehow conspiring against consumers by first raising their expectations and then dashing them. But this surely would be contrary to, not in conformity with, the interests of TNCs and the TCC behind them. A lack of purchasing power on the part of consumers does not auger well for TNC profitability.

The Decline of the State?

In the literature on globalisation, and world politics generally, one finds at work two concepts of the state. These concepts are rarely distinguished. Indeed there is a tendency, especially in the socio-logical literature, for analysts to slide from one conceptualisation to the other with seemingly little awareness that they are doing so.

The first concept is the 'coercive' or 'institutional' state. This is the state we have in mind when we refer to 'state-owned enterprises', or 'state education', or 'state regulation of industry'. The institutional or coercive state is the state that taxes us, binds us with laws and conscripts us, or at least some of us, into the armed forces. The second concept is the 'territorial' or 'nation' state (sometimes known as the 'Westphalian' or 'sovereign' state).[7] This is the state we have in mind when we talk of states signing a treaty, conducting diplomacy, or when we refer to the 'powers' or the 'great powers'. The territorial or nation-state is the state that joins international organisations, is bound by international law, and which from time to time goes to war.[8]

The failure to distinguish between these two concepts of state has generated much confusion and misunderstanding. The decline, or failure or retreat of the state in one sense has been taken as evidence of the decline, failure, or retreat of the state in the other. But this is not so. The retreat of the institutional/coercive state from economic affairs in recent decades does not necessarily mean that the territorial/nation-state is in decline. It is true that states around the world have engaged in privatisation of state-owned enterprises, have liberalised their financial markets, have become increasingly wary of their ability to manipulate exchange rates, have sought to encourage private investment and private enterprise, have abandoned Keynesian policies of demand management in favour of more orthodox 'supply side' economics, and so on. The institutional/coercive state, in other words, has withdrawn from a range of economic activities in which it used to participate as a matter of course. The lesson has been learnt, it is said, the world over. States simply do not make good businessmen. The state cannot buck the market. Economies perform best when allowed to operate as freely as possible.

But the strategic retreat of the institutional/coercive state from the economic domain, in the wake of the widespread economic failures of the 1970s, does not mean that the territorial/nation-state is in decline, and that the world is inexorably heading in a 'transnational' direction in which the state (in this second sense) is no longer central. On the contrary, the territorial/nation-state, as a mode of political organisation, is today more popular than ever. The UN now has a bigger membership than at any time in its 50-year history. There are numerous ethnic groups, national liberation organisations and secessionist movements that seek their salvation through the acquisition of their own nation-state.

Moreover, by making the economy more prosperous, the retreat of the state in the first sense may enhance, not diminish, the viability of the state in the second. A strong economy gives the state (in the second sense) more influence abroad, enhances its domestic legitimacy and strengthens its ability to prevail in war. This was certainly the impulse that drove the Conservative governments of Margaret Thatcher in Britain in the 1980s. More than any other individual, it was Thatcher who reversed the tide of Keynesianism, state and trade-union corporatism, and the control of large swathes of the economy by public-sector monopolies. She strove to reduce the role of the state in the economy, to 'get the state off the people's backs', to restore the role and reputation of private enterprise, and generally to shift the balance of power away from the state towards the individual. Yet Thatcher was also a great patriot. Her political hero was the great war leader, diehard imperialist and disastrous Chancellor of the Exchequer (1925–9), Winston Churchill. She wanted to restore Britain's place in the world, to make her strong again, to put the 'Great', as the popular saying of the time went, back into 'Britain'. It might be said that these two goals are contradictory. On the one hand, she wanted to strengthen the power and influence of the state. On the other hand, she wanted to weaken it. But this is only a contradiction if one fails to distinguish between the two different concepts of state. Britain, the territorial/nation-state, had become economically and politically weak because of the unchecked growth in the power of the institutional/coercive state over its energetic and creative citizens. As a result of the overweening power of the institutional/coercive state, this energy and creativity had been sapped. Thatcher hoped, in essence, to restore the power and prestige of the territorial/nation-state by putting the institutional/coercive state back in its place.

Conceptual Clarity?

Given these facts, it might be asked, is 'globalisation' anything more than a buzz-word of financial journalists, management science gurus, pop-economists and faddish sociologists? One might be forgiven for having one or two reservations. Few analysts have taken the trouble to define clearly what they mean by it. Those who have, have found themselves falling into errors of tautology. For example, globalisation is sometimes defined as 'the reduction in the geographical constraints on social arrangements' or 'the emergence of a borderless, de-territorialised, though not necessarily homogeneous, world'. But the same writers then go on to make the important claim that 'globalisation is rapidly eroding the power and authority of the nation-state'. But given their definition, globalisation is the erosion of the power and authority of the nation-state. The statement is tautologous. It is true by definition.

In addition, many analysts fail to distinguish between globalisation and related concepts such as transnationalism or internationalisation. Sometimes they use these terms interchangeably. Sometimes they imply that globalisation is significantly different: a special, more advanced, or more profound form of transnationalism or internationalisation. This lack of conceptual precision is a serious impediment to clear understanding.

In mitigation, it might be said that the concept of globalisation and theories about it are still in their infancy. The Industrial Revolution of the late eighteenth century had a profound effect on the social, economic and political organisation of the world and virtually every aspect of the daily lives of its inhabitants. Many of its effects are still being felt today. The microchip revolution of the late twentieth century may prove equally profound in its consequences. Though they can be criticised for lack of a conceptual clarity, globalisation theorists are to be congratulated for attempting to grapple with the multifarious and potentially profound implications of the present revolution.

Notes on Chapter 11

1   The phrases are Carr's. See E.H. Carr, *The Twenty Years' Crisis*, 1st ed. (London, Macmillan, 1939), 17–19.

2   Malcolm Waters, *Globalization* (London, Routledge, 1995), 53. In fairness to Waters, in this passage he is summarising the argument of Lash and Urry (*Economies of Signs and Space* [London, Sage, 1994]). The fault may, therefore, be theirs more than his.

3   Rousseau was perhaps the first philosopher to note the dangers of increased contact and communication between sovereign states acknowledging no superior authority. 'The historic union of the nations of Europe,' he said, 'has entangled their rights and interests

in a thousand complications: they touch each other at so many points that not one of them can move without giving a jar to all the rest; their variances are all the more deadly, as their ties are the more closely woven; their frequent quarrels are almost as savage as civil wars.' Jean-Jacques Rousseau, 'Abstract of the Abbé de Saint-Pierre's Project for Perpetual Peace', in M.G. Forsyth, H.M.A. Keens-Soper and P. Savigear (eds), *The Theory of International Relations: Selected Texts from Gentili to Treitschke* (London, George Allen and Unwin, 1970), 136.

4 Karl Marx and Friedrich Engels, *Manifesto of the Communist Party* (Moscow, Progress Publishers, 1977 [1848]), 39–40.

5 See Meghnad Desai, 'Global Governance', in Meghnad Desai and Paul Redfern (eds), *Global Governance: Ethics and Economics of the World Order* (London, Pinter, 1995), 6–21.

6 The Dutch international lawyer Hugo Grotius (1583–1645) characterised international relations as an essentially co-operative realm, regulated by law, managed by diplomacy, and typified by international trade. His contemporary, the English political philosopher Thomas Hobbes (1588–1679), on the other hand, characterised international relations as an anarchical 'war of all against all', in which peace was merely the interlude between wars, and life was 'solitary, poor, nasty, brutish, and short'. See Martin Wight *International Theory: The Three Traditions*, Gabriele Wight and Brian Porter (eds), (London, Leicester University Press, 1991), especially 7–24. See also Barry Buzan, 'From International System to International Society: Structural Realism and Regime Theory meet the English School', *International Organization* 47, 3 (1993); Max Singer and Aaron Wildavsky, *The Real World Order: Zones of Peace/Zones of Turmoil* (Chatham, MA, Chatham House, 1993).

7 'Westphalian' after the Congress (and subsequently Treaties) of Westphalia which brought to an end the internecine Christian wars of 1618–48. Unable to agree on 'first principles', the delegates arrived at the formula *cuius regio, eius religio* (in the region of the prince, the religion of the prince) as a *modus vivendi*. This laid the basis for the modern principle of non-intervention. See James Mayall, 'International Society and International Theory', in Michael Donelan (ed.), *The Reason of States: A Study in International Political Theory* (London, George Allen and Unwin, 1978), 122–41;

Andrew Linklater, *The Transformation of Political Community: Ethical Foundations of the Post-Westphalian Era* (Cambridge, Polity, 1998).

8 For an important general analysis, see Fred Halliday, 'State and Society in International Relations: A Second Agenda', *Millennium: Journal of International Studies* 16, 2 (1987).

Select Bibliography

Clark, Ian, *Globalization and Fragmentation: International Relations in the Twentieth Century* (Oxford, Oxford University Press, 1997). Lucid introduction to twentieth-century international relations from a post-Cold-War perspective.

Cox, Robert, *Production, Power, and World Order: Social Forces in the Making of History* (New York, NY, Columbia University Press, 1987). Broad-ranging theoretical account of the relations between states, world orders and social forces. Major statement from the leading critical theorist in IR.

Giddens, Anthony, *The Consequences of Modernity* (Cambridge, Polity, 1990). Broad-ranging sociological account of the modern world from the leading theorist of globalisation.

Giddens, Anthony, *The Third Way: The Renewal of Social Democracy* (Oxford, Polity Press, 1998). The leading theorist of globalisation sets out his practical stall.

Held, D., A.G. McGrew, D. Goldblatt and J. Perraton, *Global Transformations: Politics, Economics, Culture* (Cambridge, Polity Press, 1999). The Introduction provides a most helpful overview of the contending theoretical positions.

Helleiner, Eric, 'States and the Future of Global Finance', *Review of International Studies* 18, 1 (1992). Sophisticated analysis of the role of states in international financial markets.

Hurst, Paul and Grahame Thompson, *Globalization in Question: The International Economy and the Possibilities of Governance* (Cambridge, Polity Press, 1996). Exacting analysis of globalisation theory. The most thorough work of criticism in the field.

Hurst, Paul, 'The Global Economy: Myths and Realities', *International Affairs* 73, 3 (1997).

Linklater, Andrew, *The Transformation of Political Community: Ethical Foundations of the Post-Westphalian Era* (Cambridge, Polity Press,

1998). Account of the possibilities for progressive change immanent within the current international system. Inspired by the critical theory of Jurgen Habermas, especially his notion of 'dialogic communities'.

Lipshutz, R.D., 'Restructuring World Politics: The Emergence of a Global Civil Society', *Millennium: Journal of International Studies* 21, 3 (1992).

Luard, Evan, *The Globalization of Politics: The Changed Focus of Political Action in the Modern World* (London, Macmillan, 1990). Lucid analysis from left-liberal perspective.

Ohmae, Kenichi, *The Borderless World: Power and Strategy in The Interlinked Economy* (London, Collins, 1996). Former nuclear engineer and Senior Partner in McKinsey sets out fast and furiously the 'hyper-globalist' position. Fierce attack on nationalism, the nation-state, 'politicians', 'bureaucrats', regulation, 'regulators' and anything else which prevents firms 'adding value' (i.e. making money). Constantly mixes up 'is' and 'ought'. Has sold millions to the already converted.

Sjolander, C.T., 'The Rhetoric of Globalization: What's in a Wor(l)d?', *International Journal* 11, (1996).

Sklair, Leslie, *Sociology of the Global System* (Hemel Hempstead, Harvester Wheatsheaf, 1991). Provides systematic account of the Sociology of the global systems model. Clear, systematic and provocative.

Spegele, Roger, 'Is Robust Globalism a Mistake?', *Review of International Studies* 23, 2 (1997).

Strange, Susan, *The Retreat of the State: The Diffusion of Power in the World Economy* (Cambridge, Cambridge University Press, 1996). Typically profane, innovative and thought-provoking analysis from pioneer of IPE. Imprecise at crucial junctures.

Robertson, R., *Globalization: Social Theory and Global Culture* (London, Sage, 1992). Important statement from sociologist who sees globalisation as primarily a cultural phenomenon.

CONCLUSION

The Borderful World

The relationship between economics and politics at the international level is complex and multifaceted. It cannot be reduced to a simple formula or dictum. Only by doing great violence to the complexity of the subject matter can such grand assertions as those with which this book opened be sustained. The notion of 'economic factors' is itself not so innocent, nor so unbeguiling, as its simple, everyday usage suggests. As we discovered in Chapter 1, this term commonly denotes one or more of four things. It can mean: the economic causes of a particular event or phenomenon; the economic means used to achieve a particular end; economic ends themselves; and the economic implications of any given action or event. In popular writing on world politics, these four possibilities often lie hidden. Little if any attempt is made to distinguish them. This may serve the propagandist purpose of the writer. It may make good copy. But it does little to aid or advance genuine understanding.

The purpose of this volume has been to lay the foundations for a more subtle understanding of the role of the economic factor in international relations. The first and most elementary foundation stone is precisely this kind of critical conceptual analysis. Not for the first time in history, there has been an outcrop in recent years of works that prophesy the end of the state. Information technology, it is said, is rendering the state obsolete. MNCs act as if they operate in a borderless world. Economic interdependence has become so great in the 'inter-linked economy' of Europe, Japan and North America that traditional national borders within and between them have effectively disappeared. Nation-states are no longer meaningful units of economic activity. The meaningful units are now 'regions'. These 'regions' cut across states and arise spontaneously in response to market forces. Chief among these market forces are the desires and preferences of the ever more sophisticated and 'sovereign' individual consumer, liberated by the information revolution and shorn of his or her national and cultural allegiances (except when whipped up by self-interested, backward-looking, 'bureaucrats' and 'politicians'). The increasing empowerment of the consumer signals the victory of utility over ideology. Consumers want the best products at the lowest price and have little regard for 'country of origin'. But governments continue to frustrate the interests of consumers by putting producers and other 'special interests' first. Their natural inclination is to protect and subsidise. They see themselves as economic providers rather than facilitators. In so doing, they preserve their power and continue to exercise the central controls which do so much to impede full integration of national economies into the global marketplace. 'Old-fashioned bureaucrats', in the words of one leading commentator, 'create barriers and artificial controls over what should be the free flow of goods and money'.[1] States have become unnatural, even dysfunctional, forms of economic organisation.

As we saw in Chapter 11 there is a tendency in such arguments to conflate and confuse two quite distinct concepts of the state. It may be the case that the involvement of the institutional/coercive state in a wide range of economic activities is in retreat. But this does not mean that the territorial/nation-state is in retreat as a mode of political organisation. Nor does it mean that the involvement of the institutional/coercive state in economic activity is still not high and significant. Indeed the doom merchants of the state tacitly admit this. They acknowledge that the neo-protectionism of the 1980s was a major factor in the growth of foreign direct investment. Unable to export their products in quantity to the lucrative markets of the EU and North America, companies such as Hitachi, Sony, Toshiba, Toyota, Nissan, Honda and many other household names began to set up plants in the markets themselves. In this they were encouraged by host governments eager to reap the political and economic rewards of large-scale job creation. Trade policy thus had a major impact on the pattern of international investment. The nature and shape of the various government-created environments within which global economic activity was increasingly taking place became a key factor in corporate decision-making. Contingency plans for dealing with changes in these environments now had to be at the very heart of corporate global strategy.[2]

This acknowledgement that governments or public authorities can and do have a dramatic effect on economic behaviour sits uneasily with the 'decline of the state' thesis. But there is a broader problem from which this one partly springs. The decline of the state thesis is, in fact, not one thesis but several. If one looks carefully at the writings of those who predict the end of the state, one finds a number of different contentions at work. Firstly, there is the question of which concept of 'state' is being invoked. As demonstrated above, the decline or retreat of the institutional/coercive state does not necessarily imply the decline or retreat of the territorial/nation-state. Secondly, there is a difference between saying that the state is 'declining' and saying that it is 'retreating'. The former suggests inevitability, the triumph of 'structure' over 'agency'. The latter suggests an element (perhaps large) of choice, the mutual conditioning of agency and structure. Thirdly, to say that the state is becoming obsolete is not the same as saying that it *is* obsolete. Similarly, to claim the world is *becoming* borderless is not the same as claiming that it is borderless. Both differ from the claim that MNCs, among others, *act* as if the world is borderless. Fourthly, to say that states (or governments, or politicians, or bureaucrats) are losing their power and authority is significantly different from saying that their role is becoming 'dysfunctional'. The former suggests that their ability to shape outcomes intentionally, whether positively or negatively, is waning. The latter presumes that the power and authority of these entities remains intact (at least to a significant degree) but that the exercise of such power and authority is increasingly leading to negative outcomes. Fifthly, the claim that states *are* declining (or retreating, or becoming obsolete) is light years away from the assertion that they *should* be. This is the most serious flaw in the decline of the state thesis: the constant mixing-up of 'is' and 'ought'. In Ohmae's writings, one cannot help thinking that his empirical assertions are the slave of his normative convictions. Ohmae says the state is declining not because he has discovered incontrovertible evidence of its decline but because he wants it to decline. It is, to revert back to Carr's phrase, an optative proposition couched in the indicative mood: a wish dressed up as a fact. In true classical liberal fashion, Ohmae believes in the free flow of goods and money. Anything that gets in the way of this flow is a hindrance to economic growth, to the 'adding of value', and therefore 'unnatural'. His approach is highly 'economistic'. He wishes away the complex interplay of economic and political factors that have been the subject of this book. In his writings, individual human beings are consumers but rarely citizens. Their national and cultural allegiances are seen as irrational if they run contrary to their ability to maximise economic utility. Similarly, the rationality of their behaviour in the marketplace is nowhere questioned. The ability of firms to manipulate demand through ever more sophisticated marketing and sales techniques is not examined. Nor is their ability to utilise the latest developments in information technology in order to create ever wider markets for their high value-added (that is highly profitable) products.[3] The communications revolution strengthens the hand of the consumer, never weakens it. No concerns are expressed about the homogenisation of tastes and values worldwide. The extension of Western-style consumerism around the world is not seen as a subject worthy of critical study.

Similarly the state (either institutional/coercive or territorial/ nation) is seen in exclusively economic terms. The assertion that it is no longer a meaningful unit of economic activity makes no sense unless it is assumed that once it was such a unit. But this can be questioned. The nation-state is a territorially based mode of political organisation possessing a government and a people. Not everyone in the state shares the same identity or outlook, but they have enough in common to generate a sense of fraternity, of 'togetherness', and concomitantly 'separateness' from others. The institutional/coercive state is an institutional apparatus erected and maintained to implement government policy, enforce the law, and encourage compliance with a social and ethical code. The nation-state has never been a 'unit' (meaningful or not) of economic activity. Rather it is an arena, or a socio-political setting, or a 'space' within which economic activity of various kinds takes place. Similarly, the role that the institutional/coercive state plays in economic affairs has varied from country to country and from period to period. Was Bolshevik Russia once 'a meaningful unit of economic activity'? The slave economy of the southern states of the US? The Nazi 'New Order' in Europe 1940–5? The Ottoman Empire? Japan before the Meiji restoration? Contemporary North Korea and Burma? Revolutionary Iran? In some periods and in some countries the state has played a major role in economic affairs, even to the point of seeking control of every aspect of the economic life of the nation. But in other periods and in other countries the state has taken a much lesser role, seeking instead to provide a legal framework and a secure social and political environment within which predominantly private economic intercourse can take place. The mix of public and private is infinitely variable. Attempts to control the whole economic life of the nation have been the exception rather than the rule. The exceptional case, totalitarianism, Ohmae and other critics of the state seem to take as normal.

This example illustrates the caution with which many broad statements about the relationship between politics and economics have to be taken. Behind them often lies a political purpose or 'agenda'. Consciousness of this purpose or agenda is not necessary for it to exist. Societies have a way of shaping individual values, interests and outlooks that few people fully appreciate. It is with a careful analysis of the structure of arguments and the conceptual tools and materials with which they are built that any such appreciation must begin. This book has shown that states, governments and borders are still crucially important features of the economic and political landscape. The rapid erosion of the significance of national borders is not an empirical fact but a liberal dream.

Notes on Conclusion

1   Kenichi Ohmae, *The Borderless World* (London, HarperCollins, 1990), xi–xii.
2   Ibid., 2–3.
3   In fairness, one does find the beginnings of such an analysis in Ohmae's most recent book, *The Invisible Continent: Four Strategic Imperatives of the New Economy* (London, Nicholas Brealey Publishing, 2000)), though the generation of demand for new products is always seen as a rational and natural thing, never a form of manipulation or psychological disarmament.

BIOGRAPHICAL GLOSSARY

ANGELL, NORMAN (1872–1967). Journalist, publicist and campaigner for peace. Educated at the Lycée de St Omer, a business school in London, and briefly at the University of Geneva. He emigrated to America in the 1890s and pursued a variety of occupations, including that of cowboy. On his return to England seven years later, he entered journalism, rising rapidly to become the General Manager of the *Paris Daily Mail* in 1905. His first book, prompted by the contemporaneous Dreyfus Case, the Spanish–American War and the South African War, was *Patriotism Under Three Flags: A Plea for Rationalism in Politics* (1903). It had little impact. His next book, *Europe's Optical Illusion* (1908) fared little better. However, an expanded version under the title *The Great Illusion* (1909) captured the public mood. Angell argued that 'modern economic civilization' was incompatible with indemnities, colonies and war. In various editions it went on to sell over two million copies, making it the best selling IR text ever. Angell was a founder member of the Union of Democratic Control, a radical body set up to campaign against the 'old' aristocratic diplomacy of the nineteenth century, the notorious 'secret treaties' in particular. He was a staunch supporter of the League of Nations. He was a Labour MP from 1929 to 1931; knighted in 1930; and awarded the Nobel Prize for Peace in 1933. He spent most of the 1930s vigorously promoting the idea of collective security, a facet of the League of Nations he had previously played down.

BUKHARIN, NIKOLAI IVANOVICH (1888–1938). Bolshevik, social scientist and economist. A close friend and collaborator of Lenin, he played an active part in the October Revolution and was rewarded with the editorship of *Pravda*. His *Imperialism and the World Economy* (1917) established his reputation as an important, or useful, thinker. He became the official theorist of Soviet communism with works such as the much reprinted *ABC of Communism* (1925) and *The Economic Theory of the Leisure Class* (1927). He was co-leader, with Stalin, of the Communist Party between 1925 and 1928, and Chairman of the Executive Committee of the Third International (or 'Comintern') between 1926 and 1929. Although he initially supported Stalin against Trotsky, who held him in contempt, he broke with the former over his attempt to abandon the relatively liberal New Economic Policy in favour of mass collectivisation. From this point he became Stalin's chief opponent. He was put on trial for treason in 1938 and shot.

CARR, EDWARD HALLET (1892–1982). Historian and professor of international relations. He studied classics at Trinity College, Cambridge, where he was much influenced by the formidable classicist and poet, A.E. Housman. He joined the British Foreign Office in 1916, serving most notably in Paris, during the Peace Conference, and Riga. In 1936, he became Woodrow Wilson Professor of International Politics at the University College of Wales, Aberystwyth. It was during his tenure at Aberystwyth that he wrote a series of elegant and trenchant books on the international situation, culminating in *The Twenty Years' Crisis* (1939). During the war he served briefly, and controversially, as the director of the foreign publicity department of the Ministry of Information, and as deputy editor of the London *Times*. Here his forensic mind and literary skill were used to full effect in the writing of provocative and influential leading articles. He became known as 'the red professor of Printing House Square', due to his unorthodox but readily apparent left-wing views. In the 1950s he returned to Trinity, though was never offered a chair, and began work on his monumental 14-volume *History of the Bolshevik Revolution* (1950–71) and his influential and bestselling *What is History?* (1961).

COBDEN, RICHARD (1804–65). English radical thinker and campaigner. Raised in a poor Sussex farming community, he started a calico wholesale business in 1828, becoming sufficiently wealthy to support extensive travel between 1833 and 1839. In two influential pamphlets written during this period, *England, Ireland and America* (1835) and *Russia* (1836), he argued for a new approach to foreign policy based on non-intervention, free trade and an end to power politics. Between 1839 and 1846 he championed the campaign against the Corn Laws. He founded and lead the Anti-Corn Law League, one of the most successful pressure groups of the nineteenth century. He entered parliament in 1841 in order to engage the Prime Minister, Sir Robert Peel, directly in debate. On Peel's conversion, the laws were duly repealed in 1846. With non-conformist John Bright, he became leader of what became known as the Manchester School of economic and political radicals, arguing for a reduction in taxation, the establishment of a universal system of education, a reduction in national armaments, and an end to imperial expansion. He opposed the Crimean War and for a time became highly unpopular, briefly losing his parliamentary seat in 1857. In the last decade of his life he dedicated himself to improving Anglo–French relations. The Commercial ('Cobden–Chevalier') Treaty of 1860, in which the 'most favoured nation' clause first appeared, owed much to Cobden's efforts.

COLBERT, JEAN BAPTISTE (1619–83). Finance Minister and Secretary of State for the Navy under Louis XIV. From a family of merchants, he rose to prominence under the patronage of Cardinal Mazarin, for a time the most powerful figure in France. After skilfully discrediting the incumbent, Nicholas Fouquet, he achieved one of his ambitions in becoming Comptroller General of the Council of Finance in 1665. In this post he restored the health of the public finances by clawing back excessive profits made from the government by private financiers. He reformed the chaotic tax system by reducing the overall burden, but putting in place a strict system of enforcement. He also increased France's share of international trade by encouraging foreign tradesmen to bring their skills to France, expanding the merchant marine through a system of subsidies and privileges, introducing a system of national quality control for manufactures, and establishing state manufacturing and trading companies. Not all his policies were successful. The policy of building up French industry behind high tariff walls led to retaliation and resulted in the Dutch War of 1672–78. He became Secretary of State for the Navy in 1668, setting about making France a great sea power. The arsenal at Toulon was reconstructed and a new one founded at Rochefort. Naval schools were established at Rochefort, Dieppe and St Malo. Dunkirk, Brest and Le Havre were fortified. Magistrates were encouraged to sentence common criminals to serve on the galley ships of the Mediterranean fleet. Other sources of manpower included Protestants, political prisoners and slaves seized from Africa and Canada. Ships built at home attracted a premium, those built abroad a penalty. His achievements were all the more impressive given that during this time prices throughout the world were generally falling, and his employer embroiled France in a series of unnecessary and costly wars.

FICHTE, JOHANN GOTTLEIB (1762–1814). German idealist philosopher. Educated at the universities of Jena and Leipzig. His first work, *An Attempt at a Critique of All Revelation* (1792), built on the work and was published with the help of Kant, whom Fichte had visited in Königsberg a year earlier. In 1793, he entered the realm of political thought with his anonymously published *Contribution to the Correction of the Public's Judgements Regarding the French Revolution*. In this work, Fichte asserted that the right to liberty was inextricably linked to the existence of man as an intelligent being. He also asserted that the state was inherently progressive, with modification and reform being a normal and necessary activity. His appointment to a chair in philosophy at the University of Jena in 1793 inaugurated his most productive period. Over the next five years he published his most important philosophical works, including *The Vocation of the Scholar* (1794), *The Science of Rights* (1796), and *The Science of Ethics as Based on the Science of Knowledge* (1798). These works fundamentally challenged Western philosophy by putting forward the uncompromising idealist view that everything, even experience itself, is created by the human subject. He thus asserted the primacy of the will over the intellect, and creation over discovery. In 1798, he ran into trouble with the authorities when a short essay defining God as the moral order of the universe was condemned as atheistic. The *Philosophical Journal*, for which he wrote, was suppressed, and he was forced to resign his chair. While residing in Berlin during the next seven years he became closely attached to the German romantic movement. He published *The Vocation of Man* (1800), *Der Geschlossene Handelsstadt* (1800), which kindled his reputation as an extreme economic nationalist, and *The Characteristics of the Present Age* (1806), in which he defined the place of the Enlightenment in the evolution of consciousness. His *Addresses to the German Nation* (1808) contain the first explicit formulation of the doctrine of nationalism.

FRANK, ANDRE GUNDER (b. 1929). German economist and historical sociologist. Educated at Swarthmore College and the University of Chicago. Frank spent the early part of his career in Latin America, where he developed his concept of 'underdevelopment' and his 'metropole–satellite' model of capitalist development. Forced to flee Chile after the Pinochet coup in 1973, he subsequently held posts at the Max Planck Institute, Starnberg, the Free University of Berlin, the University of Paris, the University of East Anglia and the University of Amsterdam. The author of some 40 books and numerous articles, he is chiefly known for his *Capitalism and Underdevelopment in Latin America* (1967), *On Capitalist Underdevelopment* (1975), and *World Accumulation: 1492–1789* (1978). His most important recent study is a detailed analysis of the rise of the Asian economies, *ReOrient: The Global Economy in the Asian Age* (1998).

FRIEDMAN, MILTON (b. 1912). American economist and advocate of *laissez-faire*. Educated at Rutgers, Chicago and Columbia Universities, he joined the National Bureau of Economic Research in 1937, served in the Tax Research Division of the US Treasury during the war, and became Professor of Economics at the University of Chicago in 1946. As a formative member of what became known as the 'Chicago School', he pioneered monetarist economics. According to this approach, the business cycle is determined primarily by the money supply and interest rates, not by fiscal policy. This was the first major challenge to the ascendancy of Keynesianism and the post-war consensus on 'demand management'. In *Capitalism and Freedom*, written in 1962 with his wife, Rose D. Friedman, he argued for a 'negative income tax' to replace central provision of welfare services by the state. According to Friedman, such services are inimical to individual responsibility and thrift. He brilliantly developed these themes for a popular audience in his best-selling *Free to Choose* (1980, also with Rose D. Friedman). Other important works of a more technical nature include *A Theory of the Consumption Function* (1957), *Price Theory* (1962), *A Monetary History of the United States, 1867–1960* (1963), *The Great Contraction* (1965), and *Monetary Trends in the United States and the United Kingdom* (1982). He was awarded the Nobel Prize for Economics in 1976.

GALBRAITH, JOHN KENNETH (b. 1908). Paul M. Warburg Professor of Economics Emeritus at Harvard University. Economist and liberal critic of unbridled capitalism. Educated at the universities of Toronto and California at Berkeley. He began his academic career at Harvard and Princeton. During the Second World War he held a variety of public posts, returning to Harvard in 1949. An archetypal 'engaged intellectual' he was a chief advisor to President Kennedy and served as his Ambassador to India from 1961 to 1963. By this time he had established his reputation as a writer with a rare gift for conveying complex ideas to a broad audience. His key works are *The Great Crash, 1929* (1955), *The Affluent Society* (1958), *The New Industrial State* (1967), and *The Culture of Contentment* (1993).

GALTUNG, JOHAN (b. 1930). Norwegian professor of peace studies. Educated at the University of Oslo. He has taught at a variety of institutions in Europe and America, including the universities of Columbia (1957–60), Oslo (1969–77), Princeton (1985–9) and Hawaii (from 1985). His principal publications are *Theory and Methods of Social Research* (1967), *The European Community: A Superpower in the Making* (1973), *Environment, Development, and Military Activity* (1982), and *Peace by Peaceful Means* (1996). Many of his most important scholarly essays are usefully gathered together in *Essays in Peace Research* (6 vols, 1974–88).

GILPIN, ROBERT (b. 1930). IR theorist and international political economist. Educated at the universities of Vermont, Cornell and California at Berkeley. Following brief spells at Harvard and Columbia he joined the faculty at Princeton in 1962, becoming Professor of Political Science in 1970 and Dwight D. Eisenhower Professor of International Affairs in 1975. He is the author of a number of erudite and lucid works, including *US Power and the Multinational Corporation* (1975), *War and Change in World Politics* (1981) and *The Challenge of Global Capitalism* (2000). His *Political Economy of International Relations* (1987) is the most widely used and important general work in the field.

HAMILTON, ALEXANDER (1755–1804). Politician and American 'founding father'. Forced to start work at the age of 11, and receiving little formal education, Hamilton rose to prominence with three influential pamphlets written (1774–5) in defence of the Continental Congress. He became a colonel and aide-de-camp to General Washington during the War of Independence. Under the pseudonym 'Continentalist', he wrote a series of essays for the *New York Packet* (1781–2) arguing for strong central government, and attacking the Articles of Confederation as a source of weakness and division. He was instrumental in convening the Constitutional Convention at Philadelphia in 1787. At the Convention, he again put forward his ideas for a strong centre, involving a president elected for life, an absolute presidential veto over legislation, and centrally appointed state governors (who themselves would have an absolute veto over state legislation). He nonetheless accepted the more federalist constitution that finally emerged, and with James Madison and John Jay wrote the *Federalist* series of essays defending it. The *Federalist* deeply influenced the shape of the young American republic, and became a classic of political thought. He was appointed First Secretary of the Treasury in 1789. His plan to strengthen the federal centre financially at the expense of the states led to a split in the government and the formation of political parties, a development he deplored. He nonetheless became leader of the Federalist Party, favouring closer links with England, industrialisation behind high tariffs (as set out in his influential *Report on Manufactures* of 1791), and a hierarchical society regulated by 'superior persons'. Against him stood the Democratic-Republican Party of Madison and Thomas Jefferson, favouring closer links with France, an economy based on the small independent farmer and a more egalitarian society. Hamilton failed to win the nomination of the Federalist Party following Washington's retirement in 1797. He nonetheless continued to exert considerable influence over the conduct of foreign policy, despite the suspicions of incumbent John Adams. He was killed in a duel called by Republican rival Aaron Burr in 1804.

HAYEK, FRIEDRICH AUGUST VON (1899–1992). Economist and political philosopher. Born in Vienna and educated at its university, he became director of the Austrian Institute for Economic Research in 1927. In 1931, he was appointed Tooke Professor of Economic Science and Statistics at the London School of Economics, where he made his mark, becoming a naturalised British citizen in 1938. From 1950 to 1962, he was Professor of Social and Moral Science at the University of Chicago, playing a major part in the formation of the

'Chicago School' of monetarist economists. He then professed economics at the University of Freiburg until his retirement in 1969. His most famous work is *The Road to Serfdom* (1944), an elegant and provocative critique of the totalitarianism he felt was latent in all forms of socialism, whether Marxist, Trotskyite, Fabian or social democratic. In his most ambitious work, *The Constitution of Liberty* (1960), he attempted to identify the ethical foundations of a free society, the institutions that had been most efficacious in defending individual liberty, and the constitutional framework most conducive to the successful operation of a free market. Other important works include *Prices and Production* (1931), *The Pure Theory of Capitalism* (1941), and *Law, Legislation and Liberty* (3 vols, 1973–9). He was awarded the Nobel Prize for Economics in 1974. His writings were a major source of inspiration for the free-market reforms of Margaret Thatcher, British Prime Minister 1979–90. He was one of her most cherished advisors during the 1980s.

HILFERDING, RUDOLF (1877–1941). Marxist economist and politician. Became a socialist while studying medicine in Vienna. In 1906, he became an instructor at the Social Democratic Party's training school in Berlin. His first important contribution to Marxist theory was his *Böhm-Bawerk's Criticism of Marx* (1904). His most famous work, *Finance Capital* (1910), charted the growing links between finance and industry, and the increasing pressure on banks and finance houses to find profitable outlets for surplus capital. From 1907 to 1915 he was the political editor of *Vorwarts*, the principal mouthpiece of the Social Democratic Party (SDP). Though opposed to the First World War, he was conscripted into the Austrian army and served with the medical corps on the Italian front. He became a deputy in the Reichstag in 1924, serving briefly as Finance Minister in two SDP administrations. He fled Germany when the Nazis came to power, but remained active in socialist organisation and anti-Nazi propaganda. He was found hanged in a Paris prison cell in 1941, having been turned over to the Nazis by the French police.

HOBSON, JOHN ATKINSON (1858–1940). Economist and publicist. On leaving Oxford University, where he did not excel, he became a school-teacher, then a freelance journalist, and then an extension lecturer for the universities of Oxford and London. In 1899, he was asked to go to South Africa by the *Manchester Guardian* to cover the turbulent political situation that eventually erupted into the South African War. On his return, he delivered a series of anti-war and anti-imperialist lectures. The hostile reception they received prompted his first important book, *The Psychology of Jingoism* (1901). In *Imperialism: A Study* (1902), he sought to provide a general explanation for the phenomena he had experienced in South Africa and London. This work established his reputation as a leading radical thinker and still forms the basis of his reputation today. During the First World War, his commitment to Cobdenite principles began to give way to a more interventionist position. He became a major proponent of economic management and 'international economic government' following the war. He was a member of the Bryce Committee, set up to examine plans to create a new international order. His *Towards International Government* (1917) was a dissenting opinion. He was fiercely critical of the economic provisions of the Versailles Treaty and also of the British government's policy of appeasement in the 1930s.

HULL, CORDELL (1871–1955). American statesman. He was a Democratic member of Congress from 1907 to 1921 and from 1924 to 1931. He was elected to the Senate in 1931, resigning in 1934 to become President Roosevelt's Secretary of State. In his early years of office he dedicated himself to reviving world trade. His overwhelming belief in the economic and political virtues of free trade informed his entire period in office. He successfully steered the Reciprocal Trade Agreements Act through a largely protectionist Congress in 1934. In providing for the reciprocal reduction of tariff walls, and the use of the 'most favoured nation' principle, this agreement was a forerunner of GATT. During the war, he opposed Keynes's plans for a more restrictive and centrally directed trading and monetary order, and had a large impact on the shape of the Bretton Woods Agreement. He had a large hand in the foundation of the UN, believing that the failure of the League of Nations, and America's refusal to join it, had been a major cause of instability during the inter-war period. He retired from office on grounds of ill-health in 1944. In 1945 he was awarded the Nobel Prize for Peace.

KEOHANE, ROBERT (b. 1941). Theorist of international co-operation and pioneer of regime theory. Educated at Shimer College and

Harvard University. He began his career at Swarthmore College (1965–73), subsequently professing at Stanford (1973–81), Brandeis (1981–5), Harvard (1985–96) and Duke (from 1996) universities. He is the author of numerous books and articles on the nature and theory of international co-operation, including the influential *Transnational Relations and World Politics* (edited with Joseph S. Nye, 1972), *Power and Interdependence* (with Joseph S. Nye, 1977), *International Institutions and State Power* (1989), and *Neorealism and its Critics* (editor, 1986). In his most important work, *After Hegemony* (1984), he argued that the relative economic and political decline of the US in the 1960s and 1970s did not spell the end of the liberal international economic order that that country had helped erect in 1945. In place of American hegemony, a network of co-operative 'regimes' had arisen. These regimes are defined as 'sets of implicit or explicit principles, norms, rules and decision-making procedures around which actors' expectations converge in a given area of international relations'. In effect, they lock states into co-operative patterns of behaviour.

KEYNES, JOHN MAYNARD (1883–1946). Economist and civil servant. Educated at King's College, Cambridge. He became a civil servant in the India Office in 1906, but returned to Cambridge in 1908 to lecture on economics. His first book was *Indian Currency and Finance* (1913). He left academia to join the Treasury in 1915, serving as the chief Treasury representative at the Paris Peace Conference of 1919. He achieved fame with his brilliant critique of the reparations clauses of the Versailles Treaty in *The Economic Consequences of the Peace* (1919). But in the face of persistent financial difficulties which dogged Britain and Europe in the 1920s, Keynes began to modify his earlier classical liberal convictions, as elegantly recounted in his eulogistic *The End of Laissez Faire* (1925). He denounced the 'return to gold' at the pre-war parity in *The Economic Consequences of Mr Churchill* (1925). In the same vein, he helped to write the Liberal 'Yellow Book' of 1928, arguing for a programme of large-scale public investment and state management of the economy. He continued to attack orthodox economic policy in the 1930s, and provided a full theoretical defence of his revolutionary 'demand-side' economics in his seminal *General Theory of Employment, Interest and Money* (1936). He became Special Advisor to the Chancellor of the Exchequer in 1940, playing a major role in the negotiations that led to the foundation of the IMF and the World Bank.

LIST, FRIEDRICH (1789–1846). German–American political economist. Largely self-educated, List rose to national prominence as founder of and secretary to an association of south German industrialists, advocating abolition of the numerous tariff barriers which at that time divided the German nation. In 1827, he was exiled for his liberal views, settling in America, where he became editor of a German-language newspaper in Pennsylvania. In *Outlines of American Political Economy* (1827), he first put forward his argument that a national economy at an early stage of its development requires tariff protection. The costs of protection, he claimed, should be viewed as an investment in the nation's industrial potential. He returned to Germany in 1834 as US consul in Leipzig. Following inadequate returns from heavy investments he made in the Leipzig-to-Dresden railway line, he moved to France. There he wrote his most famous work, *The National System of Political Economy* (1841). Plagued by financial difficulties all his life, he committed suicide in 1846.

LUXEMBURG, ROSA (1870–1919). German socialist and revolutionary. She was born in Poland and educated in Warsaw and at Zürich University. Forced to flee Poland because of her revolutionary activities, she settled in Germany, becoming a German citizen in 1898 through a marriage of convenience. With Karl Liebknecht (1871–1919), she established the syndicalist wing of the Social Democratic Party in 1905. She vigorously attacked the 'revisionism' of the leader of the party, Eduard Bernstein. In 1913, she set out her ideas about the nature of capitalism and the inevitability of imperialist war in *The Accumulation of Capital*. On the outbreak of the inevitable imperialist war in 1914, she established the Spartakist group of socialists, dedicated to stopping the war through direct action. She was imprisoned for her trouble, but managed to continue the fight through smuggling letters calling for mass revolutionary action. She was one of the first Marxists to recognise the authoritarian tendencies within Bolshevism. She attacked Lenin for his unscrupulousness, and for imposing a dictatorship over the proletariat rather than of the proletariat. She was murdered with Liebknecht by the Freikorps in 1919.

MILL, JOHN STUART (1806–1873). Philosopher, political economist and social reformer. Perhaps the most influential English thinker of the nineteenth century. He was educated by his father, the Scottish philosopher, political economist and co-founder (with Jeremy Bentham) of University College, London, James Mill. He established his reputation with his *System of Logic* (1843), which set out to establish the rules and parameters of meaningful discourse. In *Principles of Political Economy*, published in 1848, the same year as the *Communist Manifesto*, he sought to update the classical political economy of Smith and Ricardo by taking into account the need for redistribution of wealth on the grounds of social justice. Mill's other great works include *Utilitarianism* (1863), *On Liberty* (1859), *The Subjection of Women* (1861) and *Considerations on Representative Government* (1861).

MITRANY, DAVID (1888–1975). Romanian theorist of international co-operation. Educated at the London School of Economics. He was an active member of the Union of Democratic Control, the League of Nations Society, and the Labour Party Committee on International Questions. In the 1920s, he edited the European volumes of the Carnegie Series on the history of the First World War. Failing to secure a permanent post at the London School of Economics, he spent several years as a research fellow at Harvard University and the newly established Institute for Advanced Studies at Princeton. He wrote one of the first books on economic sanctions, *The Problem of International Sanctions* (1925) and, influenced by Leonard Woolf, Harold Laski and G.D.H. Cole, one of the first studies of the growth of international organisation from the point of view of the functions they perform, *The Progress of International Government* (1933). Drawing on his American experience of the New Deal, particularly the design and function of the Tennessee Valley Authority, which he much admired, he elaborated his ideas in a short treatise, *A Working Peace System* (1943). Essentially a critique of political realism, it proved remarkably influential for so slim a volume. He spent the post-war years promoting and defending his functional approach, often fiercely attacking European federalists and 'neo-functionalists' who tried to claim him as one of their own.

MORGENTHAU, HANS JOACHIM (1904–1980). American theorist of international relations and analyst of US foreign policy. Born in Germany and educated at Berlin, Frankfurt and Munich universities, and the Graduate Institute of International Studies, Geneva. Admitted to the bar in 1927, he went to Geneva to teach public law in 1932, staying until 1935 due to Hitler's acquisition of power in Germany in 1933. He then taught briefly in Spain, and at a variety of colleges in America, before settling down as Professor of Political Science at the University of Chicago (1943–71). His first major work, *Scientific Man vs Power Politics* (1948), was a philosophical essay elegantly assailing the scientific or 'rationalist' approach to the study and practice of international relations. In his celebrated *Politics Among Nations* (1948), based on his lectures at Chicago, he reasserted the centrality of power in international relations, upholding the moral sanctity of the national interest but also skilfully delineating the limits of power and foreign policy. He was an early and consistent critic of American involvement in the Vietnam War, on the grounds that it conflicted with US national interest. One of the most influential political scientists of the twentieth century, his other important books include *In Defence of National Interest* (1951) and *The Purpose of American Politics* (1960).

NOEL-BAKER, PHILIP (1889-1982). Athlete, academic and politician. Educated at King's College, Cambridge. He was the first student to combine Presidency of the Cambridge Union with that of the University Athletic Club. Running in Cambridge colours in the 1500 metres in the 1912 Olympics, he helped his Oxford rival win the gold medal. In the 1920 Olympics he won the silver medal, again acting as pacemaker for the British winner. He captained the British Olympic team in 1924. In the same year, he became the first professor of international relations at the London School of Economics. During his tenure, he wrote several books on the League of Nations and international law, including *The League of Nations at Work* (1926), *Disarmament* (1926), and *The Present Juridical Status of the British Dominions in International Law* (1929). He resigned in 1929 to become an MP (1929–31, 1936–70). He was Parliamentary Private Secretary to the Foreign Secretary, Arthur Henderson, from 1929 to 1931. When Henderson became Chairman of the World Disarmament Conference in 1932, he took Noel-Baker with him as his assistant. Shortly afterwards, Noel-Baker wrote his detailed *The Private Manufacture of Armaments* (1936). During the war, he was Parliamentary Secretary of the Ministry of War Transport, finally entering the Cabinet in 1947 as Secretary of State for Commonwealth Relations. In 1959 he was awarded the Nobel Prize for Peace for his *The Arms Race* (1958).

PREBISCH, RAUL (1901-86). Argentine economist. Educated at the University of Buenos Aires, he was Executive Director of the UN Economic Commission for Latin America, 1950–63, and Secretary-General of UNCTAD, 1963–69. In these posts Prebisch did much to promote research into the problems of Third World development, particularly with regard to the impact of the industrial 'core' on the primary producing 'periphery'. He was a major participant in the campaign for a NIEO, greatly influencing its agenda. His most important works include *Una Nueva Politica Commercial para el Desarrollo* (1964), *Transformacion y Desarrollo* (1965), and *Capitalismo Periferico* (1981).

RICARDO, DAVID (1772-1823). Businessman, economist and politician. He entered his father's business on the London Stock Exchange at the age of 14. Showing great aptitude, he soon became a member of the Exchange, and amassed a sufficient fortune, trading principally in government securities, to enable him to retire at 42 and indulge his scientific and cultural interests. His interest in economics was sparked by Smith's *Wealth of Nations*. In his first book, *The High Price of Bullion, a Proof of the Depreciation of Bank Notes* (1810), he demonstrated that there was a close correspondence between the volume of bank notes in circulation and the level of prices. His findings prompted the setting up of a House of Commons Committee of Enquiry, which re-commended the repeal of the act enabling banks to issue notes not backed by gold. In another controversial work, *Essay on the Influence of a Low Price of Corn on the Profits of Stock* (1815), he argued that raising the tariff on imported corn only served to increase the rents of country gentlemen and depress the profits of manufacturers. Ricardo became an MP in 1819 and did much to enhance the respectability of free trade. In *Principles of Political Economy and Taxation* (1817), he developed his labour theory of value and law of comparative advantage. These ideas greatly influenced the work of later thinkers, including Marx and Mill, and his abstract approach had a major impact on the develop-ment of economics as a science.

RUGGIE, JOHN GERRARD (b. 1944). Austrian-born American theorist of international co-operation and pioneer of regime theory. Educated at McMaster University and the University of California at Berkeley, at which he began his academic career, he became

Professor of Political Science and International Affairs at Columbia University in 1991. He is the author of many articles and several books on international co-operation, including *The Antinomies of Interdependence* (editor, 1983), *Winning the Peace* (1996), and *Constructing the World Polity* (1998). He is credited with inventing the term 'international regimes' in his article 'International Responses to Technology: Concepts and Trends' (*World Politics*, 1975).

SCHACHT, HJALMAR (1877–1970). German banker. Vice-director of Dresdner Bank, 1908. Financial consultant to the German army of occupation in Brussels, 1914–15. Appointed director of German National Bank, 1916. He rose to prominence with the strict monetary policy he implemented to tackle rampant inflation in Germany while currency commissioner at the Finance Ministry in 1923. Later the same year he was appointed President of the Reichsbank. He resigned in 1930 over Germany's acceptance of the Young Plan for the re-scheduling of reparation payments. Over the next few years he edged closer to the Nazis. When they seized power in 1933 he was re-appointed to the presidency of the Reichsbank. As Minister for Economics (from 1934), he was in charge of the Nazi un-employment and rearmament programmes. He successfully enticed neighbouring countries into the complex web of Nazi finance and trade. Unhappy with the scale of rearmament, and the dictatorial rule over the economy of Herman Goering, he resigned as Minister for Economics in 1937, and was dismissed from the Reichsbank in 1939. In 1944 he was suspected of plotting against Hitler and sent to a con-centration camp. He was brought before the Nuremberg War Crimes Tribunal in 1946 and acquitted. He resumed his career as a banker, became an advisor to several governments, and died prosperous in 1970.

SCHUMPETER, JOSEPH ALOIS (1883–1950). Moravian-born American economist. Educated at the University of Vienna, he lectured at the universities of Czernowitz, Graz and Bonn before becoming Professor of Economics at Harvard in 1932. In his best-known work, *Capitalism, Socialism, and Democracy* (1942), he argued that capitalism would eventually become a victim of its own success and give way to some kind of social control. Several factors were paving the way for socialism: constant increases in the scale of production and organisation; the growth of bureaucratic forms of management; the decline of the individual entrepreneur; the loosening of family ties, leading to a reduction in the incentive to accumulate; and the corrosive role of intellectuals who always backed 'society' against the 'individual'. His *History of Economic Analysis* (1954) is a detailed study of the evolution of analytical methods in economics. His *Business Cycles: A Theoretical, Historical, and Statistical Analysis of the Capitalist Process* (1939) pioneered the theory of the business cycle.

SMITH, ADAM (1723–90). Political economist and moral philosopher. Founder of classical political economy. Educated at Glasgow and Oxford Universities. While at Edinburgh University (1748–51), he delivered his lectures on Rhetoric, which did much to establish his reputation. In 1751, he became Professor of Logic at Glasgow University, becoming Professor of Moral Philosophy a year later. It was during this time that he wrote his first major work, *The Theory of Moral Sentiments* (1759). In 1764, he resigned his professorship to become tutor to the young Duke of Buccleuch. It was while touring France with his charge that he met some of the leading thinkers of the day, notably Voltaire and Quesnai, and began work on his masterpiece, *An Enquiry into the Nature and Causes of the Wealth of Nations*. This was published in 1776, after which he enjoyed a sinecure as Commissioner of Customs in Edinburgh until his death in 1790.

STRANGE, SUSAN (1923–98). International political economist and founder of the British International Studies Association. Educated at the Université de Caen and the London School of Economics. In 1944, she became an editorial assistant with the *Economist*, becoming Washington correspondent for the *Observer* in 1946, moving to New York shortly after to cover the incipient workings of the UN. She returned to London in 1949 to take up a lectureship in international relations at University College, continuing her work for the *Observer* as an economics correspondent and leader-writer for a further 10 years. In 1965, she became a research fellow at the Royal Institute of International Affairs ('Chatham House'), concentrating on transnational relations. It was during this period that she produced her first important book, *Sterling and British Policy* (1971). Strange was one of the first observers to note the uncertainty that flexible exchange rates would bring, and the increasing rapidity with which money could circulate around the world due to technical change.

These developments were fully explored in her *Casino Capitalism* (1986). In 1978, she became Montague Burton Professor of International Relations at the London School of Economics. It was here that she produced the major statement of her position, *States and Markets* (1988). *Contra* Political Science, she argued that economic factors were an ever-present, if not always visible, fact of international life. *Contra* Marxists, she argued that production was not the only structure of power: security, finance and knowledge were also important. *Contra* Economics, she argued that every economic arrangement, however *laissez-faire*, rested on a particular distribution of political and military power. Following her retirement from the London School of Economics in 1988, she spent six years at the European University Institute, Florence, producing (with John Stopford) her important *Rival States, Rival Firms* (1991). She took up a professorship at the University of Warwick at the age of 70. Her last book, published two weeks before her death, was *Mad Money* (1998).

TRIFFIN, ROBERT (1911–93). Belgian–American economist. Educated at the universities of Louvain and Harvard, Triffin spent the early part of his career with the Federal Reserve Board (1942–6), the IMF (1946–9), and the European Recovery Administration in Paris (1949–51). From 1958 to 1980, he professed Economics and Social Science at Yale. His interest in economics was sparked by the ease with which Hitler capitalised on economic instability in the 1930s. Inspired by the example of Einstein, he dedicated his career to the promotion of international peace and stability through world monetary reform and regional monetary integration. He designed the European Payments Union in the 1940s. He was an advisor on monetary and banking issues to many governments, especially Latin American, in the 1950s and 1960s. His warnings about the inherent instability of the Bretton Woods system in the early 1960s went unheeded. Among his numerous works are *Monopolist Competition and General Equilibrium Theory* (1942), *Gold and the Dollar Crisis* (1960), *The World Money Maze* (1966), and *Maintaining and Restoring Balance in International Payments* (with W. Fellner et al., 1966).

VINER, JACOB (1892–1970). Canadian-born American economist and economic historian. Educated at McGill and Harvard Universities, he was a Professor of Economics at Chicago (1925–46) and at

Princeton (1946–60). Viner published numerous works on the history and theory of international trade, including *Canada's Balance of International Indebtedness* (1924), *Studies in the Theory of International Trade* (1937), and *The Customs Union Issue* (1950). The latter book introduced the now familiar distinction between trade-creating and trade-diverting economic arrangements. His essays on foreign policy objectives during the mercantilist era, and the emergence of the doctrines of free trade and *laissez-faire*, are seminal contributions to the literature. These and other important writings are usefully gathered together in *The Long View and the Short* (1958), and *Essays on the Intellectual History of Economics* (1991).

WALLERSTEIN, IMMANUEL (b. 1930). American Sociologist. Educated at Columbia University. He has lectured at the universities of Columbia, McGill and the Ecôle des Hautes Etudes en Sciences Sociales, Paris. With Fernand Braudel he has done much to restore the credibility of 'macro-history' (variously called historical sociology, philosophical history and 'broad-brush' history). His major work is his three-volume *Modern World System* (1974, 1980, 1989), in which he most fully develops his 'world system' theory of the origins and impact of capitalism. Other important works include *The Capitalist World Economy* (1979) and *Unthinking Social Science* (1991).

WALTZ, KENNETH (b. 1924). Professor of International Relations. Educated at Oberlin College and the University of Columbia. In a wide-ranging career on both sides of the Atlantic he has taught at Columbia (1953–7), Swarthmore College (1957–66), Brandeis University (1966–71) and the University of California at Berkeley (1971–94). He has held research fellowships at Harvard (1963–4, 1968–9, 1972), Kings College, London (1986–7), the London School of Economics (1976–7), the Australian National University (1978), and the University of Peking (1982, 1991, 1996). His *Man, the State, and War* (1959), based on his Columbia PhD thesis and written partly behind the lines in the Korean War, is widely regarded as a classic. Through a broad survey of the history of Western political thought, he sought to show that it was the anarchical nature of the international system, rather than the corrupt nature of man, or the aggressive or dysfunctional nature of particular states, that was chiefly responsible for the occurrence of war. He later attempted to demonstrate this hypothesis scientifically in his celebrated *Theory of International Politics* (1979). Other important works include his polemical essay *The Spread of Nuclear Weapons: Why More May be Better* (1981) and *Foreign Policy and the Democratic Process* (1967).

WOOLF, LEONARD (1880–1969). Colonial administrator, publisher and political writer. Educated at Trinity College, Cambridge, where he was much influenced (as was his friend Keynes) by the philosopher G.E. Moore. From 1904 to 1911, he was a colonial administrator in Ceylon. He returned to London to marry the young author Virginia Stephen. He threw himself into the heady circle of friends known as Bloomsbury and the more sober activities of the Fabian Society. His first book was a novel critical of imperialism, *The Village in the Jungle* (1913). In 1916, he published a report for the Fabian Society entitled *International Government*. This established his reputation as the Fabian 'expert' on international affairs. Three years later, he published his influential *Empire and Commerce in Africa*. He was a member of the Union of Democratic Control and a founder member of the League of Nations Society. With his wife he founded the celebrated Hogarth Press in 1917. From 1918 to 1945, he was Secretary of the Labour Party Advisory Committee on International Questions. From 1924 to 1945, he chaired the party's sister committee on international questions. In his long career he wrote over 20 books and thousands of articles and reviews. His masterful five-volume autobiography was completed shortly before his death.

INDEX

Mohammed Al-Helal